Ticket to Ride

Inside the Beatles'
1964 Tour
that Changed the World

by Larry Kane

9   8   7   6   5   4   3   2
Digit on the right indicates the number of this printing

Library of Congress Control Number 2002096414

ISBN 0-7624-1592-4

Cover designed by Whitney Cookman
Interior designed by Bill Jones & Jan Greenberg
Edited by Greg Jones
Typography: Palatino

CD produced by Tom Power

This book may be ordered by mail from the publisher. Please include
$2.50 for postage and handling.
But try your bookstore first!

Running Press Book Publishers
125 South Twenty-second Street
Philadelphia, Pennsylvania 19103-4399

Visit us on the web!
www.runningpress.com

Dedicated to Donna,
Michael, and Alexandra

And to John, Paul, George, and Ringo

Contents

FOREWORD   6

ACKNOWLEDGMENTS   7

PROLOGUE: *If That Was Fab . . .*   10

PART ONE: *1964*

Chapter 1: A Ticket to Ride   17
Chapter 2: A Stranger in the Bedroom   25
Chapter 3: Seventy-two Hours of Madness   31
Chapter 4: Fishing for Trouble   41
Chapter 5: A Hollywood Fantasy 53
Chapter 6: Beatle Frights and Beatle Nights   63
Chapter 7: A Juicy Piece of the Apple   69
Chapter 8: Surf and Sex at the Jersey Shore   75
Chapter 9: Rockin' at the Birthplace of Freedom   83
Chapter 10: High-Speed Beatlemania   89
Chapter 11: Guns, Palm Trees, and a Rock-and-Roll Hurricane   99
Chapter 12: North to Boston: Does Anyone Have a Compass?   115
Chapter 13: Memories from the Fans   119
Chapter 14: Catfight in Cleveland, Wild Horses in New Orleans   123
Chapter 15: Word War in Kansas City, Fear in Dallas   145
Chapter 16: A Rolling Stone on the Beatles' Doorstep   153

Part Two: *Life on Tour*

Chapter 17: A Plane Life   159

Chapter 18: Flirtatious Mothers and Candy Kisses   165

Chapter 19: What Were They Really Like?   171

Chapter 20: The Late Show: Free Love and Free Parking   181

Chapter 21: The Beatles' Inner Circle   185

Part Three: *1965*

Chapter 22: Help! In the Bahamas   195

Chapter 23: The Beatles Have Landed!   201

Chapter 24: Mugs and Drugs in Maple Leaf Country   215

Chapter 25: A Few Hours of Heaven   219

Chapter 26: Mayhem and Music in Texas   225

Chapter 27: Air Wars and the Beatles' Radio Daze   231

Chapter 28: Engine on Fire: John! Don't Jump!   237

Chapter 29: Back to Hollywood: Famous Face in the Bedroom   243

Chapter 30: "We Are the Beatles, That's What We Are"   255

Epilogue: *Beyond the Tours*   261

Appendix: *Complete 1964 and 1965 Tour Schedules*   271

Foreword

Like yours truly, Larry Kane flourished in the Philadelphia television market, where he has broadcast as an anchor for 37 years. But before Larry came to Philadelphia, he had a magical ride with the Beatles. In 1964 and 1965, he was the only American reporter, broadcast or newspaper, to travel with the fab four on every stop of their two groundbreaking North American tours.

Now, Larry tells the story of what it was like to literally live with the four young men who would leave a daunting impression on the landscape of contemporary music.

This is a story of high drama and high notes. Larry, through the descriptions of a young and eager journalist, fills the reader with the mindset of four superstars, and the sometimes-controversial people around them. No book on the Beatles has ever been written from this perspective, and no book ever will be again. How many of us would have liked to be a fly on the wall during the Beatles hectic and triumphant night-and-day marathon through the United States and Canada? Written tastefully, with the voices of the Beatles telling their story, Larry Kane brings us to the real world of the Beatles and the sixties.

There are other stories here: fanatic teenagers, flirtatious mothers, nights full of music and love, and most of all, a passionate love affair with momentous music.

Ticket to Ride is a ticket punched for a wild ride that will bring you closer than ever to the Beatles and music history. The accompanying CD brings the voices and sounds of the Beatles up close and personal.

So, brace yourself for moments of revelation and joy, and memories that will last forever.

—Dick Clark

Acknowledgments

There are many people to thank for helping me in this project, but no one more than Joe Johnson, host of the Beatle Brunch program on Westwood One. Joe is also producer of the syndicated show. His knowledge and tape input has been extraordinary. I would urge the reader to visit his website at www.beatlebrunch.com.

Janet Benton, who served as special editor for this project, was invaluable with her expertise and energy. Tom Power was awesome in the production skills he brought to the accompanying CD.

My former travelers on the Beatles' tours were so helpful in recalling the past. Ivor Davis, Art Schreiber, Jim Staggs and Long John Wade gave me immeasurable support. Talking to former Beatles Press Secretary Tony Barrow helped bring back stories of the 1965 tour. Tony is a virtual treasure of information in the entertainment industry. Rick Friedman, my good friend and fellow broadcaster, provided valuable insight, along with Bob Bernstein, aka Scott Regan. Gary Stevens, former star deejay in New York, and current radio broker, was invaluable. Gary and I go back some 44 years, so it was great to connect with him again.

Denny Somach, former deejay and current impresario of many entertainment projects, was extremely helpful to me. Denny's knowledge of the entertainment industry is unparalleled.

I'd also like to thank *Philadelphia Daily News* writer Rose DeWolf, Don Shelby of WCCO in Minneapolis, Mark Lapidos of the Fest for Beatles Fans, and researchers Jon McGlinchey, Tim Archer, Adam McKibbin, as well as court reporter and transcriber Pat Lipski.

Along the way, the following people helped me with insight and materials: former promotions executive Doug Jones, Larry Solitrin and the art department at KYW TV, Damon Sinclair, a talented and respected producer, Bev Aaron of WPVI TV, and KYW intern Jane Song, KYW TV cameramen Mike Teiper, who recorded my last interview with

Ringo Starr, deserves a big thank you. Legendary concert promoter Sid Bernstein helped me link some important information.

I would like to acknowledge the help of Dave Davis, the general manager of WPVI TV, where I worked during John Lennon's visit to Philadelphia in 1975.

My gratitude to producer Traci Benjamin at CN8 News, and to all the people at Comcast.

My special thanks to the Beatles fans who shared their memories: Anne Gottehrer, Kristina Monaco, Tina Camma, Bradley Arthur, Nancy McFadden-Lloyd, Pam Trujillo, Jim Morin, Nancy I. Moore, Stephen C. Hall, Mary Horvath, Judy Kline, John Moore, Lynn Angelo, Gordy Partridge, Barbara Singer, Mary Troumouhis, Phyllis Cambria, Jeff Hammond, Jill Sutton Finan, Debbie Taylor, June Champion, Beverly Griffith, and Kathryn Osmondson.

It is difficult to write a book while working full time, and for their support, I especially want to thank my KYW co-anchor Denise Saunders and sports director Beasely Reece. The radio people were wonderful. Special thanks to Roy Shapiro and Steve Butler of KYW Radio, and Tim Sabean of WYSP Radio for their assistance. The technical advice of Dave Harris is always welcome. My thanks go to fellow author Bob Spitz. And thanks also to Temple Universtiy Press.

A special thank-you to Dick Clark for graciously writing the foreword to this book, and to Al Roker for his support. Lew Klein, the national broadcast legend, was also instrumental.

My friends played a helpful role—especially Paul Gluck of WHYY Television, Joanne Calabria, the Communications Director of KYW TV, and Misti Tindiglia.

The man who represents me, Alfred Geller, forged a wonderful alliance with Running Press to make this book possible. The Running Press staff must be commended for its level of expertise and support. Greg Jones edited this work with talent and fervor. His encouragement and input was powerful and creative. Susan Oyama found the pictures to bring it to life. Sam Caggiula prepared a masterful publicity plan. John Whalen prepared the sales plan. Associate Publisher Carlo DeVito was inspiring all the way through, and Publisher Buz Teacher made it all happen. Tina Camma, who works for Buz, was the first person interviewed as a 1964 Beatles fan. She gets a second credit for being the guardian of Beatles pictures and memorabilia that contributed to this book.

Finally, it all comes back to the most important people in my life.

Donna, my wife, never ceases to amaze me with her brilliance and vision. Her love and help in this project were critical and key to its success. Our son Michael and daughter Alexandra, besides being sensational human beings, are smart and talented professionals, and their support has been invaluable. During the early part of the project, our future son-in-law, Douglas Weiss, acted as a great sounding board.

And thanks to all of you who are reading *Ticket to Ride*. I hope you enjoy it as much as I enjoyed writing it.

Photography Credits

Prologue
If *That* Was Fab...

She was beautiful, her sandy blonde hair swirling in the chill summer wind, her embroidered dress draping over a thin frame, her eyes welling with tears. She held an autograph book, and her hands shook with anticipation. I didn't know her name, but my instincts told me she had not yet reached her fourteenth birthday.

We stood trapped in a field of grass between a remote airport runway and a California freeway. Unknown to us at the time, we also stood at a pivotal moment in history. This innocent girl would almost certainly be humming a different tune by 1968, but how could we see that coming on the afternoon of August 19, 1964—the day the Beatles invaded America?

The cab I had taken to meet the Beatles when their plane touched down had mistakenly dropped me off at a perimeter road, and it appeared I would have to wait to see them later at the hotel, where they would be expecting me. I'd interviewed them earlier in the year, but in several months' time they had begun the transformation into legend, and my assignment had also taken on a much grander scope. As I stood with the trembling young fan, the Pan Am Clipper that carried the Beatles to America was not 150 yards away. But a large wire fence stood between us and the plane, and there was no way over or around it. We walked back to the road together. I carried my tape recorder; she grasped the autograph book and a single flower for Paul.

The wind from San Francisco Bay was howling, and yet above it was another sound, a shrieking wail, that almost reached the decibel level of an airplane engine. The extraordinary roar erupted from the huge crowd gathered on the other side of the barricades. It was the sound of children screaming in excitement, joy, and frustration, and the Beatles would hear it in on thirty-two separate occasions over the next thirty-one days.

My walking companion glanced over and said, "I've got to meet Paul. I love him. He's so fab. I need him, and he needs me."

So fab. I need him. He needs me. Such was the rapture of the always desiring, absolutely obsessed, and daringly frank phenomenon known as the Beatles fan. Each one eminently convinced that theirs was a true bond with the suave, debonair Paul; the gutsy, outspoken John; the mysterious Ringo; and of course George, the man with that eternally just-past-puberty face.

I was awestruck when this girl informed me that, if I could help her meet any one of them, she would do "anything" for me. (I didn't even want to think about what she and others just like her planned to do to the Beatles themselves.) Her unmistakable offer struck a chill through my body as I came to the realization that I was talking to a teenager. There would be similar offers made over the course of the madness that would follow—and, as far as the Beatles were concerned, some of these offers would be made good—but in life you always remember the first time. This first offer was unexpected and quite disturbing, but I would get used to girls routinely offering me their money, their clothing, and their bodies in a reckless attempt to get close to the Beatles. If *that* was fab, I wanted to know what came after fab.

Finally we parted, she with her dream, I with my doubts about why I had come this far. It was not a good time for me—I was not particularly thrilled to be covering what I considered to be "soft news" and, besides, my world had just changed forever. Meanwhile, the rest of the world was experiencing a seismic shift of its own.

It was, after all, the summer of 1964. The nation was bracing for the looming dark shadows of war, racial unrest, a lurid love affair with drugs, and a sometimes-violent crusade of social protest. The news was rife with the political rhetoric of President Lyndon Johnson on the left and his challenger, Senator Barry Goldwater, on the right. Many young innocents in the middle would soon receive that awful letter from the draft board that, in a jaded twist of irony, would begin with the word, "Greetings."

In my life, I was saying goodbye. My mother died in the summer of 1964, and the night before her death, I told her about this unusual opportunity that had come my way. Even as we talked, President Johnson was speaking to the nation, declaring hostilities against North Vietnam. The signs were ominous. Meanwhile, in what would be our final conversation, I traced the roots of my coming adventure back to February of that year.

A group of singers had taken the world by storm. They were described as "mopheads," "freaks," and "slobs" by media mavens and those offended by change. Yet their music was sticking, their joint and individual personalities were resonating, and their style was informing the dramatic cultural change that was already underway. I had covered their airport arrival in February as Miami police rushed to hold the barricades at the gate. Hours later, I interviewed the Beatles during a hurried news conference at a Miami Beach hotel. Later that month, news had reached my radio station that the Beatles would embark that summer on the biggest tour in the history of music. Their closest stop to my town, Miami, would be Jacksonville. There, my station management decided, I would secure an exclusive interview with the Beatles.

I wrote to the Beatles' manager, Brian Epstein. In months to come, I would get to know Mr. Epstein well, even becoming an object of his affection. But at that time he knew me only as the news director of WFUN Radio in Miami. He was duly impressed, and perhaps somewhat misled, by my letter, and invited me to travel coast to coast and across Canada in the official Beatles traveling press party. The management at WFUN quickly decided to syndicate the reports to forty-five radio stations; that would pay my way. I would not only see the continent, but my work would be featured on a nationwide radio network.

At the age of twenty-one it was a wonderful opportunity, though to take it would mean leaving home during a critical time. My mother said, "Honey, it's so wonderful. It's so exciting. Make the most of it." I did.

Since then I have covered war, natural disasters, presidents and popes, mayors and martyrs, paupers and princes. I have chronicled murder, mayhem, love and hate, birth and death, and everyday happenings. I have spent thirty-seven years anchoring the good and bad news of Philadelphia, a city that I love, and raising a family with a brilliant and beautiful woman. Life has been full of memories. Reporters remember what they want to remember. I remember a lot, and I have forgotten much more.

But I will never forget the summers of 1964 and 1965 and my time with the Beatles. Most of the people who tried to get close to them were deejays and promoters. A few genuine journalists made their way into the circle. For some reason, I was able to penetrate beyond the facade and the imagery to explore their thoughts, frustrations, and deeper views of the world around them. John, Paul, George, and Ringo became real people to me, and I think I became real to them.

This reporter was the only American broadcast journalist who covered every stop of the 1964 and 1965 tours of North America. And the journey you are about to take with me, forty years later, is an inside account of the greatest event in the history of rock-and-roll. It seems like only yesterday, yet the images come back to me with clarity. . . .

Light bulbs flash in the dark of the night. Legs break under the crush of a crowd. Sirens wail. Feathers and food fly in the passenger cabin. Newsmen ask the same silly questions from town to town. Jellybeans fly like missiles onto stages nationwide, and an airplane goes up in flames. Help! I need somebody! Struggling to breathe in the crush of the crowd. Is that really Jayne Mansfield? McCartney wears a boyish grin after meeting Elvis. Oh, Canada, with so many machine guns in Montreal.

Ringo in tears after a fan crashes through a plate-glass window. Brian Epstein invites me to his room—Lennon says, "Watch out, Larry." George blushes during our private screening of A Hard Day's Night. The fish truck heads into Philadelphia. The guy in the hotel lobby looks like Bob Dylan; is Bob Dylan. Monopoly for money? Sittin' on the dock of the bay in Nassau. Starlets in Hollywood. Harlots in Atlantic City. John's growing anger at the war. Frenzied fans everywhere. Conversations about race relations and politics. An ethnic slur from the back of the airplane. An incredible offer from Ed Sullivan. Madness in Manhattan. The music growing on me, slowly but surely. A problem mother in Las Vegas. Technical problems, a broken tape recorder, and an unexpected show of support from "the Boys." A soiled carpet in Seattle. The famous beauty in the bathroom....

And the memories flow. This story moves briskly as the Beatles' love affair with America keeps growing, and they keep giving. The days of fab may now be gone, but the music, ever vibrant and always relevant, comes alive with every new generation that comes along. And the impact the Beatles had continues to ripple. If you loved the Beatles in 1964, chances are you are now fifty-something, older in body but still a teenager at heart. Chances are your children and theirs are spellbound by the music, fascinated by the legend, and enriched by the memories that you've shared. And memories like these are meant to be retold, and relived.

So climb aboard the Electra, buckle up that seat belt, and get ready for a thrill ride of historic proportions. Join me on the amazing Beatles tours of North America in 1964 and '65. Experience the fun and joy they left behind, and get to know the generation they helped to shape, almost forty years ago today.

—Larry Kane
Philadelphia
August 2003

PART ONE:
1964

CHAPTER 1:
A Ticket to Ride

LARRY KANE: Is there any particular memory you would like to cherish from this trip?

JOHN LENNON: Well, just the whole thing. It's been fantastic. We will probably never do another tour like it. It could never be the same as this one and it's probably something we will remember the rest of our days. It's just been marvelous.

John Lennon was right: The Beatles never did another tour like the one in 1964. But then again, neither did anyone else. We all know now that the first Beatles tour of America stands as the greatest tour in rock-and-roll history, and that it was an event of great musical and social magnitude. But few know that the tour may never have happened if an earlier visit to America hadn't gone the way it did....

It really all started on February 7, 1964, when the Beatles landed in New York City and were greeted by an unprecedented crowd of more than 3,000 hysterical fans. After making an historic appearance on the *Ed Sullivan Show* two days later, and giving their first live stateside performance in Washington, D.C. two days after that, the Beatles headed south for the sunny shores of Miami. That's where I would meet the band for the first time.

The records show that February 13 was a sunny day in Miami, with outside temperatures in the low eighties. But inside Concourse 3, the National Airlines hub at Miami International Airport, where an estimated 5,000 youngsters had gathered to greet the Beatles, spectators said the temperature was unbearable.

I stood on the asphalt below the concourse, waiting for the Beatles' arrival. Although the crowd was in an eager and anticipatory mood, I was anything but. As news director of WFUN Radio in Miami, my beat was covering the news of the streets, the courthouse, politics, and in 1964, the mass exodus of Cuban refugees to South Florida. The Beatles were not exactly in the front of my mind. In contemporary radio, there were record spinners, or "jocks" as we called them, and there were newsmen. The two groups rarely met, except in the hallway or at the water cooler. Assigning me to cover the Beatles in Miami was the idea of the deejays and the program department. To be honest, I wasn't exactly thrilled with the assignment.

In February 1964, jaded and skeptical, I and many others viewed the Beatles as just another quickie phenomenon, a distraction. But that was before I came to fully appreciate the band's music and social impact. It would be convenient and sly to tell you that I knew the Beatles were going to be megastars the minute I heard them, or that from early on I had realized they would be the most significant entertainment force in the twentieth century. But the truth is, I didn't have a clue.

Hollywood reporter Ivor Davis, a traveling companion on the 1964 tour, says now, "I was too young to appreciate it. Who knew the Beatles and their tour of 1964 would be the benchmark for all time? After all, this was just a rock-and-roll group. You could feel the insanity, but you didn't feel the history then. After that experience, almost every other was downhill for me."

Davis, who has interviewed hundreds of stars and is a scion of the Hollywood entertainment beat, was as skeptical as I was in February 1964. After all, it was only rock-and-roll, right? But soon enough we would learn that it was much more. And so on that hot February afternoon, I reluctantly reported on the Beatles' landing at Miami, the final stop of their first visit to America.

National's Flight 11 landed like any other scheduled flight. But the welcome given to its passengers was unlike any other in the history of the Miami airport. For one thing, the crowd in the concourse was so big and restless that their force and fervor caused plate-glass windows to start falling out onto the field where the plane was landing. Dade County sheriff's deputies were hardly prepared, and as the Beatles stepped off the plane, the surging crowd erupted in screams and pressed even harder against the windows. From my position on the asphalt, I looked up and saw arms reaching out of the openings, hands flailing in the air, young women climbing over each other to get one desperate look, and several ambulances positioning themselves on the other side of the tarmac.

I spoke into the tape recorder: "Larry Kane here at Miami International, where the Beatles have invaded South Florida. Thousands of fans have packed the airport." As I spoke, my words were drowned out by the high-pitched roar of the crowd. Then my taping was interrupted by the Beatles' walk down the steps. I ran toward them but was stiff-armed by a private detective who gave me a good jolt. The Beatles hurried into a limo and drove off to Miami Beach.

I ran up the steps and into the concourse. Several girls were hyperventilating on the floor. Others were bloodied from jostling in the close crowd. Some of the girls were crying, but I couldn't tell whether they were tears of happiness or terror. To say that the authorities were not prepared is only half the story; no one was prepared for such madness. In my life and career before and since, I never saw anything quite like that airport welcome.

One of the girls in the concourse, 15-year-old Kristina Monaco, had joined four of her friends and hired a taxi to take them from Palmetto High School in Southwest Miami to the airport. Almost forty years later, I found Kristina still living in the Miami area. Kristina says she has never forgotten the scene in that concourse: "We were all squashed together. You couldn't move your body until the entire group moved. There was no room to breathe. It was like living a fantasy, all of us there, watching them come off that plane. I only caught a glimpse but it was worth it, believe me."

I asked her what had drawn her to the Beatles. "Well, it was right after the assassination of the president. When I heard 'I Wanna Hold Your Hand,' it was something special, foreign. I connected to it right away. And I was drawn to Paul. I guess it was a hormonal reaction, but it was really strong. We all started wearing British-style pants and things. And they [the Beatles] were special. Eventually I outgrew the hero worship, but then another obsession took over—I was wild about their music." And she says she still is.

To millions of fans across the globe today, the music of Lennon and McCartney, along with the legend of the Beatles, is still vibrant. Despite death and change, time stands still for the Beatles. But in February of '64, I was convinced they were a passing fad and a footnote to history, even as I witnessed the surreal and powerful scene at Miami International.

Two hours after their arrival, I met the Beatles for the first time in a sparsely attended news conference at the Deauville Hotel in Miami Beach, their home for a week. When I walked into the room, the four were smoking, drinking Coke and chatting. I asked them about the airport reception. Paul McCartney answered, "We thought no one would be there to greet us. Wasn't it great?" That's the only answer I remember, but I do recall how surprised I was by their physical appearance and demeanor.

John Lennon, Paul McCartney, George Harrison, and Ringo Starr looked like boys. In fact, they were close to boyhood. George was twenty, Ringo twenty-three, John twenty-three, and Paul twenty-one. My age. And their hair startled me. Tame by today's standards, the length of it seemed odd, almost manufactured for effect. But it was real hair all right, as real and genuine as the people I was meeting for the first time. That's what surprised me the most—the difference between my expectation of meeting star entertainers and the actual experience of finding in these young men a naturalness rarely seen in the world of famous people.

When I returned to my radio station in Miami, the jocks were eagerly waiting for the tape of my initial interviews with the Beatles. They played segments of it every hour on the hour for days. We had suddenly become "Your Beatles station in Miami."

The Beatles were on a hastily scheduled first trip to America. Their canny, brilliant manager, Brian Epstein, told me a year later that this inaugural journey had been a "test run," a step designed to chart the waters in America. Epstein said, "We really didn't know what to expect. Would Americans take to the boys? Certainly, I didn't want a failure. So everything had to be right, planned. We had to look good." He wasn't disappointed with the outcome.

In mid-January of '64 the Beatles song "I Want to Hold Your Hand" topped the American charts. Epstein suddenly felt better about the dramatic gamble he made earlier—signing a contract to have his four stars appear on the *Ed Sullivan Show* on three consecutive Sunday nights. And when the Beatles landed in America on February 7 for the first time, amid thousands of screaming fans, the gamble immediately looked like a good one. Now the Beatles just had to deliver.

Their February concert schedule was limited. They performed live on the *Ed Sullivan Show* on February 9th (in New York City) and 16th (broadcast live from the Deauville Hotel in Miami Beach), and on tape the 23rd. The final performance was actually taped prior to their first live performance in New York. They also performed in concert at the Coliseum Theater in Washington, D.C. and at Carnegie Hall in Manhattan. Miami was mostly a vacation stop for the Beatles, except for dress rehearsals and that live Miami Beach performance on Sunday the 16th.

I attended the evening performance at the Deauville. It was my first time seeing the Beatles perform, and I expected them to sound much different in person. After all, what group could duplicate the intricate sound of a produced recording? What I saw, along with millions of others watching at home, was a brilliant performance, unaccompanied by the embellishments of pre-taped music or the flourishes of extra musicians. It was plain and simple—four band members striking notes of harmony and grace. That twelve-minute segment on *Sullivan*, combined with the first appearance the week before, drew a television audience of 150 million people. In both performances, the Beatles were electric. For the first time, Americans, always wary of advance billing and over-hyped "phenomena," had seen the artists and heard their rather wholesome sound live and with no technical enhancement. Suddenly, the stereotype of "mop-tops" singing meaningless music vanished. For three Sunday nights, the Beatles owned the American television audience, satisfying their loyal fans beyond all expectation and instantly welcoming millions of new fans.

Sullivan had played a major role in the success of the Beatles' "American gamble" by offering them the platform of prime time television. He would also, a year later, extend a special offer to me as a journalist. In August 1965, Sullivan, on the recommendation of Brian Epstein, hired me to do interviews for a special called "The Beatles at Shea Stadium," produced by Sullivan Productions. I sat in the New York Mets' dugout at Shea as Sullivan, the grand master of live television, watched the Beatles sing for their biggest audience yet. Sullivan sat there beaming. Just days before, I had stood backstage at CBS Studio 50 on Broadway, an old theater, watching the Beatles tape their single 1965 appearance on Sullivan's show. The marriage of Sullivan and the Beatles was a wonderful one. The world superstars benefited from the exposure, and the aging king of prime time resuscitated his program again and again with Beatles magic.

The Beatles, of course, also had a big impact on my own career as a broadcast journalist. It's an unlikely story, and it starts with the simple question: How did a twenty-one year-old radio news director at a small-market station become the only American journalist to travel with the

Beatles' official party to every stop on their first two tours of America?

It is a remarkable tale of fate mixed with some personal enterprise, and bares a lesson that anyone in the news business understands: No news story waits to find you; if you want to be in the game, you have to just stand up and play. The irony is that I did not want to be involved with what I considered a fad—I was just doing my job.

Weeks after the Beatles' trip to Miami in February 1964, word leaked out that the group would launch the biggest tour in history come August. There was a tentative concert date set for Jacksonville, Florida. WFUN Radio's program director, a young and sophisticated deejay named Dick Starr, urged me to secure an interview with the Beatles at the Jacksonville venue, the closest location to Miami.

I wrote a letter to Brian Epstein and included some letters written to our station by devoted Beatles fans. The letter simply outlined the reasons why I was requesting this one-time interview: fans' dedication, the impact of the Beatles, and the role of radio in supporting the Beatles' music. To my shock and utter disbelief, I received the following letter, dated July 10, 1964:

Dear Mr. Kane,

The Beatles would be pleased to have you join us in our traveling press party during the tour commencing August 19 in San Francisco.

The sum of $2500.00 will cover hotel, ground transportation and other services.

Derek Taylor, our press secretary, will be in touch regarding further arrangements.

We look forward to seeing you on the journey across America,

Brian Epstein

I had asked for one interview. In return, I was invited to travel with the band and be granted unimaginable access! Station management was flabbergasted at our good fortune, though there was the concern of money; after all, WFUN was tiny. Dick Starr solved that problem by signing up forty-plus stations in a network that would pay to receive reports I would feed to WFUN. Suddenly, it was a go. A most unusual assignment had been placed in my lap.

I was nervous and conflicted about the assignment. I knew little about entertainment and, from a professional point of view, cared even less. "Why not send a jock?" I said. But Starr and higher management wanted a newsperson. They wanted me. There was no turning back. I had to say yes. And with some reluctance, I did.

My immediate task was to prepare myself for a journey that no one had ever taken. And in early August, I received the following letter from the secretary to Derek Taylor, the Beatles' press secretary.

Dear Mr. Kane,

Further to our telephone conversation of last week, I have the pleasure of confirming the arrangements for the charter flight with the Beatles during the American tour.

The plane will depart from San Francisco on August 20th. The cost of the seat will be 350 pounds [approximately $1,250] for the whole trip. I am enclosing a list of hotels. I hope this covers everything.

With best wishes for a very good trip.

Diana Vero
Secretary to Derek Taylor

Much later, I would discover that a standard business card I had enclosed in my letter to Epstein was the reason for my good luck. The card listed our station, WFUN, and six other stations owned by our group. The six others were mostly gospel and rhythm-and-blues stations designed to appeal to an African-American audience, yet Brian Epstein was none the wiser. Because of the design of the card, Epstein was under the false impression that I was the news boss of seven stations! Duly impressed, he invited me to join the Beatles' official party.

As I said, in the life of a reporter, you can't get the story unless you're willing to ask for it. But you might get more than you bargained for. The die was cast. I would leave behind the streets of Miami for thirty-three days and make a journey across North America. Untold adventure awaited me, I was sure.

I left Miami for San Francisco on August 19, 1964, with anxiety and apprehension. I came back with an unexpectedly rich education, a self-styled master's degree in contemporary culture. This trip would also take me to the outer limits of human behavior at a time when American life was changing. I would see things and experience events that seemed shocking at the time. Yes, there is sex, drugs, and a lot of rock-and-roll in this story. But there is also revelation threaded throughout about the way we were and the world we lived in.

It was 1964. America was about to slide into an abyss of war and division. The times would test us. But first, the Beatles and the generation of Americans who adored them would join in a relationship, a love affair between entertainers and fans that would last into the next century.

And back there, in the beginning, before we all realized the power of their presence and the impact of their music, this naïve but curious reporter got the gift of a generation—I had a ticket to ride.

CHAPTER 2:
A Stranger in the Bedroom

Reporters' denials not withstanding, attitude can play a pivotal role in covering a story. My attitude on that first day in San Francisco—the day I met the fab flower girl near the airport—was one of cynicism. After all, I was a reporter of the hard news bent, more comfortable covering the courthouse and the coroner's office than traipsing around with a bunch of entertainers. I viewed this assignment with anxiety and trepidation and was prepared not to like the Beatles. That was probably just a defense mechanism.

The first event in San Francisco was a press conference, with several hundred news hounds crowding into a small meeting room. One press conference was scheduled for each city, and these sessions were clear evidence of why the Beatles would come to disdain most reporters. The questions in almost all cities were dull-witted and fired off in disrespect, telegraphing that some news people thought the Beatles were brainless. Their answers were a perfect match.

San Francisco Press Conference:

Q: How was your trip?
LENNON: It was like a plane trip, you know.
Q: How often do you get haircuts?
LENNON: Uh, about once every three weeks.
Q: Who is your tailor?
McCARTNEY: A fella called Millings.
Q: Savile Row?

LENNON: No.

Q: Where?

McCARTNEY: A little back street in London.

Q: How frightened were you getting in that cage today?

LENNON: What cage?

McCARTNEY: At the airport. [The reference is to a cage used to protect the Beatles from fans and flying objects while allowing fans to see them.]

JOHN: Uh, it wasn't bad, 'cuz somebody had been up there and tested it.

STARR: In fact, all the press went up and tested it.

Q: Why did you leave so soon?

McCARTNEY: They told us to go and so we got off, you know. We're very obedient.

LENNON: Oh, we are! Arf arf!

Q: Your hair looks red.

LENNON: Well, I just had me a shower, and you never know how it's going to look . . . hee hee.

Q: What did you have to eat today?

LENNON: Corn flakes with jelly beans and chips.

Q: Is your hair real?

McCARTNEY: Is yours?

The trivial interrogation would continue at every stop, and looking into their eyes at their first press conference encounter, I realized that they were hungry for normal discourse. That would come later and would help me to bond with them. But first, it was time to go to my room and prepare for the worst.

The hotel check-in was easy. The Beatles' advance traveling party was pre-registered, and I took the elevator to the top floor. This was the headquarters floor, as it would be in most hotels. Brian Epstein, Derek Taylor and the official party members were all housed here, just yards away from the rooms of the reporters and photographers. Road managers Malcolm Evans and Neil Aspinall paced up and down the hallway, looking for intruders. Evans, I would learn, was also always looking for women. Emerging from the elevator, I introduced myself. They were polite, but kept their eyes on the emergency exits where local police helped guard the doors. They were determined to stop intruders. They missed one.

At the turn of the key, my door opened to a small studio room with a convertible bed. Sitting on the bed was a woman dressed in a blue uniform with a skirt that slid well above her knees. I was surprised. I asked, "Am I in the wrong room?"

"No," she said. "I am."

She stood and looked out the window at a vacant parking lot below. My mind was racing. Was she alone? Was I about to be robbed? Even worse, I thought, would there be violence? Getting more shaky by the second, I blurted, "So what are you doing here?"

She sat down. That's when I noticed the silver wings above the left pocket of her blouse, and the familiarity of her smile.

The phone rang. It was Derek Taylor, inviting me and the other press travelers to a large room on the same floor. It was an important meeting—an introduction for the small cadre of newsmen who would be sending most of the intimate details of this first-of-its-kind tour to the world.

I grabbed my tape recorder and notepad. The intruder reached over and put her hand on my arm. She said, "I'm a stewardess from your plane. I heard you talking about being with the Beatles. So I looked up your room. I want to meet them in the worst way, if you know what I mean."

I replied, "I'll be back in a while, but maybe you should get out of here."

She answered, "I'll just stay for a while."

I raced down the hallway; how I would deal with my uninvited guest would have to wait. This was an important meeting, a chance to meet the other media people on the tour. Ivor Davis was a young reporter for the *London Daily Express*. Art Schreiber, a national correspondent for Westinghouse Radio, would join us in New York. Ron Gunther and Ron Joy were photographers. Jim Stagg was a deejay for KYW radio in Cleveland. Later in the tour, a Hartford deejay, Long John Wade, would join us, along with other personalities who jumped on for a stop or two.

Derek Taylor, a slim, handsome, thirty-something former journalist, greeted us at the door. After the customary introductions, Taylor outlined the daily regimen, including instructions on security, communications on travel arrangements and rules of engagement.

Taylor would try to make "the boys" available to us daily, whether at the hotels and dressing rooms, on the plane or on the fly. We would, he said, allow them as much privacy as possible, and in return, he would guarantee access. It was the first time I had heard anyone describe the Beatles as "the boys." Taylor, Brian Epstein and most of their intimates called them the boys. It was an appropriate moniker, since it might have been awkward to refer to intimates as the Beatles. The boys was a convenient designation.

The boys were in different parts of the suite. George Harrison, sipping a rum and Coke and appearing wasted from a seventeen-hour trip, stared into space. George's complexion was marred by a bad case of headlights, a code word for pimples. Ringo was sitting quietly in a chair across from John Lennon, who looked like he was in a coma with his eyes open. Paul McCartney was combing his hair, something he would do many times over in the days ahead.

I introduced myself to Paul, George and Ringo, and then heard the words, "What's your problem, man?" It was Lennon.

"What do you mean?"

"Why are you dressed like a fag ass, man? What's with that. How old are you?" Lennon was not joking. From the corner of my eye, I could see a look of revulsion on the face of Brian Epstein.

Awkwardly, I retorted, "Well, it's better than looking scruffy and messed up like you." I smiled, but he didn't.

My face felt like it drained of its color. Adrenaline rushed through my body with a tinge of depression, and my body reacted instantly. I moved across the room, grabbed my tape recorder and proceeded to do three short interviews with Paul, George and Ringo. Finally, I could avoid the confrontation no more. I asked my antagonist to talk.

I shifted the theme and asked Lennon about the undeclared war in Vietnam. It was a strange question to ask, and it caught him by surprise. His face lit up, and he launched a scathing diatribe against the *Gulf of Tonkin Resolution* and the escalating conflict. I was taken aback by the intensity of his anger and knowledge base, and also by the eloquence of his protest.

So I had met John Lennon, observing for the first time that angry energy that would allow him to make beautiful and poignant music, fight for the needs of the hungry, make love in public, and prophesy doom for America in Vietnam all during a sixteen-year period that would end on a grim night in the shadow of Central Park in New York City.

With the session over, I faced reality. My tape was packed with some decent interviews, but my mind was filled with dark thoughts. Mainly, I had managed to insult John Lennon. This was not a good start. Plus, there was the haunting thought of my causing a security breach by not evicting the flight attendant from my spartan hotel room. I could be the first person ever expelled from a Beatles tour.

As I walked back to my room, two abrupt events changed the course of day one. First came a tap on my shoulder. I turned around and John Lennon was there. He said, "Hey, really enjoyed the interview, 'specially about the war in Asia. Liked the talk. Look forward to more stuff. Sorry about the clothes bullshit."

"John, it was great meeting you," was all I said.

Lennon had shown me real emotion there. That and the sight at the far end of the hall lifted my spirits. There was Malcolm Evans, the Beatles' happy-go-lucky road manager, arm in arm with an attractive woman, chatting it up like old friends. The body language was unmistakable. It was the woman with the flight wings and the short skirt. I never saw her again.

Chapter 3:
Seventy-two Hours of Madness

In its storied history, the Cow Palace in San Francisco has housed political conventions, car shows, business expositions and, yes, cows. It was built in 1941 as a hall for livestock expositions and quickly evolved into a staging point for troops preparing for combat in World War II.

The venerable hall scored many firsts, but no one was quite ready for the first that happened at 8 p.m. on August 19, 1964. It would be the Beatles' first concert on their great tour of America—their largest concert to date at that point—and they would play before 17,130 fevered and frenzied fans.

The backstage area was actually a long hallway lined with several trailers. The Beatles were in and about their trailer, looking nervous. I paced outside the mobile green room, getting ready to see the action in the crowd. The boys were smoking and joking with each other inside. They wore blue suits and stayed close to the guitars. George was leaning against the trailer, shaking. Malcolm Evans and Neil Aspinall peeked out front to stake out the crowd. The road managers emerged from the curtains with worried looks. Brian Epstein then decided to have a look at the crowd himself. I followed him with my tape recorder.

Inside the arena we witnessed entertainment futility. The Bill Black Combo, Jackie DeShannon, and the Righteous Brothers (backed by the Exciters) were the opening acts. When Epstein and I made our way to the rear of the arena, we could see rows and rows of hyperactivity. Already, teenagers were stomping their feet on the ground, creating a rumble that resembled thunderclaps. Jackie DeShannon, a mere twenty years old, animated and excited, was trying to sing over the din. Her voice was drowned out in a sea of noise.

From the rear, a group of fanatics started screaming in unison, "We want the Beatles! We want the Beatles! We want the Beatles!" The chants lasted through Jackie and the Righteous Brothers.

Down the narrow walkways between sections, I glanced at the security people by the stage. Evans and Aspinall took their places at stage right and left, the last lines of defense against fans who might get too close.

Getting the real picture would require some quick movement. I ran to the trailer area where the boys, now holding their instruments, stood ready to climb up the steps. It was hot. They looked nervous. George was biting his lip. I was beginning to feel queasy and edgy myself. After all, who knew what to expect? I returned to the inside of the Cow Palace to experience the Beatles' entrance from the fans' point of view. The Righteous Brothers were wrapping up as I walked to the rear of the hall and kneeled next to a row of fans. My timing was unfortunate.

A minute or two passed. Suddenly, led by John, the Beatles bounded onto the stage looking buoyant and thrilled to be there. As they began the concert with "Twist and Shout," I felt a hammer-like strike to the back of my neck and rolled into the middle of an aisle, where I was trampled by a stampede of girls and boys who were using my body as a stepping stone to get closer to the stage. I tried to get up, even using my tape recorder as a shield, but every time I stood up I was sent back to the canvas, which, in this case, was solid concrete. Crawling into a row of seats, I parked myself on the lap of a rather heavy boy, who then stood up and gave me his seat. The youngster was so involved in the surrounding Beatlemania that he had forgotten the ice cream cone in his hand, which was melting and dripping into the zipper section of my pants. I was out of breath, bruised in the rear end, wet and sticky from melted ice cream, and annoyed that I had decided to do my duty and experience my first moments of Beatles insanity with the crowd.

Trying to catch my breath, sweating bullets and fearing another surge, I glanced to the left where a young woman was screaming, but not for the Beatles. Her leg was twisted and she was writhing in pain. Her elbows were scraped to the bone. When the guys with the stretcher arrived, they diagnosed a broken leg. Before you knew it, the arena had turned into a triage center. The girl was whisked away, and over in the right section of seats, nurses were carrying out three girls who fainted. A number of kids felled by exhaustion and the heat were sprawled on the floor.

By the time the Beatles began "All My Loving," I was carefully making my way to the front of the crowd to watch the action. That's when the jellybeans started flying. Undoubtedly, it was George's fault. In press interviews, he had been complaining that Ringo was stealing his "jelly babies"—much softer candies sold in England. This had prompted American fans to load up on jellybeans—the much harder American variety. The jellybeans were flying across the Cow Palace. One hit me in the neck, but my troubles were minor. Some fans had been sitting in a section behind the Beatles and were firing them at the band from behind. John looked irritated as he joined in perfect harmony with Paul on "She Loves You." The next day, Ringo and I talked jellybeans:

> KANE: How did you like the jellybeans?
> STARR: They hurt. Hey, America . . . don't throw them jelly-
> beans. Streamers are good, you know. They don't hurt. Get
> me some streamers. Jellybeans are too hard. Do you have any,
> Larry?

The Beatles' concert performances were to last thirty-three minutes, but the first concert at the Cow Palace lasted thirty-eight minutes. It was stopped twice because of the jellybean jamboree. The police took it upon themselves to call for the short breaks, hoping to get the message to the fans that the jellybeans were dangerous. It didn't help. The concert ended with "Long Tall Sally." I ran in back of the curtain to watch the guys exit the stage. Ringo came down first. He looked relieved and he waved as he came by. John, Paul, and George ran off, and the race to escape the Cow Palace began. Derek Taylor had advised us to run immediately out the exit door for the cars when the performance ended. We would head directly to the airport.

But I had to get one last look at the arena. I ran to the stage area, where the crush of the crowd was growing. In the rear, a squad of medics was carrying injured kids to a first aid station by hand and by stretcher. I recorded what I saw on tape, then, adrenaline flowing, I ran as fast as I could toward the cars. When I reached the trailer area, an ambitious police officer stopped me in my tracks. I remember his words well: "Get out of here now. Who are you? Get the hell out." I frantically tried to plead my case as I noticed, through the opening at the end of trailers' row, that the motorcade was ready to roll. I begged the officer. For some reason, he let me go, and with my heavy load I galloped down the rear of the Cow Palace, reaching the last car of the convoy just in time.

I sweated all the way to the airport as my companions in the car—fellow newsies and the Beatles' assistant press secretary, Bess Coleman—chuckled over my self-imposed misadventures at the Cow Palace. The motorcade made its way to a remote area of San Francisco International Airport. And what a sight! The boys were exiting an ambulance—a deception used to get them safely away from onrushing fans at the concert site and the airport. The ambulance tactic would become a favorite on the tour until fans became wise to it. Eventually, other devices (a fish truck, for example) would be used.

Getting in and out safely would become a challenge in each city, and it wouldn't get easier for the band members. For the people with them, it would become a nightmare. The Beatles' organization was hardly prepared for the everyday surprises of the American tours. The credentials required to identify us as traveling members of the Beatles' press party changed in every city. There was almost constant confusion. And although they were totally devoted to protecting their friends from Liverpool, road managers Neil Aspinall and Malcolm Evans were not security experts and were novices at crowd control. Still, they were experts at protecting the boys from the potentially scandalous situations that lay ahead.

Climbing up the steps of the aircraft, I got my first look at the American Flyers Electra that would carry the Beatles across the United States and Canada. It was a sleek aircraft for those days, a turboprop that, depending on its configuration, could hold up to 130 passengers. The reporters were urged to sit in the rear, close to Derek Taylor and Brian Epstein. The other entertainers, including Jackie DeShannon and the Righteous Brothers, stayed in front, along with technicians and equipment handlers. Unlike the sophisticated, high-tech road shows of today, most of the equipment was loaded and unloaded from this single aircraft.

I found a window seat four rows from the rear and the small alcove where the Beatles sat. Glancing back, I could see Ringo reading a *Green Hornet* comic book. John and Paul were just sitting there, in the recovery zone. George was sipping the official drink of the Beatles' tour, rum and Coke.

The flight to Las Vegas would last less than one hour. Two friend-ly flight attendants brought snacks and drinks around. Fifteen min-utes into the flight, I decided to visit the rear, but without my tape recorder. It was important to make it clear to the Beatles that I wasn't always going to drop around, tape recorder in hand, hounding them for interviews. Otherwise, I would be treated like a pariah. We talked about the night.

"How did it feel out there?" I asked.

John replied, "Not safe. Can't sing when you're scared for your life."

I described my escapade in the aisle, which prompted a pretty good laugh all around.

"Good luck in Vegas," I said, and that was that. It was a simple hello and goodbye. There would be time to learn their real characters later. In fact, the next day would provide the genuine test.

Arrival at Las Vegas was uneventful; that is, until the cars pulled up to the Sahara Hotel. Hundreds of girls standing at the entrance set a beeline for the caravan as it rolled in. Private detectives escorted the Beatles inside, hugging the boys' bodies as they bumbled through the crowd. The man assigned to John covered his body so completely that they looked like conjoined twins hopping their way into the hotel complex.

Dragging my feet, grasping my monster of a tape recorder and hoping for quiet, I entered my room on the twenty-third floor of the Sahara—the Beatles' floor. It was time for rest. In forty-eight hours of sheer madness, I had managed to turn off a Beatle, unwittingly harbor a strange woman in a hotel room, get stomped on by a delirious crowd at the Cow Palace, and nearly miss the car to the airport. I drifted off to sleep, excited to be there but apprehensive about what might come next. Of course, what would happen in the next twenty-four hours would actually make the first day seem like a day at the beach.

The heavy knock on the door came around 5 a.m. The face in the doorway was that of Malcolm Evans, a face that would cheer anyone up, even in the middle of the night.

I will never forget his words: "We need you. Can you put on a tie and jacket?" I had known Malcolm Evans for less than forty-eight hours, but I knew he was worried about something.

Evans waited outside while I got myself together. What could it be? I couldn't imagine, but I knew that whatever it was, the stakes were high. It turned out that the stakes were so high in the strato-sphere, the entire Beatles tour was at stake.

In the hallway, Evans was joined by Derek Taylor and Neil Aspinall. They explained that a dangerous situation was afoot. Twin sisters were in John Lennon's room, catching autographs and posing for pictures with Lennon. They were part of a group of fans who had penetrated security. Most of the visitors had left, but these girls were sleeping on the second bed in John's room.

"It's all okay," Derek said. "Not a damn thing happened in there."

I scrutinized his face for hidden meanings and to gauge his sincerity.

Derek added, "Their mother is in the lobby, demanding to know what they're doing up there, and we need you to go and tell her everything is proper."

"Where are the girls?" I asked. Malcolm grinned. Neil said nothing. Derek gave me the answer.

"They're in the room," he said.

"Why me? I'm not going to be part of any lying," I replied.

"There's nothing to lie about. They just came in to visit," Derek insisted.

"Okay, but send the girls down," I replied. I made it clear that I would trust his word but not be part of any whitewash.

Finally, I turned and said again, "Why me?"

Derek answered, "You're a reporter. You look trustworthy."

Mal Evans and I took the elevator to the lobby, where we approached a woman in her mid-thirties who appeared to be in the grip of worry; although she did have casino chips in her hand. Where had she been while her daughters were sneaking past security to join a party in an upstairs room? Besides the casino chips, this woman also held in her hands the power to destroy the wholesome image of the Beatles. Even the appearance of impropriety in the climate of America in August 1964 would be devastating to them.

Taking Taylor's word, I identified myself to the mother and explained the girls' visit as an innocent quest for pictures and autographs. She wasn't convinced. But when the elevators opened a minute later, the girls came out, smiling broadly and with innocent looks, relaying the details of John's kindness. The girls looked about fourteen or fifteen. A police officer was with them, looking concerned in that police-officer sort of way. He said nothing. His role in their exit remains unclear to this day.

As dawn was breaking, mother and daughters left the premises. Malcolm Evans grinned. Derek Taylor called up to Brian Epstein with a status report, and then Derek and Malcolm thanked me warmly. Still, I didn't feel good about it.

"Was John messing with those kids?" I asked

Derek said, "No."

Was I naïve or uncaring? Neither. I just couldn't believe that a Beatle would risk his future by getting involved with young girls in that way. Lennon, who wasn't aware of my involvement, professed his innocence to me. To this day, I don't know what happened in that hotel room. I do know that, a day later, the Las Vegas authorities investigated a report that a member of the Beatles' official party had had underage girls in his room. The investigation turned up nothing. Rumors have circulated for years that Brian Epstein paid off the mother after conferences with her lawyers in Los Angeles. Though no legal action has ever been confirmed, like many legends of Beatles history, this episode remains a subject of speculation.

In 1967, Derek Taylor confided to me that he was convinced the entire episode had been a setup designed to generate cash by extorting the Beatles. The real story will never be known, but the incident, real or manufactured, was a close call for the boys, placing them in high jeopardy.

Celebrities can be strange creatures. Some believe their own positive press clippings and act liked spoiled children, demanding that they be treated differently because of who they think they have become. The next day, I learned that the Beatles, at that point in time, had no such rose-colored vision of superstardom. Derek Taylor invited all the traveling press into a session with the boys in their room. Ivor Davis, writer for the *London Daily Express* and ghostwriter for George Harrison's daily column, had come up from his Hollywood beat to join the tour. Waiting for the Beatles to arrive, Ivor commented, "You know, Larry, they're really nice guys. I like them. How about you?"

I replied, "Really don't know yet."

The Beatles walked in, looking tired from the Cow Palace concert. Lennon and McCartney plopped themselves down on the sides of the bed, with Ringo and George choosing chairs. I approached Ringo first, then George, Paul and John. The sessions were more casual than the first, with a good sign—they remembered my first name. Ivor and deejay Jim Staggs from Cleveland stood beside me, firing away their own questions.

I was quite happy with myself. That feeling lasted all of two minutes. Returning to my room, I pressed the rewind button on my tape recorder. Next, I pressed play. There was a silence, the terrifying sound of hum, and the truth sinking in that the entire session was gone. Feverishly, I pressed rewind and play again and again. Still, I heard nothing. My morning's work had vanished into the dark hole known as "technical difficulties."

Over the next several hours, I toured the streets of Las Vegas and its suburbs, searching in vain for a new tape recorder or someone who could fix the monster I had. No luck. I was stuck in broadcast quicksand—no tape recorder, no interviews. "The Sound" with the Beatles was already a part of my daily filings to my station, which distributed the reports to all of our subscribing stations. It was essential material. Dejected, I slumped in the cab, glancing at the passing stores. Then I saw it. The sign read: "Discount Appliances." In that shabby little store, I found a smaller, used tape recorder that actually worked.

A bigger problem remained—how to recoup the lost interviews. Time was running out—the first of two shows at the Las Vegas Convention Center was set for 4 p.m. The Beatles had also scheduled a photo op with a one-armed bandit. They couldn't get to the casino floor because of crowd issues, so hotel management brought the floor to them. When would I get my interview?

I called Derek Taylor, who said he would try to work it out. Deejay Jim Staggs heard about my dilemma and offered me some of his tape, a kind gesture considering that our little network was feeding his competitor in Cleveland. Staggs' material was good, but I needed more and I needed it fast. Time was running out as I left for the concert.

The Las Vegas Convention Center was small by today's standards. A little more than eight thousand people jammed into the complex for the afternoon show, many of them children and teens driven to Las Vegas by their parents from California locales. The crowd was crazed, but there was a difference in the hall this time: Police and highway patrolmen surrounded the stage. I interviewed a few fans, making my first interview contact with the "Beatles-obsessed." This group would surface in every city.

I knew Beatles-obsessed people the minute I saw them. Not mere members of the normal Beatles fan club, they filled a special place in their psyches with the band. The Beatles-obsessed were typically female fans who truly believed they were married to one of the boys, or deserved to be. The "obsessed" also included young men who held the belief that they were related to one of the Beatles, resembled them, or deserved to be in their presence. Unlike the normally dedicated fans, the obsessed were quieter and not as obvious in their quest to get close. Therefore, they were more dangerous and looked less suspicious.

The one I met in Las Vegas trailed behind me as I walked to the backstage area hoping to resurrect my lost interview. I turned around and said, "Where are you headed?" The girl, looking rather normal, answered, "I'm looking for the bathroom."

"It's back in the lobby area," I replied. At that point, at Olympian speed, she raced past me and two security guards, making a beeline for the dressing room. Within seconds, Malcolm Evans, standing by the door, scooped her up and carried her in his arms out to the exit. Passing by me, she said, quite calmly, "Paul is waiting for me. I'm late. He'll want to know where I am." I think she believed it.

The incident would make a good item for my next reports, but without Beatles interviews, the reports would be boring. I needed to find Derek Taylor, and fast. My filing deadline was only hours away.

Taylor emerged from the dressing room minutes later. He invited me in, and with great compassion for my dilemma, the boys agreed to sit for another interview. They all expressed sympathy for my technical mishap, with Ringo even saying, "What a bummer, man." Considering that we were just getting to know each other and that they had literally just finished their second concert in the past eighteen hours, it was a wonderful gesture. That interview session would also help me develop a fascinating story that would culminate two thousand miles away on the tail end of a major hurricane.

A newspaper account had quoted Paul McCartney as saying the Beatles would never play before a segregated crowd. His comment addressed a timely subject, with the civil rights movement coming into its own in America. I decided to introduce the subject: a report that promoters had ordered seating by race inside the Gator Bowl at a concert scheduled for September 11 in Jacksonville, Florida.

KANE: What about this comment I heard from you, Paul, about racial integration at the various concerts?
McCARTNEY: We don't like it if there's any segregation or anything, because we're not used to it, you know . . . it just seems daft to me. I mean it may seem right to some people, but to us, it just seems a bit daft.
KANE: Well, you're gonna play Jacksonville, Florida. Do you anticipate any difference of opinion?

McCARTNEY: I don't know really, y'know, because I don't
know what people in America are like. I think they'd be a bit
silly to segregate people . . . cause you know . . . I don't think
colored people are any different, y'know, they're just the same
as anyone else. But, y'know, over here there are some people
who think that they're sorta animals or something, and I just
think it's stupid, y'know.
KANE: Yeah . . .
McCARTNEY: You can't treat other people like animals. And
so, y'know—I wouldn't mind 'em sitting next to me. Great,
y'know, 'cause some of our best friends are colored people . . .

It was the first in a series of references to the Jacksonville concert.
Paul's comments may seem patronizing now, but even in 1964 the
word "colored" was still being used by many people. His reference—
"some of my best friends are colored"—was a telltale phrase of subtle
prejudice used by people who were itching to profess their tolerance
by claims of association with minorities. Did that coded meaning
apply in Paul's case? I can't be certain, but his comments naturally
made me wonder.

The Beatles' views on race would come into play at the Gator Bowl
in Jacksonville. But even sooner, in some caustic moments aboard the
airplane, I would personally face some contradictions in the areas of
tolerance and prejudice. The aftermath of those disturbing moments
would give me a clear view of the four Beatles as real people, deeply
affected by the impact of human behavior and the consequences of
pain and hurt.

CHAPTER 4:
Fishing for Trouble

The flight from Las Vegas to Seattle was a daytime affair, allowing for spectacular views of the Cascade Range of Oregon and Washington, its rolling hills and mountain peaks jutting into a blue sky. The Beatles, especially a quiet and meditative George, looked out the windows of their rear compartment to contemplate the view. While they feasted on the sights, a large portable reel-to-reel tape player was spinning away, playing music for them, rock instrumentals with a heavy backbeat. With the music in the background, I read the Las Vegas newspapers.

About an hour into the flight, a word reached my ears that I couldn't ignore. In everyone's life, there are certain words that spark instant revulsion. I raised my head from my book, and my mind raced quickly, along with the beat of my heart, when I heard the word *kike*. Worse yet, the ethnic slur came from the rear, where the Beatles and Derek Taylor were sitting. I didn't race to conclusions. After all, I could have misunderstood what was being said. I bit my lip and hoped I was wrong. Then I heard the word again, this time in part of a sentence. "The kike did—," I heard, though I couldn't be sure whose voice had said it. Although it's hardly a part of the current hate vernacular, the word was used generously by bigots in the 1960s.

Irritated, disappointed and agitated, I got up from my seat and approached the rear, about five rows back. My growing-up years, especially those I had spent in suburban Miami, had sensitized me to words that hurt. And *this* hurt, especially at this time and place.

I approached the opening to the Beatles' small compartment, stuck my head in and blurted out, "Listen. I just want to say that I heard a word that really pisses me off. I'm Jewish, and I won't stand for that crap. I mean, whoever said it, can't you think before you talk?"

The Beatles, Derek Taylor and Malcolm Evans looked startled. Sheepishly, without the courage to wait for an answer, I returned to my seat, figuring that the outburst would end my travels with the band, or at the least would rupture the rapport I had established in just a few days.

Minutes passed. Then Derek Taylor came forward and knelt alongside my aisle seat. He said, "Look, I'm really sorry. It came from me. It's just a word that is used quite casually in English life, and I didn't mean anything."

I replied, "But you didn't say it." I knew the voice hadn't been his. "What do you mean?"

"I mean, *you* didn't say it."

Derek smiled. "Doesn't matter. It was said nonetheless. I'm sorry."

At that point, I felt foolish about the whole thing. But I also knew that if I had let it go and ignored the slight, I could not have lived with myself the rest of the tour.

Minutes later, Lennon came over and sat down. I don't remember our exact words, but we had a relaxed and compassionate conversation about the roots of prejudice in Liverpool. It was a good talk. As we spoke, Ringo and George walked by. Ringo gave a wink, and George just said, "How you doing, Larry?"

Paul didn't make a special trip. He did pass by on the way to the bathroom and said, "Great working with you, Larry." It was, I interpreted, his way of smoothing the episode over. I felt good, but still self-conscious that I had responded so aggressively.

Whatever the roots of the prejudice, and whatever the reasons someone had spoken that word, I knew I would never hear it again for the remainder of the tour. And this incident did something else; it showed me that the Beatles possessed genuine compassion and feeling.

Two years later, Derek, who was by then the former Beatles press secretary (he was released after the 1964 tour by Brian Epstein), accompanied another rock group, the Byrds, on a publicity tour to Miami. At a private dinner with me, he brought up the subject. I had long forgotten, but Derek had not. He confirmed that he wasn't the one who had said the word and that the boys had been embarrassed. When I asked him who'd said it, he changed the subject.

In a strange way, this episode added to the familiarity developing between the Beatles and me. Certainly such episodes weren't the best way to get acquainted, but sometimes adversity can bring people closer.

Back on the Electra, my heart was still racing over the confrontation, and my ears were popping as the plane began a gradual descent. The next stop came into view. Seattle was more ready than Las Vegas had been for the Beatles' arrival, or so it seemed at first. I was learning quickly that, traveling with the Beatles, things weren't always what they seemed to be. The crowd at the Seattle-Tacoma airport was loud but under control. This all changed when the Beatles' party arrived at the low-rise Edgewater Inn Hotel in downtown Seattle.

Edgewater was an appropriate name, as the hotel's west side faced the water. In fact, our rooms were on the water, giving us not just a water view, but Elliott Bay and its currents splashing up to the base of the hotel's walls. You could fish from the window of your hotel room, which several of the Beatles tried to do, unsuccessfully.

Fearing a waterfront assault, the local harbor patrol had motorboats in the area. A small navy stood anchored just outside my hotel window. In front of the hotel, a barrier of wood and barbed wire had been set up, preventing fans from a frontal attack. Such extravagant security was an absolute necessity. Seattle's legions of Beatles followers were some of the most aggressive in the nation. So were Seattle's profiteers.

I got a sense of all this during a brief interview session at the Edgewater, when John Lennon indicated that the boys had received some prior intelligence.

KANE: What are your plans for Seattle?
LENNON: Well, y'know, we got some word that some hoodlums are goin' to sell some of the sheets, and towels, and carpet. We've got some plans, too.

The Beatles, four people who had great empathy for other human beings, devised a mean plot of their own in Seattle upon learning they were being used by unscrupulous business people to "cut" a profit. But before that piece of business would be carried out, there was a concert at hand, and no ordinary concert at that.

The Seattle Center Coliseum held about 14,000 people, but anyone who was there will tell you it felt and sounded like 140,000. The coliseum was modern before its time, and was a remarkable sound chamber with unusual acoustics. The screaming from the fans created a wail that reverberated from wall to wall of the oval coliseum, a sound resembling a jet engine or, I could imagine, the legions at the Roman Coliseum screaming for the gladiators. It was so intense and so filled with guttural passion that it took your breath away—and, temporarily, your hearing.

While I took in the roar of the crowd, I was missing a big backstage incident. Things were always flying and falling at Beatles concerts, but never had a person done so until Seattle. Walking to the dressing room before the concert, Ringo Starr heard a thump. To his right, a female fan was suddenly sprawled on the floor, having fallen twenty-five feet from an air vent overhead. I spoke to him about it later.

> KANE: So what happened?
> STARR: Well, y'know, I was walking to the dressing area
> [and] I heard the noise . . . saw this girl just laying on the floor
> kinda looking up in sorta disbelief. So I said, "You okay?" and
> she didn't say a thing, just got up and ran into the arena and
> into the crowd. It was scary, Larry.

The entire scene at Seattle Center Coliseum was scary. Only about fifty police officers and security guards stood on patrol surrounding the stage. The opening acts were drowned out completely by the hysteria. Jackie DeShannon was into her final song, which was, appropriately, the hard-rocking "Shout." The screams were now at such a pitch that for the first time on the tour I had to hold my hands over my ears and grasp my tape recorder between my elbows. Actual pain had set in. And it was just beginning.

When Jackie moved offstage, a local deejay introduced the Beatles. Standing alongside the riser, I could see abject fear in the eyes of Paul McCartney. Paul always had an upbeat look, but his lips pursed and his brows tightened in signs of obvious tension. Then I saw the first girl lunge at the stage, running fast and seemingly trying to pull her hair out of her own scalp. A security guard managed to take her down with a tackle around the legs. The combination of noise, onrushing fans, and jellybeans flying randomly about the small stage made me feel that I was in the middle of a psychotic ward with fourteen thousand crazies. In fact, these were children who had mothers, fathers, teachers, and, I presume, normal lives. In no time, you could see trauma on both sides of the stage. To my left, three girls were stretched out on the ground and were receiving oxygen from nurses. To my right, some sailors were helping police fend off a heaving and hollering crowd of kids who had broken through police lines.

John Lennon was sweating profusely as the band members began their set, yet he forced a steady smile for the crowd. He was, as always, an incredible showman. Unlike future rock stars, the Beatles in 1964 did not jump up and down around the stage. Their movements were minimal, but John was certainly the most animated, often nodding a smile at a section of the crowd, blinking his eyes or winking at a fan. As I looked up at the riser, the realization set in that John and Paul were frightened. The scene was quickly getting out of control. Neil Aspinall was standing stage left, checking his watch. Could the band take thirty-three minutes of this chaos? Could I stand watching it? Could the young and vulnerable crowd survive it?

The concert proceeded with bodies lunging randomly, voices wailing from every direction, and policemen rushing about. Finally there was a short lull when the Beatles slowed down to play "If I Fell." "Long Tall Sally," which the band alternated with "Twist and Shout" as the final number on this tour, wasn't a favorite of mine, but when I heard the band play the first notes, I figured the rest of the evening would unfold without complications. But in the land of the Beatles, you were never safe until you locked the door of your hotel room, and even then, as I had learned in San Francisco, there might be strangers lurking.

The Beatles bowed in thanks to the audience and ran for the back, heading straight into an ambulance. There were three cars waiting for the rest of us, all Cadillacs. While a few of us reached for the rear doors, the crowd surged around us, boys and girls searching for their prey. This human tidal wave numbered in the thousands. The Seattle police, although valiant in their effort to keep the crowds away from the backstage doors, had simply been outnumbered.

The ambulance carrying the Beatles was long gone by the time the car I was in had all its passengers and was locked securely. And then again, as in the trampling rampage in San Francisco, I got the shakes. That howling crowd was surrounding the car in front of us, jumping on the roof and causing it to sway back and forth. The driver got out just in time—just before the roof caved in from the sheer weight. Thankfully, there were no passengers in the car yet as it was completely destroyed under the weight of frenzied fanatics. Several kids were bleeding from the shattered glass. The marauding fans had thought the Beatles were inside. Thank God they hadn't been.

Clearly, the hysterics were getting more dangerous at each stop. This was not a scene from the movie *A Hard Day's Night*; this was real life, and with the potential for calamity we had all just gotten a taste of, security would have to be reassessed.

Back at the hotel, safely resting in my waterfront room with the waves slowly splashing against the wall outside, I wrote some notes about the Seattle concert to prepare for my radio reports. And I wondered what the next stop would bring. Tired, but parched from the heat, I headed downstairs for a drink. In the lobby, I met up with Derek Taylor, who was not amused by the events of the day, especially the riotous car demolition I had witnessed earlier. Derek had watched the destruction from the Beatles ambulance on its way out of the coliseum. "Total bullshit," he said. "A bloody amateur hour."

In the weeks to come, I would learn that blame was an easy game in the security business. The promoters blamed the local police; the police blamed the promoters. Epstein and his staff, control freaks but unable to control security, soon realized that they would have to make certain demands to keep their charges healthy. While security challenges were discussed late into the night, the Beatles gathered in another room to hatch their plan for a parting shot.

The next morning I discovered that the Beatles, or someone in their party, had urinated on the carpets of their suite at the Edgewater. This was the apparent "plan" Lennon had mentioned to have the last laugh—or in this case the last drop—against local merchants who had planned to cut the rug up and sell it.

Takeoff from Seattle-Tacoma airport was smooth, but about forty-five minutes into the flight, the American Flyers charter turned around. Apparently, the proper customs forms had not been filled out. The problem was fixed when we arrived back in Seattle, and the plane took off again. The Beatles were on their way to Vancouver, their first Canadian stop, a breathtakingly beautiful city and a community that would test the limits of Beatlemania.

Prior to landing, the Beatles were visibly excited. They had been told that Vancouver would offer a visual treat. As the plane descended, I saw the late afternoon sun fading to the west, casting the mountains in hues of blue and gray. I was in the last row and could see Ringo Starr glancing out at the view, smiling widely. Ringo's smile was a wonder to watch. There were those who described him as "the sad Beatle," but they were mistaken. There was no more optimistic Beatle than Ringo Starr. From my perspective, he was the un-celebrity, the everyman among them. He looked at small pleasures with glee. I yelled back to him, "What a sight down there!" He replied, "Man, it is just beyond great, isn't it?"

Once the trip was over, I would remember Vancouver as a beautiful sight but an ugly night—a night of difficulty that even the best intentions couldn't have prevented. Sociologists might now read into what happened there as a precursor of events to come, beyond the Beatles. And as a reporter who has since covered the civil rights and antiwar revolutions of the sixties, hindsight tells me, too, that the events at Empire Stadium reflected not only the public's obsession with the Beatles, but also a simmering youthful unrest and defiance against the establishment. While most adults across America felt the Beatles were a bad influence on their children, certainly the delight and joyfulness inspired by the Beatles and their performances also provoked and would provoke maddening reactions and potential violence among their charged fans. But what I witnessed in Vancouver went far beyond the norm.

The first ominous reports filtered through our motorcade shortly after we'd deplaned and set out toward the Hotel Georgia in downtown Vancouver. We never saw the hotel. Advised of unruly crowds out front, and wary from the close calls of the night before, Brian Epstein decided to make it a marathon evening. The Beatles would go directly to Empire Stadium, play the concert, and then fly to Los Angeles in the middle of the night.

The motorcade took a back route to Empire Stadium, giving us a guided tour of various neighborhoods and the scenic mountains surrounding them. Eventually, Empire Stadium came into view. Empire was a relatively new stadium that housed professional soccer and football teams. It had not been designed for a concert of the Beatles kind. Of course, up until this point, there was no stadium or arena that had encountered Beatlemania. And so, when promoters and stadium officials drew up security plans for the Beatles concert, they called for the same number of police officers that cover baseball and football games. The official records show that a force of a hundred police officers was in the stadium on the night of Saturday, August 22, 1964. Soon, they were facing far more than they could handle.

The mood was upbeat as the Beatles arrived beneath the rafters of Empire. Why not? It seemed that the coast was clear, at least compared to the near-disaster in Seattle. For the first time, I saw George looking totally relaxed before a concert, playing his guitar and joking with Derek, with whom he seemed to have a close relationship. John and Paul, prepping backstage by combing their hair and straightening their thin ties, seemed excited, animated and primed for their first North American concert in an outdoor stadium. Walking down the tunnel that led out to the field as the Bill Black Combo took the stage, I could hear the pounding of feet and the beginning of the screaming.

As I arrived on the turf, I noticed the green grass and the stadium lights begin to blend in with the fading sunlight. The air was cool. It was wonderful to stand there on the field and watch the crowd, a far less claustrophobic experience than I'd had indoors in Seattle.

It was 8 p.m. and I hadn't had dinner; I was hungry. I walked up into the stands and onto the stadium ramps, and noticed a familiar sight—a vendor behind a stand with no customers in line out front. Few Beatles fans would ever leave their seats to buy something; they were afraid of being left behind, abandoned, of getting lost in the crush, and of missing their favorite song. Food concession operators did not make out well at Beatles concerts. But this was good for me, as I quickly grabbed my hot dog and headed back through the stands to a field gate, where a security guard let me through.

My reporter's sense started tingling. I began to witness a slow but steady movement of bodies down into the aisles of the middle stands just above the field. Mal Evans was surveying the scene from behind the platform stage. I walked over to the stage, and over the noise, I whispered in his ear, "They're going to storm the field." He took his heavy glasses off, wiped his eyes and just smiled, an indication that he thought it couldn't happen. The field area, with the exception of some ground-level seats, was at that point still secure.

It was after nine when the Beatles took the stage, and five minutes later when about six thousand spectators (as police would estimate) started swarming onto the field, making a mad rush for the stage...and the Beatles. Adding to the mayhem were fans without tickets running in from outside the complex, using the force of sheer numbers to batter down the gates. This invasion and chaos would continue for a few minutes, until a local deejay tried to calm down the crowd.

Gordy Patridge, now fifty years old, watched it from the field seats. As he tells me, his memories of that night are still vibrant:

"The Fab Four ran onto the stage to the deafening scream of the fans. A rather large young woman in a white dress with large black polka dots wormed her way in front of us and was blocking our view of the stage. A couple of fellas beside us brought jellybeans to throw at the Beatles. These boys were throwing the jellybeans at the polka-dot girl, and she soon moved out of our way. The Beatles no sooner started playing and there was a surge towards the stage. At one point, the evening's emcee, radio announcer Red Robinson, stepped out on the stage to ask the crowd to calm down and sit down. John Lennon seemed quite incensed by this intrusion and was swearing at Red to 'get off the fucking bloody stage!' John was just the coolest! The concert didn't last long, and it was hard to make out any of the tunes with the screaming, but that didn't matter, I was at a Beatles concert!"

Another ominous pattern was beginning. The police were standing in lines to blockade the fans, but those lines kept falling back under the weight of the fans. After the third song, "All My Loving," John looked at Paul and they both shook their heads, signaling over the roar of the crowd that they would move from one song to another without waiting for the audience to react. No small talk or chitchat in this concert. By the time they reached the seventh song, "Can't Buy Me Love," there was hardly a pause to breathe. They were segueing briskly from song to song, their eyes moving steadily to survey the situation on the field.

Meanwhile, down on the field, I had moved close in behind the lines of police. The Vancouver police were extraordinary, heroically forming lines of resistance around the barriers that were meant to prevent the stampede that was happening nevertheless. Nightsticks or batons were never touched, but about mid-concert, the cops brought in the dogs. This had become a riot, pure and simple.

A few feet away from where I stood, several girls disappeared underneath the rampaging crowd. One of them screamed, "Help me . . . God help me!" I saw her legs and arms flailing out from all the legs that were walking over her. She and others were being trampled, forcing the police officers to break their line of defense and run into the crowd to pick up anyone who could be suffocating under the press of people. When the victims were retrieved, they bore the signs of Beatles-induced combat—bloody lips and noses, bruises, welts, abrasions and contusions.

Nurses and medical crews were racing in all directions. I remember seeing the litter on the ground—gauze, bandages, bottles of medicinal alcohol—and another eerie sight: lost shoes scattered on the grass. Adding to the hysteria, the lights of the stadium flashed on and off in an attempt to shock the crowd to their senses. Combined with thousands of flashbulbs popping, the light show was enough to make you see stars. All attempts to restore normalcy failed.

Finally, the second-to-last song, "A Hard Day's Night," meant the end was in sight. By this point I had retreated to the rear of the stage to prepare for what was becoming a routine moment of concert anxiety—the race to get out. Neil Aspinall was screaming to everybody that we would make a run for the exits after the final song ended. I decided to get there early, so I moved backstage to make what could have been a very dangerous footrace.

Once outside the stadium, I saw victims of the madness sprawled on the pavement, and there was a MASH unit on premises and ambulances standing by. I turned and saw the Beatles racing through the exit and toward the car, an operation lasting thirty seconds from start to finish. For the first time on the tour, they looked to me like they were running for their lives. They looked like they were in a fifty-yard dash, their legs moving in long strides, their hair streaking behind their necks. Fear was written in their expressions.

On the ride out of the stadium, a couple of kids tried to block the motorcade but fell to the side. A mangled bicycle at the edge of the road spoke of some earlier tragedy. But the drive to the airport was filled with relief. My head was still aching from the combination of music, screaming, sirens wailing, and the sound of the motorcycles that formed a moving ring around our cars like fighter-plane escorts. Yet once we had gotten safely onto our airplane, the Beatles were as loose as I had seen them to date, moving up and down the aisle freely and chatting up a storm. I took the chance to ask a few questions.

> KANE: Were you ever worried out there?
> LENNON: Not a good scene, would you agree? We decided
> early on to keep it short between songs, y'know, to make it
> easier for the police.
> KANE: Were you scared?
> LENNON: Were you?
> KANE: Well, yeah.
> LENNON: Imagine how we felt. Guess we'll have to get a
> plane or something.

His reference to a plane was symbolic of his hope to fly away from dangerous scenes. Inspired by Lennon, Epstein would soon try to hire special squads of private security guards in every city where they might be available. The scene at Empire Stadium had been enough to convince him that the threat to the band's safety was real, and real serious.

The long flight from Vancouver to Los Angeles offered an evening of release. After dinner, a pillow fight and a food fight added some harmless and hilarious entertainment to the general atmosphere of jocularity. The Beatles looked happy. Even George was rollicking up and down the aisles like a flight attendant, comically checking on the passengers. The Beatles' faces were those of people who had seen real danger and lived to sing another day.

Yet as I drifted into sleep in my airplane seat, I was haunted by the other faces, those on the soccer field in Vancouver. When I arrived at my Los Angeles hotel room at 4:50 a.m., I placed a call back to a Vancouver radio station to get an updated report on what had happened in the crowds. I would broadcast to my stations later that 135 people had been treated for a variety of injuries, including broken limbs and head trauma. According to local observers, that was one of the most difficult nights in the history of the Vancouver Police Department.

Chapter 5:
A Hollywood Fantasy

KANE: With me is Ivor Davis, correspondent for the *London Daily Express*. Ivor, what do you think of the Beatles tour so far?

DAVIS: There is only one word: incredible. We've used it a lot, and we're only going to use it a lot more. Every morning when I wake up, and every morning we go into a new town, I say, 'Well, it can't get any more hectic, more fantastic'—and it does!

And it did.

The Beatles were ready for Hollywood, but the town was not quite prepared for them. The Ambassador Hotel, fearing chaos, cancelled the party's reservations. Luckily, entertainment agent Roy Gerber, who had heavy societal connections, reserved a mansion for them in ritzy Bel Air. Most of the other entertainers and the crew stayed at the Beverly Hillcrest Hotel. Rooms were scarce even there, so a few of us wound up in a hotel on a small, almost-deserted street called Rodeo Drive.

Years before it became chic, Rodeo Drive was just a sleepy street in Beverly Hills. A small hotel in the middle of the street, the Beverly Rodeo, was my lodging during that 1964 trip to Los Angeles. Surrounded by parking lots and a solitary Polynesian restaurant, it was the perfect refuge from the chaotic events that would follow. It was mostly quiet and unassuming, with the exception of Sunday night when I found myself eating dinner at a table across from Bob Hope and his wife. This was Hollywood, after all!

And while Hollywood had plenty of weird and wild adventures in store for the boys and the rest of us, the main event was still, as always, the music. The Beatles' performance at the Hollywood Bowl would stand out as one of their best. Let me take you there....

As the brilliant sun descended over the treetops, thousands of fans gathered at the rear and sides of the Bowl, desperate to get even a brief glimpse of history. Yet the ticket holders weren't the only ones soaking up the sights and the scene. When I arrived before the concert, Ringo was hovering behind the stage watching the people coming through the turnstiles. I said to him, "You know, walking in, I saw hundreds of older fans, men and women in their twenties and thirties."

"No surprise," he replied. "In time, you'll find out what we knew months ago—the music brings 'em in."

He was right on target that night. The Hollywood Bowl was the first concert where hundreds of adults were sprinkled among the adoring, screaming teenage fans. I noticed this new dynamic up close when I headed out to see the concert from the fans' vantage point. I climbed to the top of the bowl—a steep climb—and looked down at a gorgeous scene: the Beatles on an outdoor stage under the stars, a phenomenon that would be repeated nights later at the Red Rocks Amphitheater outside of Denver. But the Hollywood Bowl was the best. Something in the air and atmosphere allowed the listener to hear the words as well as the music. Of course, one big reason for the unusually clear sound was that the slightly more mature crowd wasn't screaming so loud. They were simply enjoying the Beatles' concert for the same reason Ringo mentioned—the music.

And like these "older" fans in the audience, I was beginning to appreciate the music for its melodies. As I listened to the words of "If I Fell," a beautiful song, and watched the moonlight glow on the faces of the seventeen-thousand gathered at the Hollywood Bowl, I realized for the first time that this skeptical, cynical reporter was beginning to fall for the music of the Beatles. I was even humming out loud along with the tune, and I continued to do so throughout the evening. Was it the repetition, the hearing of these songs over and over, or was the music beginning to stir my spirits? Whatever the reason, listening to the music was making me feel happy. Is there a better reason to enjoy someone's talent and artistry? From my high perch, it was also a visual treat. The fans were holding their hands high, as if reaching out for manna from heaven, hoping to make a connection with their idols. As I moved down the far aisle, and closer to the stage, I noticed a second, smaller crowd. The Beatles were looking far and wide, enjoying *their* view. From the rear, Ringo, not missing a cadence as he struck hard at his drums, seemed to rubber neck, his face moving up higher to catch the view. George, guitar down lower than usual, almost below his hips, seemed to enjoy it the most. It was a beautiful sight. Both the singers and the screamers were in a state of gratification.

The Beatles' producer, George Martin, had arranged to record this performance and to release it as a live album, but when he heard the master tape, he decided not to go ahead with it. The reason, ironically, was because the crowd noise seriously compromised the clarity of the music and lyrics. As Martin would say later, "It was like putting a microphone by the end of a 747 jet." More than a decade after the performance, however, Martin dug up the old master tapes and, with newer technology, was able to diminish the crowd noise and cut an album from the live Hollywood Bowl show that was released in 1977, called *The Beatles at the Hollywood Bowl*.

Hollywood brought several surprises, but none was more enlightening than a party following the Beatles' concert at the Bowl. That night, our first full night in Los Angeles, I had gone back to my hotel room after the concert, eager to turn in and get some rest. But the phone rang, and I answered it to hear the cheerful voice of Malcolm Evans inviting me to join the Beatles for a party at their secluded mansion in Beverly Hills. He said, "Hey man, we need some boys at this party. Come on over. Come on over now."

I took a cab through Beverly Hills and then through a maze of police cars, onto a long driveway, and under a wide portico to the front door of a mansion. When the big door opened, I entered a lopsided world where men were the minority. The mansion belonged to Reginald Owens; a British-born actor known for his versatility in the forties and fifties. It had been rented to the band and loaded with amenities. The foyer was huge; adjacent to it was a living room of sweeping dimensions. The overall atmosphere was incongruous as the Beatles, four rebellious musicians from Liverpool, were being housed in the grandeur of an F. Scott Fitzgerald novel.

My eyes darted about, quickly scanning the scene. In one corner, Paul was sitting at a baby grand piano entertaining an eager and entranced group of young women. The large living room was filled with women. Most were clinging to the few present men like magnets to metal. Everyone seemed to be involved in the same activity: "putting on the make."

I asked Neil Aspinall, "Who are they?" Neil replied, "Mostly some chicks that Capitol Records sent over. Right now, we're waiting for the others to come over and pay their respects." It turned out that the "others" referred to a parade of stars who eventually dropped by, mostly musicians. Like teenagers across America, these famous folk were themselves overwhelmed by the need to get close; they simply wanted to meet and touch the Beatles. And, as I would learn that night and the following day, the Beatles were just as wide-eyed at meeting some of the other celebrities as the celebrities were at meeting them. The first to enter was Sandra Dee. Actress Peggy Lipton followed. Ushered in by Malcolm, they were treated like royalty by the boys.

While all the stars were doing huggy and kissy, I unwittingly got involved in a little drama of my own in the corner of the room. This little spectacle would be very difficult to live down in the weeks ahead, especially in the company of four men and their cohorts who viewed me, even at the age of twenty-one, as unsophisticated in the fast world of show business, with its weird social conventions.

It started innocently enough when one of the young women circulating at the party approached me with the question, "So, what are YOU doing here?" I answered, "I'm a reporter traveling with them." She said, "I'm an actress." I asked, "What kind of acting?"

At that point, the actress let out a wild, guttural shriek that caught the entire room's attention.

"Help!" she continued. "Please! Oh my God! Someone help me! Get him away from me!" The people in the living room turned around and stared with looks of shock. Then, to my added horror and astonishment, she continued screaming so loud and so long that I considered running for the door. But she suddenly stopped as quickly as she had begun. Then, very softly, she explained, "That's what I do. I scream and shriek in horror movies. I'm a professional victim."

I laughed, but the people in the rest of the room continued to glance over at us with devilish curiosity.

A few minutes later, John walked over and put his arm around me, laughing and tickling me as he did. He giggled and said, "Well, Larry, my boy, I guess you just can't keep your hands to yourself. Bad boy, Larry, bad boy." My face was flushed as I wandered into the corridor, trying to make a graceful escape. I tried later to explain the whole screaming episode, but no one would buy the story.

After a brief retreat to the bathroom, I returned as a spectator to the parade of arrivals. It was a heady night for a reporter who just a few weeks earlier had been chasing fire trucks in the streets of Miami. I tried to be nonchalant about the visitors, but it was difficult not to notice, especially when Jayne Mansfield walked in. Mansfield was a recognized star, a bona fide Sixties' sex symbol who was greeted warmly and with some fanfare. She was also, to my surprise, a fanatic Beatles fan and an even bigger devotee of John Lennon.

While Mansfield circulated, Lennon was in an anteroom near the big living room sitting on a sofa bed with a young lady. But this quiet scene was soon interrupted by a nasty little episode. Long John Wade, a popular and outspoken deejay from Hartford who would join the tour at various stops, walked over to the woman with his tape recorder in hand, placed the microphone in front of her mouth, and said, "And who might you be?" This was Wade's way of being funny. But Lennon was not amused, and he drew back his right hand and punched Wade's forearm, forcing the microphone out of his hand and clear across the room. John was furious. "Are you trying to start a scandal?" he asked Wade.

Later in the tour, Lennon would make frequent overtures of friendship to Long John Wade. And even today, Wade remembers Lennon's behavior vividly. Of Lennon, he says today, "Ever since he punched me, he tried everything to make it up. I think he understood I was just joking around. He invited me to talk, and a few nights later he seemed to forget the incident when I joined him for a ride in a police car." That patrol-car ride would end in a night to remember, or forget, depending on who you were. But first let's get back to the party.

Shortly after Lennon slugged Long John Wade, he was introduced to Jayne Mansfield. It was lust at first sight. Lennon winked at me as he walked Mansfield through the room. He was pleased with himself, showing off a true American sex symbol. For her part, Mansfield was a charming, almost sweet person, whose cheesecake image may have belied a thoughtful human being. The two seemed to click, and as the party progressed late into the night, one thing was becoming clear: Mansfield wanted to see Lennon again. (She did, in grand and outrageous style, forty-eight hours later.)

The party was a late one, beginning at eleven, an hour after the end of the Hollywood Bowl concert. Returning to the hotel in the early morning, I wrote and filed my reports, then fell asleep. Wake-up was at noon, followed by one of the most unusual public events on the tour.

Alan Livingston, then chief of Capitol Records, had signed the Beatles before they were hot and was now reaping the rewards. He was hosting a garden party fundraiser that day for the Hemophilia Foundation, and the theme was: "Buy a ticket and meet the Beatles." The party, held in the fashionable Brentwood neighborhood, was spiced up by a number of curious events. Security was so heavy that Brian Epstein and Derek Taylor were initially prohibited from getting in—on time at least—making them quite upset. Epstein was also furious that day because Ringo wasn't wearing a tie. Another problem was a disgruntled neighbor, irked by the crowds descending on the street, who made the news by threatening to shoot anyone who stepped on his lawn. His gun was never used, but the hordes of people got awfully close and the situation remained tense.

The soiree was held in the backyard of the lavish home of a relative of Livingston's. There, the Beatles lined up to meet and greet Hollywood hotshots who had paid a certain amount to charity in order to meet them. Many stars had brought their children to meet the Beatles as well. It was a hit parade of personalities, and it struck me that these movie stars were, for a day, avid, eager and star-crazy themselves, all over the Beatles. This was the ultimate turnabout and was delicious to watch.

The Beatles also soaked it up, standing in a receiving line under the midday sun and pressing flesh with the likes of Lloyd Bridges and his 14-year-old son Jeff (who would become a movie star in his own right), Edward G. Robinson, Jack Palance, Stan Freberg, Hugh O'Brien, Dean Martin, Shelly Winters, Jack Lemmon, columnist Hedda Hopper, Los Angeles mayor Sam Yorty and members of all of their families.

I would never have guessed it, but Edward G. Robinson, a huge star of early Hollywood, was the Beatles' favorite movie star (not counting Jayne Mansfield). George, Ringo, and Paul were all abuzz about meeting Edward G., whom they had seen in countless black-and-white movies on TV in their growing-up years. Characteristically, John was more philosophical about the event.

> KANE: What about the party yesterday afternoon that Mr. Livingston gave you. . . . Was that a highlight?
>
> LENNON: Well . . . it was more of a job, of work, y'know. Hard—it was harder than playing [music]. You've just gotta sit on a stool and meet three hundred people of all ages.
>
> KANE: Why is that harder, John?
>
> LENNON: Because, y'know, it's unnatural . . . excuse me—it

is natural for us to play and sing. But it is unnatural to sit on a
stool and shake hands. But we can do it, y'know.
KANE: How does it feel to be sitting there and have all these
Hollywood celebrities and their children stop by just to shake
hands with the Beatles?
LENNON: We were a bit choked up. We saw Edward G.
Robinson, Jack Palance, Hugh O'Brien . . . but we were
expecting to have more fun.
KANE: I was standing right behind you and you turned
around to, I think, George, and you said, 'THIS is Hollywood.
Isn't it daffy?' Did you really mean that?
LENNON: Well, I never use the word "daffy," so it must be
something like that. It is a bit daft. It is a bit, y'know, show biz
is a bit weird. It's a bit weird for all showbiz [to be] stuck in
one area . . . maybe potty.

In any words, the party at the Livingston home was not John
Lennon's favorite event of the tour. At one point, he was overheard
asking Brian Epstein, "Who's the old bag with the funny hat?" It
turned out to be Hedda Hopper, the most powerful Hollywood
columnist of the time. Ringo was not thrilled about the session, either.
Weeks later, nursing a sore throat in Milwaukee, he said, "It does bother me, you know, that real fans don't get to see us, but people with
money can. It was fake, y'know, that party."
    While John and Ringo were unimpressed, Paul McCartney soaked
it up like a kid in a candy shop. McCartney always looked like he was
posed for a still picture. He cocked his head and pursed his lips, prepared to utterly charm the person facing him. So for him, the garden
party was a time to highlight his greatest strength on stage or off—the
ability, at a moment's notice, to strike a pose. McCartney was the ultimate charmer. As each celebrity and his or her family members posed
for pictures, John, George and Ringo seemed to be going through the
motions. Paul savored each photograph and made small talk with
almost every party guest.
    Hot and thirsty, I walked to a nearby kitchen where none other
than rugged Jack Palance poured me a soda. After brief introductions,
he asked my opinion of the Beatles. I said, "Mostly, they're pretty
decent guys." He replied, "I don't go for the idolizing crap, but I'll tell
you, the music is damn good." Shelley Winters, an Academy Award-
winning actress, then walked into the kitchen and sat down with a soft

drink. The actress, too, sang the praises of the Beatles' music. More and more, the over-18 crowd was discovering the Beatles' sound. Their music was, after all, what had brought the band to America.

The next night, our final night in Los Angeles, was passing quietly when another phone call came to my room from Mal Evans. He said that some of the boys were going to do the unthinkable that night—leave the house. Epstein wasn't with them, and I knew this would upset him when he found out. After all, the Beatles heading out into public without a security plan created tremendous potential for trouble. Nevertheless, the outing provided a rare opportunity for the Beatles, who had been trapped under the confines of their security umbrella and had only glimpsed the real America out the windows of their limos, airplanes, and high-rise hotels.

I reached the Owens mansion just in time to make the excursion. Jayne Mansfield was already at the house when I arrived. Lennon and Mansfield jumped into a police car, and John Wade, hardly shy, got in the car with them. George, Ringo, Evans and Aspinall jumped into another car. Paul stayed behind with his new friend, actress Peggy Lipton. The British reporters joined me in a cab. The driver was given the destination address—8901 Sunset Boulevard.

The Whisky A Go-Go (now known as the Whisky) is a small Hollywood nightclub that has created big lore over the years. Jim Morrison and the Doors started out there as a regular club band in 1966. It has seen the likes of Led Zeppelin, Jimi Hendrix, the Byrds and others. It has even been credited with launching the sixties' go-go dancing craze. But before any of those bands made their mark, in August of 1964, the Beatles made a scene of their own.

The arrival of the small Beatles party was no surprise. Management had been tipped off, along with local radio stations. The place was packed. Jayne Mansfield and John Lennon, according to deejay Wade, arrived first after an interesting ride over. "They were making out like kids," says Wade, who was riding with them, without his tape recorder. It seemed ironic that John, who had punched Wade earlier in the Hollywood visit, had had no qualms about his presence in the car.

By the time I got to the Whisky, George, John, Ringo, the famous actress and a few others were safely seated. They were accompanied by Roy Gerber, Derek Taylor, his trustworthy assistant Bess Coleman, Malcolm and Neil. The crowd in the club was dazzled. The few police there were wary, as was the always-nervous Neil Aspinall. The situation was rife with potential for chaos: A crowd of people crushed into a small place, heavy cigarette smoke, and, creeping out of the woodwork in the corner, a photographer was getting closer as the music from featured performer Johnny Rivers was getting louder.

The photographer was trying to maneuver into a good position but was having trouble wedging his way through the dense crowd. As he got closer, George was becoming irritated at his approach. He yelled out something to the man, something unintelligible to me. Nevertheless, the photographer kept inching closer. George's anger finally erupted, and he threw his drink at the man. The aerial assault accomplished its goal, forcing the shutterbug away. Unfortunately, the drink landed near the lap of another actress, Mamie Van Doren. And even though Van Doren was clearly miffed by the throwing error, she also seemed more intent on getting her photo taken with the Beatles.

The photographer did snap a picture of George in a moment of verbal passion aimed at the camera, his hands hurling the liquor into the air, and the picture appeared in the paper the next day. But the print press missed the real story: the budding friendship of Jayne Mansfield and John Lennon. After all, it was Jayne who had invited the band to the Whisky A Go-Go, and she sat with them most of the evening. What's more, as the Beatles exited the club, Lennon and Mansfield were hand in hand. Near the rear door, a private security guard got between them, but Mansfield raced to rejoin John in the midst of the crush. In surging forward, the actress plowed into me, forcing my body into John's, who was being pressed back into me by a zealous guard whose hands were wrapped around all of us. The surge to get out resembled a British soccer riot. But once we cleared the madness of the emergency door, we could breathe again, and I could only hope for no more freelance excursions by the Beatles. Lennon remembered the episode at the club fondly.

LENNON: Due to George's astute business brain, he offered a mighty blow [the drink toss] and swept him away . . .
STARR: Which any normal fellow would do, but just because George does it, it gets this enormous publicity because he's in the Beatles. This little photographer puts this big camera four inches from your face and blinds you . . . flashes you.
LENNON: So the guy goes away—then he comes back!
KANE: Thanks, guys.

STARR: Thank you for keeping us occupied. We'd just be sitting around doing nothing. And say hello to everyone in Miami.

This interview took place the day after the nightclub mess. Boredom would set in occasionally, and at those times I always found the Beatles eager to talk, especially in the case of John Lennon, and especially when he had something on his mind. Which was practically all the time.

The Beatles' 1964 visit to the fantasyland called Hollywood was notable in many ways: It included their first open-air American concert, the "scene" at the Whisky, the adoration of the Beatles by the American stars, and my own new awareness that there was more to John, Paul, George and Ringo than long hair, swagger and a penchant for women. They were, after all, really good musicians.

CHAPTER 6:
Beatle Frights and Beatle Nights

Sitting-duck decoys: That's what we were in Denver.

While the Beatles were obviously the primary target of screaming and reckless fans at every turn, there were some occasions in which other members of the traveling party took the brunt of the turmoil. In these moments, we were able to experience the crush of Beatlemania that the boys themselves faced constantly.

While approaching the famous Brown Palace Hotel in downtown Denver, our press car accidentally drove to the front of the motorcade. The press car was the exact same model of limousine as the lead car that carried the Beatles, and suddenly, kids from both sides of the street converged on our vehicle. Meanwhile, savvy Denver police officers brought the Beatles' car around to the other side of the hotel entrance, leaving the uncompromising but joyful horde of young people to mistakenly concentrate on our car.

This was the first time on the tour that I had experienced not just an intense fear, but the realistic possibility of injury or "death by Beatles fan." I knew we were in big trouble when the upholstery of the car's ceiling getting lower, closing in on my face. By sheer force, the eager crowd, jumping on and pressing against the roof of the car, was pushing the metal roof into a dent that evolved into a sort of sinkhole, which was getting bigger and deeper by the second. And though this crowd consisted of mere teenagers, it was truly terrifying. As I looked up, the fabric lining of the car's interior was now closing in on our heads. I rolled down a window and tried to push the invaders away, but someone grabbed my wrist and twisted it; I quickly pulled my arm back into the car. Police were trying to get the kids off the roof, but in doing so they fueled the melee that was preventing us from opening the doors and getting out. Still thinking we were actually the Beatles inside, the crowd refused to disperse.

The police, desperate to get the upper hand, wisely removed their nightsticks in a threatening gesture. But no one noticed! Inside the car we were quickly beginning to feel hopeless. Try to picture the scene from the inside looking out: faces crushed against the glass, girls screaming "Paul, Paul, I love you!", policemen's faces filled with fear, and doors that would simply not open. Claustrophobia set in. We were hostages, victims of the wrath and fury of an obsessed band of fanatics, a mob that was determined to get even a short glimpse or a brief touch of the Beatles.

Finally, the police prevailed. Worn but undaunted, we squeezed through the crowd, which was by that moment totally uninterested in us, having discovered that the Beatles were already inside. Considering the circumstances, we all deserved combat pay for our stint as decoys. But of course that wasn't forthcoming, nor would we ask for it. This was just a part of the fright-filled ritual of traveling with the boys.

Despite our horrific "welcome," Denver remains in my mind as a place of natural beauty mixed with musical delight. The concert at the Red Rocks Amphitheater was beautiful, taking place mostly in the open air and surrounded by cavernous formations of rock. Although the joy of stargazing without city lights was a desirable distraction, the music was so powerful that it pulled you back into the moment. In fact, it seemed to reverberate from cliff to cliff. I especially enjoyed "A Hard Day's Night" that evening. The guys were in perfect harmony, and John's voice seemed so powerful.

The scene was both beautiful and odd, the Beatles figures silhouetted against the red and orange rock. Modern culture collided with nature's best formations. Only the Beatles' boots fit with the western motif. The crowd was smaller, and when I inhaled the clean mountain air, I felt the familiar feel of a camp out, rather than a concert. When Lennon and McCartney sang "All My Loving," Ringo's drums seemed to be coming out in what we know now as stereo, the sound reverberating from canyon to canyon, and rock to rock. My perspective from the rear of the crowd was amazing, but a colleague wanted a better look.

During the concert, Cleveland deejay Jim Staggs decided to climb to the top of a two-hundred-foot lighting scaffold. "I wanted to get a better look at the concert scene," he said later. "It was a great night. I wanted to describe what it looked like." But when Jim reached the top of the scaffolding, he heard strong footsteps and heavy huffing and puffing behind him. He looked behind, amazed to see Beatles manager Brian Epstein finishing the climb and approaching him.

"Jim," Epstein said, "Jim, you wouldn't be taping this performance, would you, Jim?" Staggs, angry but wary since he was dealing with the Beatles' boss, said, "Now why the hell would I do something like that?"

Protecting the franchise was Epstein's motive for climbing the scaffold and confronting Staggs. Concerned about pirated tapes, Epstein had seen Jim climbing the two hundred feet and grew suspicious. The fact that he put himself at risk to make the climb himself was proof positive that Brian Epstein would do anything to protect the artistic sanctity—and profitability—of his Beatles. In the category of taking care of business, there seemed to be no equal to Brian Epstein.

At one point on the tour, as I interviewed Brian Epstein, I mentioned how he seemed so protective of the Beatles. "Well, it is a simple proposition," he explained. "They are special. I believe in them. They should not be compromised or taken advantage of in any form."

Translation: The bucks stay here! Epstein protected his "boys" by several clever prohibitions. There would be no news cameras (besides still photography) allowed in, at least for the first tour. And he took steps to prevent audio taping of the concerts (even if he had to climb a scaffold himself to enforce the rule!). Although bootleg recordings exist today, most are of poor quality. The portable tape equipment of the sixties was bulky and unreliable. There was also strict supervision of the sale of novelties, especially buttons and banners.

One aspect of the Beatles' life that Brian Epstein couldn't control was what the press wrote and said. But he could control press access to the band members. And Brian, Derek Taylor and later Tony Barrow did their best to make a good impression on the press they allowed in. Those three are right up there in the top percentile of "spinners" and handlers that I've encountered in my career. Even Epstein, shy and introverted, would carefully develop close relations with members of the press on the airplane, and in some shocking private moments, would try to develop relations beyond the usual realm of closeness.

The airplane that would take us from Denver to Cincinnati took off the next morning on the most grueling day of the 1964 tour. We'd be traveling from Denver to Cincinnati, and then Cincinnati to New York. The day had begun in Denver at 10 a.m., and it would end on Park Avenue at 3 a.m.

On the flight to Ohio, the Beatles seemed joyful. Paul walked up and down the aisle, winking that Paul wink and acting as host of the day. At one point, he stopped by some members of the group Exciter and said jokingly, "Coffee, tea or me?" On the plane, Paul was also the biggest walker. He didn't like being confined.

About a half-hour into the flight, Derek called me to the back to do a special interview with the band that would be broadcast at an awards ceremony that would be held in England. The Beatles had won the Melody Maker Award for International Music. He asked me to do the taped interview that would be played in the Beatles' absence at the Melody Maker Award luncheon in London, where they were going to be honored as the best international artists. I was gratified that, after just a week of getting to know them all, I was asked to do the interview.

KANE: This is Larry Kane, traveling with the Beatles across America. At this moment we are right over Kansas, about twenty-three thousand feet in the air, on the Beatles' chartered airliner on our way to Cincinnati, one of the stops on this exciting twenty-five-city, coast-to-coast tour. We are over Kansas on our way to Cincinnati. The boys are flying east following seven electrifying performances on the West Coast. And now, four thousand miles away from you, the guests of Melody Maker, here is John Lennon.

LENNON: Hello, people, this is John Lennon. Thanks for the award. We're flying over America, you know . . . four thousand miles from you. Thanks and have a good dinner. Paul. . . .

McCARTNEY: Hello, L and G. Paul speaking to you from four thousand miles away. Amazing what you can do with a small piece of tape. We're all sitting around here thinking about you at the Melody Maker luncheon. Like to thank you all for the award—deeply honored and all that kind of stuff. . . . Here's George. . . .

HARRISON: Hi there, Beatles people. [laughter] Bet you're wondering why we're not having lunch with you. Flying around and all that. . . . Thanks a lot for all these awards and

things. See you soon . . . Ringo?
STARR: Hello, this is Ringo speaking. Thanks for the award—
very nice of you. Hope you're all having a good time, because
we are. Great over here—no rain or anything. [laughter]
That's about it.
KANE: Boys, thank you. This is Larry Kane with the Beatles,
flying across America.

This was an unrehearsed conversation, but note the natural
sequence of speakers: John, Paul, George and Ringo. The band was
announced that way, billed that way, and always seemed to play that
way. The Beatles had found their natural pecking order. They lived by
that natural order, and it followed them, as Beatles, forever.
Interesting, isn't it, that when I offered the microphone to them, they
naturally offered their comments in that exact order?

The tape was taken to New York, shipped by airplane to London
and played to a packed house at the awards luncheon.

Cincinnati was ahead, with a concert planned at the famed
Cincinnati Gardens, an indoor sports complex best known for hosting
major boxing bouts. Its official capacity was listed as eleven thousand
five hundred, but fourteen thousand people would be packed in to see
the Beatles. We learned when we got there that there was one major
problem: the heat. The air was poorly regulated, and the usual fervor—the standard faintings and delirious crowd ecstasy—were exacerbated by the temperature.

The Cincinnati experience brought the crowd to a crescendo with
one song, "I Want To Hold Your Hand." Although forgotten in the dramatic string of Beatles success stories, that song was, to many
Americans, the first taste of Beatlemania in late 1963 and early 1964.
When Paul and John joined their heads close together and enchanted
the crowd with almost perfect harmony, their mouths almost touching
the metal of the microphone, they stirred the fans to a gutteral out-
break of high tone screaming. In the Cincinnati Gardens, security
guards shook their heads, and held their ears.

Cincinnati was a "drop-in," a stop of just five hours. And aside
from the heat issue, the Queen City was hospitable to the Beatles. Our
motorcades in and out of the city were smooth. By 11 p.m. we were
back on the Electra, heading east to New York City, the boys' most
anticipated stop on the tour, where once again police would miscalcu-
late the lure, power and force of the Beatles.

It was already Friday, August 29, 1964, when our turbo prop headed over Jamaica Bay on its approach to JFK Airport. When we heard the grind of the landing gear being released, Derek Taylor looked across the aisle and predicted a subdued arrival in the nation's biggest metropolis. After all, it was almost 2 a.m. Impossible, I thought—Beatles fans never sleep.

CHAPTER 7:
A Juicy Piece of the Apple

Amer, the beautiful. In one day we had journeyed from the purple mountains' majesty over amber waves of grain and into the core of the Big Apple. Red rock was replaced by granite, steel and asphalt. New York in the middle of the night was sparkling, its skyline shining with bright lights and palpable energy. The journey of the Beatles had taken them to what New Yorkers believe is the center of the universe—their city.

The Denver-Cincinnati-New York express arrived early in the morning. An animated John Lennon was awake, rubber-necking, reaching out to the passenger window and pressing his face against it to get an aerial look at the city that never sleeps. New York was special to the Beatles because it was the stuff of show business legends. History was made there, and they wanted to write a few chapters themselves. It would become so powerful a draw that one Beatle eventually decided to live there. He would die there.

The New York adventure we were about to embark on would be the first true test of the Beatles, onstage and off, in the world's headquarters of entertainment and media. The city would also make the scene of the largest concert in the history of entertainment, one that turned Flushing Meadows in Queens into a sound chamber of screams that reverberated throughout the music world. That would be in 1965 at Shea Stadium, but first things first.

First came an unfortunate episode soon after we arrived in New York. The crowd of four thousand at the airport didn't get close, although the Beatles heard its roar. The motorcade out of the airport was swift. But our arrival at the Delmonico Hotel on elegant Park Avenue was sloppy and dangerous.

> KANE: What happened?
> STARR: Well, it's the closest I've got to getting got, Larry. Once the police saw it, they took me away.
> McCARTNEY: One of the police didn't think Ringo was Ringo. And he lost his shirt.

Here's what happened. As the four Beatles moved through the lobby, Ringo became trapped in a small crowd of spirited girls. One ripped the St. Christopher's medal off of his neck; another ripped his shirt wide open.

In more peaceful hours the next afternoon, crowds of up to five thousand, many pouring out of subway exits all over midtown, gathered across from the Delmonico. A simple wave from a window might have satisfied their Beatles lust, but the authorities said no.

> KANE: John, rumors have it you asked to wave out the window.
> LENNON: Well, it's the least we could do. We're going to ask today to wave. They won't let us wave. They worry it will incite the crowd.

It didn't take much to incite the crowd. Like all Beatles crowds, the New Yorkers were loud and creative, but there was a different edge in Manhattan. After all, New Yorkers don't like to be denied, and someone out there had a piece of Ringo's shirt and his St. Christopher's medal. Ringo was clearly upset and made taped pleas through several radio stations for a return of his medal. The radio broadcasts encouraged a run on St. Christopher's medals at Manhattan religious stores. Within hours, calls were made to WABC radio with claims that the medal had been found. Most of the calls came from creative imposters who just wanted to get close. Finally, a sixteen-year-old girl named Angie McGowan confessed that she had pulled it off while trying to kiss Ringo. Sure enough, it was the real thing, and Angie got to meet Ringo the next afternoon.

The next day at 59th and Park Avenue was marked by assaults, frontal and otherwise. I was leaving the hotel at noon to check on the crowd when a scuffle erupted near the marquee. Daring and determined, a group of about fifteen kids had stormed the front of the hotel, becoming locked in a tug of war of arms and elbows with brave NYPD officers and hotel bellmen. One of the girls got through and made a wild dash for an elevator. She tripped on a rug and fell to the floor, trapped beneath the weight of two cops. It looked like a football scrimmage. The tape of my conversation with the girl is missing, but I will never forget some of her words. She said, "They're all scumbags, those cops. They suck." She got up, dusted herself off, left the hotel and made it to the street, where she received a round of brief applause from her soulmates.

In the meantime, skullduggery was being played out by other hotel guests and reporters. In a form of perverse humor, they began waving from hotel windows, creating an uproar on the west side of Park Avenue where the crowds had gathered. I was feeling sorry for those thousands of kids. All they wanted was a simple wave. And masqueraders were duping them.

That night, the Beatles left the Delmonico to go to their first New York concert, and so did several members of the press. My colleague, Jim Staggs, was walking out of the hotel when Derek invited him to get in the car with the band and drive to the heliport. While Jim headed to the helicopter, I boarded the subway for the ride to Queens. Both of our travel experiences, although vastly different in style, were newsworthy. Staggs remembers the chopper ride well:

"I was just happy to be in the limo with them, but when we got to the Wall Street helicopter pad, Derek invited me aboard. Wow. It was unreal. The helicopter lifted off, and I thought George was going to freak. I mean he was gripping the seat as the helicopter lifted off. Epstein, Ringo and Paul were kind of cool, enjoying the skyline view, but John and George, guitars nearby, looked around in a sort of anguish. George, fearful, at one point blurted out, 'Beatles and children first.' I laughed. I loved the ride. I loved watching them. I loved the ride until we got there."

Meanwhile, before I entered that subway, I couldn't have imagined the ramifications of traveling with a tape recorder in hand. Nor had I expected that the band's ticket-holding fans would have come to the same conclusion as I had—that the subway was the best way to get to the stadium. Inside the subway car, girls crowded around me and began touching my arms, knees and even my hair and face. One teenage terror said something like, "You know the Beatles?" Feeling a bit threatened by this army of frustrated Beatles fans dying to meet someone who had met the Beatles, I did the best thing I could: I lied. "Not really," I answered.

"What's the tape recorder for, how does it work?" one of the kids asked. In hopes of passing the time, I interviewed several fans, but I discovered on playing the tape back that the grinding roar of the subway had distorted the sound. As I spoke with them, though, I was curious. "How many of you have tickets?" Only a few raised their hands. Once again, hundreds, maybe thousands for all I knew, were traveling—and traveling without a chaperone—just to get close to the Beatles.

Remember, in those days, teenage girls traveling alone without a parent or guardian was unheard of, but on this ride they were legion. Watching these subway sirens grasping their transistor radios, holding onto plastic purses and autograph books, and clutching the hand straps to keep their balance as the subway rocked along, I realized that, for many of these young women, their love and passion for the Beatles seemed to be the beginning of liberation and the end of innocence. I also realized that perhaps their individual actions would stimulate the transformation of an entire generation.

While I sat packed in and surrounded on the elevated subway, Staggs was soaking up the sights of New York on the helicopter. He describes the scene: "George calmed down and started getting a kick out of the ride, especially when we circled the tennis stadium. John seemed more relaxed. It was noisy as hell, but what a sight. The sun was just disappearing when we touched down in semi-darkness. It was a real kick."

I emerged from the subway sweaty and a bit agitated. But after a week close up with the Beatles, it was a wonderful learning experience to spend an hour with the other half of the Beatles equation—their loving fans.

The Beatles' two New York concerts on that 1964 tour, which took place on successive nights at the old Forest Hills tennis complex, were incredible performances. Centered in the middle of this tiny stadium, surrounded on all sides and barely protected, the Beatles played their hearts out, seemingly blind to the menacing scene in front of them. From my perch on a catwalk above this dark stadium, I could see fans making it onto the stage area, crawling on and being driven back, over and over. While I watched from the catwalk, fan Phyllis Cambria, now a resident of Florida, was high in the stands. Phyllis remembers:

"We found our seats and were momentarily disappointed that we were so far away from them, but soon the energy of the crowd overtook us. Even the chance to glimpse them at a distance was all we could ask in life.

"Eventually the crowd started to chant for the Beatles to come on stage. Finally, after too long a wait, they emerged on stage. The sound was deafening as thousands of young girls squealed and screamed their names. My heart stopped as I saw Paul for the first time. They looked at each other and laughed. They seemed genuinely overwhelmed, but delighted.

"As soon as they played the first note, the screams became even louder. I don't know if it was because their sound system was inadequate or the noise of the crowd was too overwhelming, but it wasn't easy to hear them. Just enough of the melody could be heard to recognize each song, and the crowd often sang and clapped along, adding to the din. Every time they would shake their heads, the crowd went wild.

"Someone had a pair of binoculars near us, and I remember she generously handed them to me so I could see their faces more clearly. Despite being in love with Paul, I scanned them all. To this day, I'm not sure why, but as I was looking at Ringo, he pounded his drums and I screamed. It was the first time I had ever screamed in public, and I was both surprised at my reaction and a little embarrassed at my outburst. Honi and Sandy just looked at me with surprise. I blushed, shrugged, handed the binoculars back and continued to sing along with them for the rest of the concert.

"Too soon, the concert was over. I don't remember walking down the stairs. I'm not sure if I was just floating or being carried by the crowd until we reached my father's car. The ride back was a combination of us all talking at once about the experience and stunned silence as we reveled in our own private thoughts of the experience of finally seeing them perform live. It was, and always will be, one of the high points of my life and an experience I'll cherish forever."

Phyllis's memories certainly explain the thrill of the moment. But it's her final comment that has become the mantra of so many Beatles fans, then and now: "an experience I'll cherish forever." That feeling, the sense of being part of an unforgettable time, was shared by Anne Carlin, now Anne Gottehrer. She came from Brooklyn:

"We had just seen the movie, and it looked like the movie. I had won the two tickets in a radio contest, and my friend Gail Klein and I were pushed into the stadium by the crowd. It was a frenzy. It was fun, but intense. Remember, this was the first concert that anybody had been to. There were never concerts like this before.

"When they sang 'If I Fell,' that just put me away. We couldn't breathe for days. It was so 'over the moon.' I will remember that night the rest of my life.

"Of course, we got lost going home and had to walk five miles to Sheepshead Bay. We didn't care. We were walking on air."

As Anne and her friend found their way back home in the middle of the night, the Beatles trekked back to Manhattan by air; I grabbed a taxi and skipped the subway. Back in the Delmonico, a small crowd was gathered on the Beatles' floor. The group was led by Bob Dylan, an unidentified reporter and a friend. Each member of the Beatles has since made it known that Dylan and friends introduced the Beatles and Brian Epstein to marijuana in the locked confines of their suite that night. But at the time, none of us traveling with the Beatles was even aware of this possibility.

The next night, the Beatles and their entourage left New York for Atlantic City. The band would return to New York on the final night of their 1964 tour. On that night, I would meet Bob Dylan again. And of course, New York would play a central role in the band's 1965 tour, hosting the most pulsating moment in entertainment history. The drama of Shea Stadium was yet to come. But first, it was on to the city of Miss America, salt-water taffy, mysterious women and a crazy Labor Day weekend.

CHAPTER 8:
Surf and Sex at the Jersey Shore

Now Jersey's Atlantic City is now the gambling capital of the East, most notable for its bright lights and high hopes. In August of 1964, the seaside city was home first to the Democratic National Convention, and then, a few days later, the Beatles.

Ironically, the Beatles played in the Cow Palace in San Francisco shortly after the end of the Republican Convention. Now, weeks later, they would occupy the stage where Lyndon Johnson had accepted his party's nomination to run for a full four-year term as president. In the years ahead, the Beatles' growth would parallel the escalation of Johnson's albatross, the war in Vietnam. Eventually, the boys would speak out against the war, and their legions of fans would mesh their own cultural strands into the era of protest and polarity.

Coming just nine months after John F. Kennedy's assassination, the Atlantic City Democratic Convention was the most secure political gathering in American history. Unfortunately, this massive security did not carry over to the Beatles' stay.

The press party's bus went roaring down the Garden State Parkway, hours behind the boys' helicopter escape from Forest Hills, en route to Atlantic City, where the Beatles would be spending a few days. Like Hollywood, this stop would provide a chance for them to rest and rev up their engines for the final two-thirds of the tour. The thought of beaches, ocean breezes and fresh air excited the boys. Not only were the Beatles going to the shore, but they were also going to the city whose streets and landmarks formed the basis of their favorite board game, Monopoly. "Ah, a rest," Ringo said on the way out of New York.

But a rest it wasn't. Still, they did seem to have a monopoly on fun and controversy. Our hotel was the Lafayette Motor Inn on North Carolina Avenue, within eyeshot of the famous boardwalk. Within fifty yards of the hotel were the ramps leading to the boardwalk shops, with their hot dogs, pizza, cotton candy and salt-water taffy. There was no question that the Beatles were about to enjoy a slice of Americana, and much more than that.

North Carolina Avenue had been cordoned off for their arrival, but the streets around it were jammed with people, sidewalk to sidewalk. After a brief hotel reservation mix-up and an assault on a reporter named, coincidentally, George Harrison, most of us got into the hotel without incident and were assigned our rooms. The Beatles' rooms were on the top floor. Derek Taylor invited us up that first night to relax and socialize. Ivor Davis, Art Schreiber and Long John Wade and I still have vivid memories of what we witnessed in the Beatles' suite.

The door swung open. The sight was baffling. About twenty young women, most of them wearing low-cut dresses, were standing in an informal line. Some of them were smiling; others looked a bit uncomfortable. These women had a different air about them than did the semi-innocent teenagers and young women who would often be hanging around. They had that "I've been there before" look. The truth was that they were on the clock. The room was heavily perfumed. I was stunned and of course, fascinated, especially when one of the women reached down so low to light Paul's cigarette, that most of her bosom, already exposed to daring dimensions, almost fell out.

Paul and Ringo were sitting on a couch, taking in an eyeful. Derek Taylor was there, his arms folded in front of his chest as always, his constantly lit cigarette dangling from his fingers, looking a bit overwhelmed. George was sitting on the floor. Mal Evans had the look of a child on Christmas morning. John, that night at least, was about to play the cheerleader.

Art Schreiber remembers, "At first, I couldn't figure it out. What the hell was the lineup all about?"

Ivor Davis says, "Looked funny to me. But as far as this group was concerned, I always expected the unexpected."

And Long John Wade cut to the chase, saying, "Remember the promoter or whatever he was? I will never forget those words. . . ."

The words astounded me as well: "Take your pick," the man in the suit said.

"Take your pick, you heard him, take your pick," said a happy John Lennon. At that moment John was providing "leadership skills," urging everyone to make a selection. It was like a sexual automat— just point your finger and go on your way.

Hearing those words, it was evident to this clueless reporter and his travel partners that the visitors were not Beatles' fans seeking autographs or pictures. Pictures in this case would have been incriminating, because those women were not on the prowl, but on the job.

It was the first time I had ever witnessed a group of professional women delivered to the doorstep of the Beatles. Which poses the question: What's a newsman to do? Taking my pick was not an option. Rather, the dilemma I faced goes to the heart of the age-old quandary: What is news? Where do the boundaries of privacy begin and end?

In 1964, I knew it was unthinkable to report this. I couldn't see how I would get confirmation, anyway, if indeed any of the men present did "take their pick," although some people were certainly wandering off in couples. Barring an on-site inspection, which was out of the question, there was no proof, but plenty of evidence. Besides, the Beatles, trusting and fairly open, had let most of us into their private world. How could we betray them by reporting this? The Beatles were wary of the American press, but very trusting of those traveling with them. Just the day before, during an interview at the Delmonico Hotel in New York City, Paul had spoken with great candor about the press:

> KANE: Do you ever get concerned about the press and privacy?
> McCARTNEY: No, I'll tell you what. The best thing about you lot, y'know, is that on the plane, we can trust you, y'know. And we know that, for instance, if one of us wants to go to sleep, then you won't be coming up flashing cameras in our faces, y'know, or something like that. So that's, that's fine, y'know, everybody on the plane, we know now, and we, we can trust 'em to sort of think about, y'know, us a bit. Normally, it doesn't work, because people just sort of are out for all they can get, y'know, and if they catch you sleeping, they'll flash a flash right in your face, y'know. But, I mean, this isn't all of the time. Occasionally you can get sick of that, you can imagine, y'know, that can get sickening. It's much better once you get to know people.

The last thing I wanted to do was violate this growing trust. George Harrison shared his views on the press in an interview later on during our Atlantic City stay.

KANE: George, I asked you this before, in relationship to the American press. So many of them come to you in so many cities. How do you feel about this? Does it ever get to you? HARRISON: Uh, yeah, we always see the press every place we go, and we always read the papers the next day. And usually, the majority of papers, I'd say about ninety-five out of a hundred, are usually good. But the odd five, y'know, we do get that dig at us, y'know, but it's, y'know, we accept it, because it's usually written by a gang of narcs anyway. Crummy people who, who don't like us from the beginning and they're, y'know, regardless of what we say and do, y'know, they've got it in for us anyway. But it doesn't worry us.

There's no doubt that in today's news climate, after Vietnam, Watergate, the Clinton scandal and the "anything goes" climate of contemporary journalism, every minute detail of what came to be known as the "hooker incident" would be reported. But it's also doubtful that any contemporary public figures would allow any news people to share private moments like the Beatles did then.

We shared a more meaningful private moment with John, Paul, George and Ringo the next night, following a wild but organized concert at the Atlantic City Convention Hall. Eighteen thousand people filled the venerable hall, home of the Miss America Pageant. Getting the Beatles from the Lafayette Motor Inn to the concert site had been an assignment fraught with danger. Atlantic City had beaches with miles of boardwalk under which to hide. It was a security nightmare. And by the morning after our first night in the hotel, the police barriers had been removed from the street outside, and a crowd of several thousand kids stood guard at the hotel, night and day. Neil Aspinall had managed to take the Beatles through an underground network of walkways near the Lafayette Hotel and to a group of limousines, and then safely to the venue.

My difficulty that night came in the form of a deejay from my radio station, Bill Holly. Bill was on vacation in New York when he decided to drop by Atlantic City to see the Beatles. I was happy to see Bill, but his visit became problematic. Why? Bill had green hair.

On occasion, Bill would color his hair. On that Labor Day weekend, his hair was as green as the Irish countryside. His 'do turned heads on the boardwalk as we walked toward the convention hall. The special press credentials I'd acquired for Bill didn't work, since the guards were so suspicious of his green hair. It took me a half-hour of cajoling the security guards before they would let him in.

When we finally got backstage, the Beatles were settling in. I brought Bill in to meet the boys. Amazingly, they didn't look at his hair or talk about it. Their meeting him was just a routine introduction. It was ironic that the Beatles, whose hair was a constant topic of headlines and criticism, didn't care about such trivial aspects of others. Meanwhile, outside the dressing room, the fans' sound machine was reaching a crescendo.

I walked to the top level of the hall and looked down at a cavernous space, an antiquated convention center with large facades over the walls, looking more like a setting for the Mormon Tabernacle Choir than the Beatles. The crowd was loud but orderly, in striking contrast to the pandemonium on the outside, where fans were crushing against the emergency doors, trying to break them down.

Returning to the backstage area, I could hear the pounding on the doors. Police officers were running in all directions. This was beginning to look like Vancouver, except this time steel doors were keeping the mob out. Press chief Derek Taylor was shaken, and he told me about their experience in the limousine motorcade that took them to the hall.

KANE: What happened?
TAYLOR: The Beatles' car was in front. Neil Aspinall, who knows more about getting into places than any person on earth, was in the car. The car was immediately surrounded by kids. Neil guided the driver. The police bashed through. One man had his leg broken. The kids got into our car, the second car, and attacked Bess Coleman. They didn't know who we were. The police rescued us, barely.
KANE: Was it the worst you've ever seen?
TAYLOR: It was pretty bad, due to the unpredictability of a Beatles crowd. They've all seen crowds before. This city, Atlantic City, has seen conventions. What they've never seen is a Beatle crowd. This is the biggest thing that's ever happened. No question about it. It's not like Sinatra, Presley or

the late President Kennedy. It's the Beatles and it's without precedent.

I didn't get to ask the Beatles how that felt to them, but John's comments after the first concert at Forest Hills in New York—which was downright dangerous, with some fans getting on stage—explained the boys' perceptions regarding crowd situations in general. As the tour progressed, the Beatles got braver and more defiant on stage, determined to entertain without interference.

KANE: John, when they stormed the stage last night at Forest Hills, I'm sure that's happened to you before. Do you ever get worried that they might get through?
LENNON: No, y'know, we, I always have hysterics when they get onstage. 'Cause the one last night got George, and he had, I could hear all wrong notes coming out, he was trying to carry on playing, y'know. With a girl hanging 'round his neck—it was funny.
KANE: Do you ever, ever get frightened at any of these experiences on stage, or when you're being pursued, let's say?
LENNON: Not really, y'know. We get battered mostly by people trying to guard us, y'know. They get in the way half the time, and they're always grabbing us and shoving us in the wrong thing. But onstage, I always, I always feel safe even when they break through. I don't know, it must be some kind of—y'know, I just feel as though I'm all right when I'm plugged in and that. Don't feel as though they'll get me.

There were lessons learned in Vancouver and Atlantic City: Never underestimate the will of the crowd, always have more police than you think will be needed, and always presume that one or more people will break down the security. But these instructional episodes were never really studied by police at future concert sites. As Derek Taylor said, "It's the biggest thing that ever happened." How could the band really be protected, when its fans would do anything to get close?

The biggest thing that ever happened at the Atlantic City Convention Hall concluded with less trepidation than it began with. Afterward, the Beatles returned to the hotel, tired and bored. But soon, the press party would be treated to one of the most delightful experiences of tour number one.

Back at the Lafayette, whose rooms and hallways were now free of professional ladies, word was filtered to us that the Beatles had ordered a film to be shown to the entire traveling party. Showtime was midnight. At the appointed time, we entered a room surrounded by glass windows on all sides, with folding chairs set up in a theater-like formation. The screen was a small, white, fold-out version, much like Americans used for home movies in those days. After the guests had been seated, John came in first, looking a bit weary from the concert. Ringo and George sat about five rows back, in front of the row I was sitting in, and then Paul arrived with Malcolm and Neal.

What would the film be? I noticed that George was looking nervous, which struck me as odd, since George Harrison never looked nervous. He was puffing on a cigarette, drink in hand, when he leaned back toward me and said, "This is the first time we'll see the final cut with a crowd other than producers and directors. Should be fun— maybe. Tell me what ya think, Larry." That was when I realized we were getting a screening of *A Hard Day's Night,* the black-and-white gem that would come to be considered a movie classic. It had been released in U.S. theaters a few weeks before.

Refreshments in hand, we watched with wonder a movie that was an exaggerated mirror of the life we were experiencing—overflow crowds, running teenagers, Beatles on the move, great music and four guys hamming it up for the camera. I could see John and George squirming in their seats, the way many people do when they look at a photograph of themselves that they don't particularly like. Paul kept shaking his head. John whispered, "It's awful," and complained about the way he looked. At some points, George even turned away from the screen. There they were, just mere mortals, enduring a private viewing of their own cinematic performances. For ninety minutes, I was witness to the Beatles' critical views of themselves. They looked embarrassed by their remarkably genuine performances. I began to realize then why they had achieved such enormous success as entertainers and public figures: They were real, in the truest sense of the word.

Despite the Beatles' skepticism, most everyone in the room applauded loudly at the end of the film, agreeing that it would be a smash hit, which it was already turning out to be at the box office. Later, I talked over the film with the boys.

KANE: Ringo, I liked the film because it was what I was seeing for the last couple of weeks.

STARR: We tried to get as near as to what we are as we could. Some of it was real bits. Some of it was real acting. We just tried to make it as real as we possibly could. Like the bit on the train. It really happened to us, when the man came in and put the radio off. We told the fellow who wrote the script, and he put it in. That was true, real.

Paul McCartney seemed to downplay the movie experience, dismissing it as just another medium for Beatlemania. But he still had the look of pride in his eyes. John was more direct, talking about his lack of ego and difficulty in watching the film.

KANE: It was interesting watching the film with you.
LENNON: Well, last night was just about the worst. Actually the first time we saw it was the worst. When you first see yourself on the big screen, you say, 'look at my nose, look at my ear.' And each of us did that. We hated it.

While it may have been uncomfortable for its stars to watch, for me, the movie experience was fabulous, a chance to see them do a close-up on their own close-ups, reacting with smiles, grimaces and shaking heads to their own performances. It reminded me of the first time I had ever heard my voice on a tape recording and how much I hated it. I also felt like I was watching a home movie. In essence, I had been living that movie for almost two weeks—the rush, the crowds, the music, no letup, no break—just sheer excitement.

However excited I was, though, I knew that getting some good rest would be important that night. Come morning, we would be heading to a city facing a summer of crisis—Philadelphia, the birthplace of America.

CHAPTER 9:
Rockin' at the Birthplace of Freedom

The birthplace of American liberty, Philadelphia, was having a bad summer. Riots had broken out in North Philadelphia—a devastating example of the racial divide that was tearing through America. With the Beatles and their fans arriving, Philadelphia's tough and brassy police department wasn't taking any chances. Neither was Brian Epstein.

The increased caution began before we even arrived in the city. The Beatles used a surprising ruse to get them out of their Atlantic City hotel: a fish truck. It worked well. The truck carried them about five miles east of Atlantic City, where they joined the bus caravan away from the shore and into the City of Brotherly Love. Looking out the bus windows, I saw the famed Philadelphia Highway Patrol, an elite force of motorcycle cops, protecting us at the front, rear and both sides, giving us presidential-level security in a city just torched by violence.

Strangely, we did not drive toward the center of the city. Instead, the roar of the motorcycles came to an end in an underground garage at the Philadelphia Convention Center, where the concert was scheduled for later that night. Oddly, the garage was empty. Imagine—the Philadelphia police department had reserved an entire municipal garage for the safety of the Beatles. While the cleanup from the riots was still underway, the city government wanted to give the Beatles a fab experience in Philly. But they didn't yet know that this experience would last only five hours. Once again, as he had in Vancouver, Epstein had cancelled the group's reservations at the exclusive

Warwick Hotel in Center City Philadelphia. It would be a night of rock-and-roll—rock at the concert, and roll down the runway and up into the air toward Indianapolis.

As the Beatles settled into a small dressing room, I worried about a dark cloud that was suddenly and strangely hanging over the tour. Psychic Jeane Dixon had forecast the week before that the Beatles' plane would crash on the flight out of Philadelphia. Lennon had asked me about it. With a frown and a shrug, I said, "Are you kidding?" John joked about the fearful forecast but told me quietly that he obsessed about the fatal flight of Buddy Holly.

Like a virus, the fright spread throughout the traveling party, even prompting George to make a phone call to Dixon. Everyone wanted to know, 'What did she say?' George said she was "reassuring," saying that it was okay to fly.

Dixon was a newsmaker—she had forecast the death of JFK—and her alleged vision was making all the gossip columns. I normally wouldn't have introduced the subject of her dire prediction to the Beatles, but since it was already on everybody's minds, I went ahead and asked George to comment.

> KANE: George, we've been hearing things, and reading about this woman who's predicting a plane disaster.
> HARRISON: Uh, normally I just take it with a laugh and a smile and a pinch of salt. Thinking, you know, she's off her head. But, y'know, it's not a nice thing to say, especially when you're flying almost every day. But, just hope for the best, and keep a stiff upper head, and away we go. If you crash, you crash. When your number's up, that's it.

I instantly felt sleazy asking the question during down time in the garage in Philadelphia. In doing so, I raised his anxiety level, not to mention mine. This was the first time I had asked the wrong question at the wrong time. I felt dirty. George handled it well, but it wasn't my best moment.

It was time to clean up my act, as well as my travel-weary body. Art Schreiber joined me for a fast cab ride to the Warwick Hotel, where we freshened up in the rooms we had paid for but would barely use. In the cab, I had gotten my first glimpse of Philadelphia, unaware that in a few years I would begin a long career there. The city was greener than any city I'd ever seen. And hotter. What I would later remember about the concert at the Philadelphia Convention Hall was the heat, the overwhelming security and the spirit of the fans.

Thirteen thousand crazed Philadelphians packed the hall, some in balconies, most on the floor. And the hall was ornate. As I looked around, I recalled that this was the same convention hall where both Democratic and Republican parties gathered in conventions in 1948, nominating President Harry Truman and Republican challenger Thomas Dewey. The place was truly historical. Within an hour, it would become hysterical.

Hy Lit, a popular local deejay, was getting ready to introduce the band from the stage when I noticed some girls in the first few rows taking off their jewelry. When the Beatles arrived on stage, a new flying token of adoration also arrived: jewelry of all sorts, including bracelets, necklaces and—don't forget Ringo—lots of rings. The gems were accompanied by jellybeans, of course, which the Beatles eventually stomped on, primarily for safety reasons since the heat and dripping perspiration was already causing a slippery stage. The main arena was so hot, in fact, that I was beginning to feel sick to my stomach.

Moving quickly to the side corridor, I watched Philadelphia's police hauling away unruly fans. The kids were not cooperating, and neither were some parents. As one brave policeman hauled away her child, a mother screamed in anguish, "Get your goddamned hands off my kid, you punk." The cop, by this point blushing red from his inability to contain this little Dennis the Menace, dropped the child to the floor and said, "He's yours!" The policeman looked at me with a sympathetic glare and, realizing from my tape recorder that I was a newsman, sighed, "This is tough."

That episode mirrored a difficult situation that I experienced in all the venues. Police officers, aware of their responsibilities but wary of manhandling fun-loving children, were severely conflicted. It was a game of dare, and while the police protected the Beatles, it was almost impossible for them to protect themselves from the onrushing crowds, or to protect the crowds from themselves.

Veteran *Philadelphia Daily News* reporter Rose DeWolf was covering the story. Rose remembers: "If those guys were singing songs, I didn't know it. The screaming was endless, but the kids were cute and so were the Beatles. I was in the front row with other reporters, and minutes after the concert got underway, started pulling jellybeans and marshmallows from my hair. The marshmallows had messages written on them to the Beatles. Believe me, the real show wasn't just the Beatles. The show was the kids in the audience!"

During that show, I also found that the conduct and behavior of the fans was getting more of my attention than the music. Moving back from the corridor into the main hall, I surveyed the situation: Girls and some boys close together, standing, screaming, moaning, groaning, ripping at their hair, pushing, shoving, falling on the floor and crying, real tears streaming down hundreds of faces, smearing their mascara and lipstick, and mothers and fathers hiding in the back, some of them dancing to the music.

For the first time, I started wondering whether these kids were in a state of trance. What was making them go? Was this part of a bigger picture? Was there no love in their lives, or were they just "'tweeners" trapped in a time warp, caught between fantasy and reality, stuck between puberty and adulthood?

When Paul sang "I Saw Her Standing There," a girl would look at the stage and stare at Paul, her eyes fixed, no blinking, in order to make it appear that he was singing to her: "I saw YOU standing there."

Tina Camma, a Philadelphia teenager on that night, remembers:

"I became a huge Beatles fan on the night when I first watched them on the *Ed Sullivan Show* in 1964. Imagine my surprise when my aunt and uncle asked me if I would like to see the Beatles in person at their first Philadelphia concert. I couldn't say "yes" fast enough. My uncle purchased three tickets for my cousin Nancy, her cousin Diane and me. At that time, the ticket price was $5.50, but my Uncle paid a scalper the hefty sum of $35.00 per ticket. To this day, I have saved my ticket stub (Center Orchestra F–Q–seat 1)!

"My heart was pounding as we approached the entrance thinking that I was *really* going to see the Beatles, and especially Paul, my favorite. You could feel the electricity in the air.

"After what seemed an eternity, the Beatles were finally introduced, and they were right in front of me. The first song they sang was "If I Fell." I was sure that Paul was singing directly to me! Of course, you couldn't hear a word they sang since there was so much screaming by excited fans—including myself! Everyone stood on their chairs for the *entire* concert. At the conclusion of the concert, I had no voice.

"It was a night I will never forget!"

Tina Camma believed, like so many others at every show, that Paul was singing to her. To this reporter, the connection between fan and Beatle was an extraordinary phenomenon, a special link that traveled beyond idolatry and entered the world of one-to-one personal chemistry and communion. Unfortunately for those thousands of girls, the relationship between them and their favorite Beatle was always a one-way street.

Still, the mixture of the music and the musicians and the reaction to both was amazing. The experts can spend decades figuring that puzzle out, but there's one thing I know for sure—there were no hallucinatory drugs on those premises to cause this phenomenon. It was a little early in the sixties for that. Those kids were simply on a natural high, in an altered state of focused obsession.

Another obsession—that nasty forecast of an aircraft calamity—remained on our minds as we took a long post-concert bus ride to the North Philadelphia airport, the smaller of the city's two airstrips. As Beatles and company boarded the plane, the atmosphere was markedly different from that on previous flights. Neil Aspinall, the Beatles' protector and friend, and a typically serious man, was even more intense than usual. Lennon looked perturbed. Even Clarence Frogman Henry, a cheerful man who had taken the place of the Righteous Brothers as one of the opening acts, looked dour.

The flight to Indianapolis was subdued, but thankfully it was also short and uneventful. Art Schreiber, master journalist and Washington correspondent during the JFK assassination in November 1963, took it in stride, leaning over and saying to me, "Well, if shit happens, the headline will read, 'Beatles perish in crash along with unidentified reporters.' We'll just be a damn footnote to history." Art made me laugh, along with John Lennon. Traveling down the aisle later, John broke out a big smile and said, "So how are the nameless, faceless, unidentified news whores doing tonight?"

Uninfluenced by our anxiety, the Electra had a smooth-as-silk landing in Indianapolis. This airline's date with disaster would have to wait another two years. As far as Jeane Dixon goes, she gained world fame as official astrologer and psychic to First Lady Nancy Reagan in the eighties. Who knows how much she, like the Beatles, shaped history, but on that night of September 2, 1964, she was dead wrong. And that was a very good thing.

CHAPTER 10:
High-Speed Beatlemania

To many people, perception is reality. Besides George Harrison, who had visited America previously to see his sister, the Beatles' view of Americans and the nation as a whole had been distorted by preconceived ideas developed before this first tour. I asked Paul about this.

> KANE: What are your observations about the country of America? What do you think about it?
> McCARTNEY: Yeah, we knew America was big, but traveling in the plane these ridiculous distances, well, it's fantastically big. We were never too keen on American people until we got here because things you seen in films and heard on radio—I wasn't very impressed with American people until we got here, and I think they are great now.

Direct, plainspoken honesty was always a hallmark of Beatle-talk. Paul's comments could have been taken the wrong way, but he was honest enough to state that his impression of Americans hadn't been good and had changed. And the band's view of the expanse and variety of the states was reinforced with each new stop and experience. Indianapolis provided the band with a look at two American traditions: the lure of the speedway and the spirit of the old-fashioned state fair.

Our home in Indianapolis was the Speedway Motor Inn, a motel-type facility that was heavily guarded by Indiana state troopers. It was extremely quiet, except for a few stragglers outside. We woke up late, and within an hour we were following the Beatles as they took a visitors' lap at the Indianapolis Motor Speedway, location of the famed Indy 500. They loved it. So did I.

From the racetrack's infield, George looked at the grandstand with eyes of wonder, a tourist checking out a famous American venue. In a few hours, we left the Speedway for a drive to the country. The roar of the engines was replaced by the sounds of animals at the Indiana State Fair. This was Americana—cows, horses, pigs, flower and vegetable competitions, an old-fashioned carnival atmosphere and, in 1964, the Beatles. Like the Beatles, I had never been to a state fair. The smells of the farm and the bright lights of the midway were exciting and new. Walking past the attractions, I wondered how the Hoosiers of Indiana would react to the Beatles phenomenon. I soon learned that they were no different than fans anywhere else. In the two concerts in at the Indiana State Fair—one inside a coliseum, the other at the grandstand—there were the usual symptoms of onrushing crowds, fainting teenagers and breathless police. One vivid image I'll never forget is of an ice-cream vendor who stopped in place, stared at the Beatles on stage in front of the grandstand and started crying. I said to him, "Is something wrong?" He replied, "No, their music just makes me very happy."

Most people were happy to hear the Beatles. Many others expressed their love by trying to get close. And the Beatles tried, with severe frustration, to love them back. If there was one city where the Beatles demonstrated their love for their fans, it was Milwaukee, our very next stop. After performing two shows in one day in Indianapolis, and spending a short, uneventful night at the Speedway Motor Inn, we boarded the Electra the next morning and jetted off toward America's Dairyland.

Arriving in Milwaukee, the effects of the maximum security which often came between the boys and their fans really hit home.

KANE: Would you like to go and greet the fans at the various airports in America?
McCARTNEY: Yes, of course. Like today in Milwaukee, and we were told there were fans at the airport. Naturally we said, "At least let's drive past them," but the police chief said to the people in our party that we definitely couldn't do that, and there were probably about five hundred people. Five hundred people, especially when they are not a mob that is going to kill each other, they are not trying to kill us or anything. They

are just trying to see us or something, and it is the same with us. We are only trying to see them, just say hello to them.

John Lennon was more incensed by the wedges authorities drove between the band and its fans.

KANE: John, in a lot of the newspapers around the country, there has been the headline like "Beatles Dodge Their Fans." And really there's another story behind it, isn't there?
LENNON: It's usually someone comes up and says the police chief won't let you go. They say "Jump in here," and they drag us before sometimes we don't even know fans are there, because they drag us off so quickly. Even when we are allowed to wave, they give us about half a second, they just sort of shove us and drag us out—that's it.
KANE: It's not that you don't want to see the people.
LENNON: It is right, yeah. In Australia we must have seen a million people there. Because they let us go. There was good security and everybody was happy, but we still saw people everywhere we went. Nobody got hurt, and it was just as many people.

The eternal Beatles contradiction always emerged—the need for security conflicting with the desire to get close, to touch and connect with the throng of devotees. In December 1980, when John Lennon was gunned down in New York City, I remembered his comments well, and also his need to be accessible, open, just a man on the street, relating to other men and women. He seemed to fear no one, to trust everybody.

The security issue caused outrage in Milwaukee, where the press conference was dominated by questions about the Beatles' failure to drive by the fans at General Mitchell Field. Only three of the Beatles showed up at the conference—John was nursing a bad sore throat. The press gathering at the Coach House Motor Inn was hostile, to say the least. At one point, the ever-cheerful Ringo, puffing on a cigarette, glanced over at me with that "get me outta here" look.

More and more, the press was irritating the boys. The typical problems were repetition and stereotyping. I was getting sick of it, too. I mean, how many times can you hear the word "mop top" without getting sick of it?

KANE: An expression used in the newspapers in every city, mop hair—
LENNON: Mop top!
KANE: Mop top. This seems so trite to me. Does it ever get to you?
LENNON: We just break up whenever we see it. Along with the use of "Yeah, yeah, yeah."
KANE: Which has only been in one of your songs.
LENNON: Yeah. Well, we didn't mind [when] it got into the international password "Yeh yeh yeh," but it's been flogged to death, along with "mop top" and "mop-haired foursome."

The "mop tops" had only an hour after the press conference to prepare for a wild ride to the concert. In real Beatles time, a lot can be accomplished in an hour or less. That's why I noticed, with interest, the young woman who followed Paul McCartney into the elevator and the suite of rooms. She was wearing a leather skirt with a hemline well above her kneecaps. The apparel and her sensuous walking style convinced me she wasn't there for autographs.

With "recess" over, the Beatles motorcade left the rear of the Coach House en route to the Milwaukee Arena. It was a small facility with a maximum attendance of eleven thousand, although the crowd looked bigger to me. Backstage was buzzing with excitement, but not the kind you'd expect. I was the first reporter to spot the fire marshal examining the backstage area. I said, "Sir, what are you doing?" He replied, "Just making sure everyone is safe, young man." The marshal was inspecting everything, from the curtain fabric to the amplifiers on the sound stage. It looked ludicrous, and it was all a stunt. Minutes later, the uniformed official handed me a pad and pen and asked me to get autographs for his children. I brought the request to Mal Evans. He emerged from the room with the signed papers. In a flash, the fire marshal was gone.

The Milwaukee concert was sensational, with a spirited crowd but little fan interference. The trouble in this town would take place back at the hotel. Outside the Coach House, fans had picked the usual spot for hero worship: about a block away. Fearing the worst, Milwaukee police had erected ropes that kept fans at a distance. But what access they didn't get visually, the kids made up for verbally. The screams were so loud on the street that I could not sleep that night. That pattern was repeated at many venues, but Milwaukee was the worst on the 1964 tour.

The next afternoon, when we boarded the plane in Milwaukee, George looked like Count Dracula—pale, gaunt, his eyes burrowed deep into sockets surrounded by black circles. The other three, stymied by severe sore throats, looked awful too. The ravages of sleep-lessness were starting to show.

So, sleep-deprived and hoarse, the boys set sight on Chicago and another Beatles onstage first. I had begun wondering if there could be another story angle. After all, by the time I'd reached Chicago, I had seen sixteen concerts in sixteen days at thirteen locations across the country, all the while witnessing the universal language of Beatles love: a passionate hysteria mingled with a heart-throbbing movement of the body. But in Chicago, something new would come along to bring new energy to my reports. Suddenly there was the realization that the Beatles were making people happy, no small task in a year that began with the scars of assassination and the fears of war.

Chicago: What a city! Clean, organized, another great American melting pot, glistening on the shores of Lake Michigan and, with its great Midwestern flair, absolutely ready for the Beatles.

The flight from Milwaukee was the shortest on both tours, but we didn't land where we expected. Scheduled to land at O'Hare Airport, the American Flyer's turboprop touched down instead at Midway Airport. But the airport switch didn't fool several thousand fans who had been alerted by a local radio station. The Beatles, all nursing sore throats and looking wan and exhausted, moved quickly down the steps to the waiting limousines. Our motorcade moved swiftly to the Stockyard Inn, a restaurant famous for its steaks. The inn was an old building with a variety of rooms. Four of us from the press corps enjoyed a meal down the hall from the Beatles' private dining room. For once, we got to avoid the hot dogs and French fries of the concert halls.

It was looking like a pretty good day in Beatle-land until we arrived at the stage entrance to the Chicago International Amphitheater, which was adjacent to the restaurant. By September 5, it was obvious that jelly-beans, stuffed animals, flowers and stick pins were the most likely objects to fly in the direction of the Beatles. But how often do you get struck in the chest by a slice of raw filet mignon thrown by a young hurler in the tenth row? At least Paul McCartney saw the beef missile coming at him and avoided the surprise, if not the impact.

Correspondent Art Schreiber remembers the beef incident: "McCartney was just standing there, doing his thing, when the meat hit the left side of his jacket, splattering a bit of beef juice but falling to the floor, where George sort of kicked it out of the way. The most dumbfounded of all was Ringo, who stretched his neck out over the microphones on the drums to see what the hell it was. It was funny, and it was weird."

The kids in the crowd were too occupied shrieking and crying and pulling their hair out to see the UFO (*unusual* flying object). In the crowd, people like Barbara Singer were swooning with delight:

"I had just turned fourteen. Miraculously, my father managed to snare a pair of tenth-row tickets to that concert for my sixteen-year-old sister and me. My sister and I were ecstatic when we took our seats on the night of the show. We were so close to the stage that we could almost touch the microphones that had been set out in front for John, Paul and George. The air was thick with anticipation as we waited impatiently for the music to begin. Finally, the Beatles took the stage to a chorus of screams thirteen thousand strong. My sister joined the frenetic crowd and began to shriek loudly into my right ear. I realized with dismay that the pandemonium around me was drowning out the sounds coming from the stage. Frantically, I begged my sister to stop screaming so that I could hear the Beatles. My pleas fell on deaf ears. My sister continued to squeal with the crowd throughout the set. Fortunately, somewhere between 'I Saw Her Standing There' and 'Twist and Shout,' my sister overcame her frenzy just long enough to take a photo of the Fab Four with her Instamatic camera. We still have treasured copies of that singular snapshot, reminding us of the greatest concert that we never heard!"

Barbara's sister and the thousands around her provided us with the loudest reaction yet to the Beatles. The amphitheater was small, and the screaming seemed to resonate as if it were projected into a canyon. I heard not a word of lyrics. I did get an eyeful of Beatles— though I had to venture into the crowd to get it. But soon I found myself pinned between the crowd and the stage. The situation was so very tight that I had no choice but to stand in place and watch. It actually turned out to be a wonderful opportunity to take in the scene. Here are my notes, which I scribbled on the plane later that night:

"Ringo. Beating the drums so hard. Wonder how he can hear what's going on with the crowd noise. He keeps on putting the stick to the drums. Looks around. Smiling. George kicks the slab of meat off the stage. McCartney and Lennon face-to-face, cheek-to-cheek, almost in perfect harmony on "I Wanna Hold Your Hand." Girl behind me puts arms over my shoulders, reaching out to try and grab Paul's shoes. Her face is pressed against the strap of the tape recorder. Cop has arms spread out to prevent movement toward stage. Paul looks down at me with an expression that reads, "What are YOU doing down there?" He smiles. Wonder if I'll make the motorcade or get squeezed to death here. Breathing difficult. Sweating loads. Girl in rear crying. Is it pain or pleasure? "Hard Days Night" playing. This was a hard night. Being in the middle, between Beatles and fans, makes me feel closer to it—whatever "it" is. Clarence Frogman Henry is standing near the stage, taking it in. When "Hard Days Night" is over, I start pushing and shoving to get out, but some private guard holds me back. I move to the other side and reach rear entrance. No chances here. I get to the cars before the Beatles. Neil brings boys to limo. Ringo jokes about flying meat. Derek looks pissed. Hope I never see this place again. It's too hot and sticky."

I would see it again. In 1968, I covered the tumultuous Democratic Convention, the one that saw riots and fighting in the streets. Walking into the hot, smoke-filled amphitheater again, jostling between delegations, being squeezed in by television crews, I had flashbacks of my earlier claustrophobia in 1964. I reminisced about the Beatles concert with my colleagues in '68, who expressed disbelief at my experiences. In the years between 1964 and 1968, my career had taken me to scenes of racial rioting, student revolt and normal moments of everyday life. But there was something different about the Beatles tours. In my life before and since, I have never witnessed the degree of ardor, zeal and delight that I saw in Chicago and the other cities. The Beatles, on balance, were a happy story in an unhappy decade.

Of course, happy stories can have unhappy chapters. As our plane took off in a thunderstorm from Chicago at 11:30 that night, the mood was upbeat. The Beatles had conquered New York, Los Angeles and now Chicago with great performances and little real controversy. Their safety, although always a problem, was never fully compromised. That would change.

When we landed in Detroit, there were three thousand fans waiting at the airport. Motorcycle police escorted the lead cars to an expressway, but strangely, halfway into town, those police motorcycles from a suburban police department dropped off, and our cars continued without escort. The rest of the ride became a race. Cars with screaming fans leaning out the windows veered in and out of our lanes. Ivor Davis was riding with me, and the *London Daily Express* reporter was astounded. He recalls, "There we were, moving along nicely, and suddenly the cops disappeared. It was scary."

Wisely, the lead limo driver pulled into the garage of the Whittier Hotel, close to elevators that would take the traveling party up to the rooms. Some of the pursuing cars, with frenetic fans inside, drove into the garage seconds later. Davis and I got out of our car to find that, outside of Mal Evans and Neil Aspinall, there was no official security in that garage!

Paul McCartney looked concerned and yelled over to us, "Stay close, guys, we may be in trouble!" We stayed close, forming a small line of defense for the Beatles against hundreds of fans, who were getting closer and closer. The elevator doors opened, and the frightened Beatles slipped inside with Mal and Neil. We continued to face the fans, who, sensing defeat, ran out of the garage and to the front of the hotel.

That was the first and only time we were the protectors, though our responsibilities were short-term. It was an odd role, one that gave me an appreciation for the thousands of police officers who had braved the crowds to safeguard the guys. Of course, in Detroit at that moment there had been no security, which was in itself a crime.

Ironically, outside the hotel, the Detroit police department was out in force. And the department did a good job of securing Olympia Stadium during two concerts the next night. Not only did they serve and protect, but they also cleaned up, picking up hundreds of watches and pieces of jewelry thrown from the crowd toward the stage. There were forty arrests that night, mostly of girls and boys who were hurling jellybeans toward the boys. Later, Paul said he had been amused.

> KANE: Did you ever get mad at the audience?
> McCARTNEY: No, not really. Only time is if a jellybean does really hurt, which one or two have. I haven't gotten really mad, just thought, 'I wish you wouldn't' sort of thing. But you know, if you get one that's thrown from a high balcony in a theater, it comes down bang and it's going pretty fast when it hits you. It is the only time I have ever gotten a bit annoyed, but it's not worth getting mad about.

Despite the comments of the most diplomatic Beatle, I can tell you that all four were terrified of flying objects. But, as you can see, their high regard for their fans precluded any public lecturing or scolding. There were rules among the Beatles: Love and trust the fans, be wary of the press, and never, ever mention the "B" word, as in "breakup." The "B" word was something not to be taken lightly.

Of all the Beatles, George Harrison detested that word the most. In Detroit, I questioned him about rumors of a breakup.

> KANE: There are a lot of fan magazines that have rumors. Does that ever bug you?
> HARRISON: It drives you up a wall sometimes. Since we've been over here they've been asking us, 'Is John leaving?' Well, the new one today is it's me leaving. You know, that's just because some idiot in Hollywood has written in the papers that I'm leaving, so now I will have for weeks people coming up time after time and asking, 'Is it true you are leaving?'

The breakup was a long way away in 1964. The real truth was that the four individuals had become an unbreakable unit with a rare oneness that few bands would ever realize.

Unfazed by minor rivalries, disaffected so far by their enormous fame, the Beatles flew on to their next challenge, the invasion of Ontario and Quebec.

CHAPTER 11:
Guns, Palm Trees, and a Rock-and-Roll Hurricane

High winds were churning in the Caribbean, and a political storm was brewing in Montreal. As the Beatles left Detroit, they began a five-day swing that would put them face to face with machine guns, take them off course to an unscheduled destination, and finally bring them directly into the eye of racial controversy. And through a strange sequence of events, I played a principal role in their travel plans.

The short flight from Detroit to Toronto brought back memories of the tour's first Canadian melee at Empire Stadium in Vancouver. Jackie DeShannon was gleeful on the plane, kidding Paul McCartney about his great escape at the stadium in Detroit. Jackie always sat in the front rows, but she still managed to spend more time with the boys than any of the other traveling entertainers.

I was trying to get a few minutes of peace on the plane, but a news report was nagging at me. Word from my station back in Miami had it that Hurricane Dora, seventeen hundred miles away, was looking like a sure bet to skirt the Jacksonville area—the Beatles' scheduled two-day rest stop prior to a concert at the Gator Bowl. I advised Brian Epstein of the hurricane's 110-mile-an-hour winds and the potential for damage in the Jacksonville area.

As I stood face to face with Epstein, John Lennon was sitting a few feet away and listening. Epstein was clearly concerned by the prospect of the hurricane disrupting the tour. Lennon was also concerned. "Larry, can you fly into a hurricane?" he asked. I replied, "No, unless you like living on the edge." Lennon, afraid of flying in the first place, shrugged and lit a cigarette, his eyes wandering, his lids opening and closing. Hurricane Dora's path was clearly on his mind, but the man needed sleep.

Brian Epstein was a man of careful detail and strategic planning. "Larry," he said, "you're from Miami, you know the state. Is there a good spot for the boys to spend a few days quietly?" I answered, "Well, there's only one place I know of where they could have a little bit of peace. That's Key West. Key West would do it. Kind of enchanting. Three hours south of Miami." Epstein replied, "Good. Good. I'll check it out."

Toronto was minutes away when reporter Ivor Davis handed me a transcript from the Detroit press conference, which I had missed. The patter was funny—and flattering.

> REPORTER: With all these women chasing you around, who is probably the most exciting woman you've ever met?
> LENNON: Ringo's mother is pretty hot.
> REPORTER: Who are the chief competitors of the Beatles?
> McCARTNEY: Sophie Tucker.
> REPORTER: In respect to nothing, what do you like?
> STARR: I like steak. I like girls. And I like Larry Kane.

I smiled, gratified that they knew me well enough to poke fun in an open news conference, happy that after almost three weeks, I had found a comfort level with them on this amazing trip. For a change, I was relaxed. But that calm would disappear in a matter of minutes.

A crowd, estimated at seven thousand, had been waiting for twenty-four hours behind a chain-link fence at the Toronto airport, indulging in an orgy of screaming, crying and shouting. The crowd was so loud that we could hear the people screaming over the sound of the turbo-prop engines. Immigration officers came on board, and while the paperwork was being completed, tour aide Bob Bonis and Mal Evans were running up and down the aisles shouting, "Go right to the cars. Go right to the cars. Go fast." What alarmed them was the sight outside—the chain-link fence seemed to be collapsing under the weight of the crowd. Scores of police, including some members of the Royal Canadian Mounted Police, were pressing hard against the opposite side of the fence. The screaming intensified as we ran for the cars, which for safety reasons had driven up only when the plane doors opened. The good news was our quick exit. The bad news was the disappointment of the waiting kids.

The potential for a security breakdown had become a familiar fear. As the cars moved away at high speeds with a motorcycle escort close by, I wondered what was ahead at the hotel. The King Edward Hotel was in the heart of Toronto. It was almost 1 a.m. when we reached the front, but judging by the four-thousand-strong crowd it might as well have been one in the afternoon. The cars pulled under the marquee sign, and the Beatles, led by Paul, ran through a gauntlet of police and into the lobby, where just ahead of the rest of us, a crowd of kids started trailing them. The helmeted police were holding their own, but this smaller crowd had managed to break into the lobby. There, for the first time on the tour, from a few feet away, I watched the Beatles come under direct attack.

To my left, John was fighting off a young woman who was attempting an embrace but appeared to be trying to grab his neck. John, perturbed, shoved her away. On the right, Paul was having an encounter with two fans, a girl and a boy. As the police tried to break it up, Neil Aspinall rushed in. Neil and a police officer grabbed the fans, but in the process a large piece of Paul's shirt was ripped. What a souvenir that was. George had sneaked through, but Ringo was caught, surrounded by four or five fans just staring at him. Humorously, he held his hand up, smiled, said, "Nice to see ya," and made a mad dash to the elevator.

Once we were on the floor where we would be staying, several Royal Canadian Mounties took their place outside the rooms, looking stern but also offering courtesy and cheerfulness to us. In my room I freshened up and had started writing my morning summary when I heard a scuffle down the hall. I peered out. The Mounties were gently escorting a girl to the elevator. What had happened? I learned in the morning that the girl was hiding in a linen closet when the Beatles arrived in their suite of rooms.

The hour was late, but the fun was just beginning—further proof that strange happenings would confront us at the weirdest times. As I was taking care of some business in the bathroom, there was a knock-knock on the door. It was 2 a.m., and I couldn't imagine what the problem might be with so much security in place.

When I opened the door, I saw her standing there, a wisp of a woman dressed in an official-looking gray blouse and skirt and holding towels and some soap. "You called for some soap," the housekeeper said. I answered, "Well no, but I'll take some."

The woman took the soap, placed it in the soap dish in the bathroom sink, came back to the room, sat down on the bed and said, "Sir, are you a Beatle?" I said, "No, I'm not a Beatle." I asked her politely to leave.

She got up, turned toward me and said, "Where's George?"

"George?"

"George Harrison."

"I really don't know."

"I wanna say hello to George Harrison." She started giggling almost at the same time as I heard another knock on my door, as well as knocking on other doors nearby. I opened the door to find a tall, rather stern-looking woman wearing the same uniform as the girl in the room. She said that she was searching the rooms because a housekeeper's uniform was missing from the supply closet. Behind her was a man with the grim, determined eyes of a detective. I knew a cop when I saw one. While we were talking, that little wisp of a housekeeper had moved into the bathroom. In silence, I pointed my finger in the direction of the washroom. The man and the queen bee housekeeper ran across the little room and began to escort the imposter out. Unfortunately, the girl started crying, and I felt badly. Now that the event was ending, I admired her creativity. She had gotten pretty far but had knocked on the wrong door.

Finally, I was ready to sleep, but not before I called the station in Miami to get an update on Hurricane Dora. The news was not good. Dora, with top winds of 120 miles per hour, was growing in speed and might hit the greater Jacksonville area on September 9 or 10. The Gator Bowl concert was scheduled for the night of September 11.

Before the two Toronto concerts at Maple Leaf Gardens, there was time for an interview session with the Beatles, who were all agog about their close escape in the hotel lobby. I told Ringo that he had handled his encounter with a great sense of humor. Ringo explained that he hated being called the "sad" Beatle.

KANE: Hi, Ringo, how are you?

STARR: All right, Larry. How are you?

KANE: Pretty good. A lot of magazines and portraits of you depict you as being very sad. You're not a sad person, are you?

RINGO: No. It's just the face, you know. [laughter] I keep telling people at all these conferences, comes up every time, people saying, "Why are you so sad?" Y'know, I'm quite happy inside. I love to smile.

In truth, Ringo's smile was contagious. Though his facial features may have had a natural tendency to sort of droop, the sadness many noted was never evident to me. In fact, Ringo always seemed to me the most upbeat member of the group.

In the Beatles' Toronto hotel suite, as in all other cities, gifts and cards were piling up a few feet high. Most of them had been sent to the Beatles via their fan clubs, which assisted in getting pictures and signed cards, if possible, back to the fans. Many of the gifts were sent to homes for needy children and hospitals. Some would always be remembered by the Beatles.

> KANE: What about the gifts? I notice more and more you've been getting more and more gifts from fans. What was the most unusual gift you've ever received? I know there's so many—is there one that sticks out in your mind?
> LENNON: [laughs] I once received a bra—
> KANE: You did?
> LENNON: —with "I Love John" embroidered on it. I thought it was pretty original. I didn't keep it, mind you. It didn't fit.

The Canadian welcome for the Beatles was a warm one. The community was so touched by their visit that nearby Hamilton Mountain was renamed "Beatles Mountain." The downtown area was filled with people and excitement. And Toronto's hockey palace, Maple Leaf Gardens, was host to a total of more than thirty-five thousand ticket holders in two concerts on the same evening. Outside the venue, crowds of Canadians wandered the sidewalks, hoping for a glimpse.

Inside the gardens, the crowd in the first concert was on its feet. One of the Beatlemaniacs was John Moore, who somehow remembers the events of the evening:

"My older brother's girlfriend took me, since I was only three in 1964. We discovered that putting our hands over our ears would filter out the screams and allow their music to come through, although we were screaming too some of the time. When it was over, it got a bit scary. All of the thousands of ecstatic fans were trying to leave at once. The exit we were leaving through had too many fans trying to get out at once. People were getting crushed against the walls, screaming and getting trampled. I remember Nancy and I pushing on that wall very hard and rolling along to avoid injury."

During the second concert, I had the rare chance to sit and listen to the entire performance, since it was possible to hear the band in this relatively orderly crowd. And I noticed that the Beatles' guitar connoisseur, George Harrison, was switching guitars between songs. So I asked him about it later.

> KANE: Okay. The guitar you have, right—I should say the guitar you're playing—has twelve strings. Now why, before the song "If I Fell" during the act, you change guitars. What is the reason behind this?
> HARRISON: Uh, 'cause it's got a different sound, y'see. With a twelve-string, it's two sets of each—I mean, there's two lots of each string, y'see. Only, instead of it being tuned the same, they're in octaves, y'see, so instead of getting this note [plays a note] like you would on a normal one, you get [plays same note an octave higher]. So you get [high note] and [low note] both together, so it gives you that noise, y'see. It's—it's a higher sound. And with it being electric, it's a good sound, and I, so the ones I've used, um, when I've used this on a record, I use it onstage as well, y'see, that's why I'm always swapping 'round.

So I learned something new. To duplicate the sounds of their recordings in a live concert, the Beatles would use the same instruments on stage as they had in the studio. That interview in Toronto extended my musical education. And one of the unsung talents of John Lennon also came to light during a Toronto interview. We call it a harmonica. He called it a "mouth organ."

> KANE: How many other instruments do you play, if you play any?
> LENNON: A bit of piano, and a bit of mouth organ.
> KANE: Have you played the organ, um, mouth organ on any of your songs?
> LENNON: Well . . . yeah. There's quite a few we did with mouth organ. I played it on the early hits—"Please Please Me," "From Me to You," "Love Me Do," "Little Child" from the LP, "I Should Have Known Better" on the film, I stuck mouth organ on that.

After the two Toronto concerts, the Beatles returned to the King Edward Hotel in a police paddy wagon. The Toronto Police Department was determined to avoid the embarrassment of the scramble in the lobby that had caused chaos and confusion the night before. Thus far on this tour, the Beatles had had the distinction of traveling in a flower truck, a fish truck, three ambulances, and now a paddy wagon—the height of glamour.

Back in my room, knowing we were on our way to Florida after our next stop in Montreal, I decided it was time for an update on our friend Dora. Hurricane Dora was heading north-northwest at ten miles per hour. On its current course it would be in the central-northern region of Florida in thirty hours, just in time for the Beatles' mini-vacation, which had originally been scheduled for the waters off of Jacksonville. I called Brian Epstein, who told me he was "leaning" toward my recommendation of Key West. We would know tomorrow, he said, in Montreal, where another kind of storm was brewing.

The headlines in the Toronto papers held an ominous warning, along with a funny quote. Threats had been received against the Beatles in Quebec Province, where political factions had been fighting against British influence and for separation from the rest of Canada since decades before the Beatles were born. One group of extreme separatists had apparently complained about Ringo Starr, whom they called the "English Jew." Quebec had an anti-British sentiment, and some individuals from the right wing had also targeted Jews with fiery rhetoric. Ringo replied with a chuckle to a newspaper reporter: "I'm not Jewish. But I am British." Against that backdrop, Epstein had decided on another marathon plan—a flight from Toronto to Montreal, two concerts there, and a long flight to a mystery destination, presumably away from Hurricane Dora.

As the Electra taxied toward the gate at the airport in Montreal, I was sitting in a window seat, peering out to the arrival area. What I saw was awesome—local police, motorcycle patrols, the Mounties again, and something new: a couple of nondescript men in gray suits pacing back and forth.

This time, the opening acts and press deplaned first. I thought that perhaps we were guinea pigs, sent out to absorb any possible attack. But I was getting carried away; we made it out safely. Though it was a rainy day, several thousand fans had gathered in an observation deck area and were cheering the Beatles on. The band waved at the crowd and then moved to the limousine, and two of the gray-suited men also climbed in. The Beatles looked surprised. So did Derek Taylor. Later I learned that the men were Secret Service-type detectives, trained in personal protection. And there were more obvious signs of security concerns yet to come.

The first submachine guns were spotted as we arrived at the rear entrance to the Forum, Montreal's old and dusty citadel of professional hockey. The motorcade entered the rear of the Forum. A large, loading-dock type of door opened, and the Beatles' lead car moved inside. Heavily armed gendarmes surrounded the guys as they emerged from their car.

Brian Epstein's facial color transformed as he walked into the loading dock area. He remarked to me, "This is not worth it. These fucking Canadians—all the time, they shit on the Queen. Piss on them." Epstein was reacting to the press articles about their visit, which were clearly seeking to accentuate the threats to the Beatles' safety. Minutes later, when I entered the dressing room of the famed Montreal Canadians hockey club, I saw John Lennon looking gaunt and concerned. Paul McCartney, charming as usual, conducted some newspaper interviews. Ringo complained of a nagging itch. And George Harrison was buried in a *Green Hornet* comic book, grinning from ear to ear. The Beatles were looking for distractions. The anti-English newspaper articles had clearly disturbed them.

Yet despite the anti-British sentiments, the fans in Quebec gave a welcome to the Beatles that matched the emotional peak of many other concerts. But the scene was different. While the teenagers screamed and clapped their hands during "All My Loving," sharpshooters and uniformed officers of the Royal Canadian Mounted Police stood watch in the upper stands, making sure that no protesters could get in and make worldwide news by disrupting the concert with violence.

Next to the stage stood a plainclothes officer who had been assigned to cover Ringo. I walked in back of the stage and watched Ringo carefully. The drummer looked frightened and wary. As his hands played the drums, his eyes were wandering left to right, right to left. He was sweating.

During the break between shows, Epstein told me that Key West would be the site of the two-day vacation. The Beatles seemed happy, but my knowledge of the location posed a serious question for me, and I knew that Derek and Brian would be talking to me about it. Miami was three hours' driving time from Key West. I would have to make a choice about what information to report. The minute I broadcasted their upcoming whereabouts on WFUN Radio, caravans would start heading south.

Brian Epstein caught up with me in a corridor of the Montreal Forum. He said, "Larry, can you help us? If we can get a few hours in Key West without any news of where we are, we might get some real rest. If you report this tonight, we'll have a zillion kids from Miami headed there before we even arrive. What can you do?"

I replied that I would embargo the story until about nine the following morning. It was hard to hold back such a big piece of news, but the need for speed conflicted with the reality that I held in my hands the power to spoil this trip for the Beatles. Epstein was relieved. I was anxious and nervous, so concerned in fact that I decided not to call my boss. Even the slightest leak of the news might get it broadcast by one of our deejays.

With Florida in our immediate future, the escape from Montreal was flawless. On the aircraft, as official travel papers were being processed, Ringo looked like a new man. John commented on all the guns in Montreal and warned me not to let the cat out of the bag. I told him, "The cat is in the bag till tomorrow morning." The other reporters had also agreed to hold the story.

The flight to Key West was smooth as silk for about a half-hour. But as we reached the eastern seaboard, winds from Dora started playing with our balance. I looked to the rear and saw John and Paul slumped in deep sleep. I couldn't sleep, as I was so worried that word would get out about the destination. Just when I was feeling gloomy, Ringo broke the mood by hurling pillows down the center of the plane. George did him one better by sending a roll of toilet paper down the rear aisle, touching off pandemonium and some real laughter. Laughter in the middle of that insanity was a prescription for better health.

Our arrival at Key West was the strangest to date, simply because it was so different from the others. Not a creature was stirring at 4 a.m. when the plane touched down, other than a few police officers, a representative from the hotel and a handful of fans, who kept their distance. Finally, the wild ride had temporarily stopped and we were ready for a real rest.

John Lennon slept till four the next day, then emerged in a bullfighter's shirt on a terrace at the Key Wester Motel, a colony of cottages located across from the turquoise water of the Atlantic Ocean. Ringo came out in pajamas, delighting a small group of fans watching from across the street.

I walked up to John and made a proposition. "Why don't you come with me to Miami? We'll just take a drive home, I'll pick up some clothes and I'll take you on a tour. No interviews. No one will know, and you'll escape the crowds headed here." Mal Evans loved the idea. John seemed really interested. But Derek thought it was too risky. So I rented a car and drove home alone.

What I saw on the way out was a cavalcade of cars headed in. Six hours after my report on WFUN, the kids of Miami were descending upon Key West. I felt guilty about reporting the arrival, but a deal was a deal, and I had kept my part of the bargain. It was strange to be on home turf again. Suddenly, I had a few hours of normalcy—no security, no crowds, noise or hoopla. And the three hours I spent driving to Miami, along with the return trip, provided some free time for thinking.

There was no question in my mind that the Beatles tour, the assignment I had loathed earlier in the year, was part of a bigger picture in American society that I was just starting to understand. The men themselves were a wonderful story—there was no shortage of news. But in the crowds and along the police barriers, and mostly in the tenor of the experience, I could see my generation and even younger people moving in a new direction. From forty years later looking back, this observation seems obvious, but the new perspective I was gaining then was fresh and illuminating. News people try to become instant analysts, but sometimes you have to take a step back to see the real, underlying story, and my pause in South Florida helped me to focus. There was no question—immense cultural changes were underway.

The way the fans across the country expressed their defiance of authority was the first thing worth noting. Crowds of middle-class kids forging ahead and piercing police lines had been unheard of in the fifties. The almost sexual openness of the Beatles fans was also startling. Suddenly, normal, polite teenagers were showing their passion and pleasure in a very public way. This was shocking to an older generation, but sensuality was replacing sensibility, and the road was opening to an expanded liberation. The impact of the Beatles' style on their fans, too, was enormous. The hairstyle that many listeners adopted to copy the bands' hair was especially notable. The style looked primitive by 1964 standards, but it was a precursor of the long-haired look that would soon accompany the antiwar protests.

While Berkeley (California) was exploding in campus revolution, and open defiance against discrimination had surfaced in the South and elsewhere, the so-called mainstream followers of the Beatles were experiencing their own sea change, abandoning the structured forms of the fifties and exploring a new and public passion. And by 1968, many of them would be facing police barricades once again as they joined in antiwar and civil-rights protests.

When the Beatles had first begun to play their beautiful music, Americans were still building bomb shelters, but Cold War rhetoric was taking a back seat as a hot war was incubating in Southeast Asia. The mid-sixties was a strange time. We were headed into outer space, but there seemed little space at home for a real debate on civil rights, war and peace, and the politics of violence.

As I drove to and from Miami, I reflected on the headlines of September 1964, which often had ominous overtones. The White House Chief of Staff had resigned after a dubious liaison with a man in a Washington restroom. This scandal for President Lyndon Johnson occurred during the same month that China detonated its first nuclear weapon. Less than a year after a president was murdered, more storm clouds were gathering over America. LBJ was publicly dead set against expanding the conflict in Vietnam, while he was quietly planning a post-election escalation.

My very short visit home also awakened me to the reality of my personal loss—the death of my mother, the impact of which was not yet clear, considering the vacuum I had been living in on the tour. As I drove back to Key West, I thought how sad it was that I couldn't share these experiences with her. She was an open-minded person, and the experiences of the tour would have really amused her. I guess that inability to be able to talk to her brought home the reality of her death. I missed her. Changes. We are never quite ready for them, are we?

More changes were evident when I arrived back in Key West. Crowds, some unruly, were gathered in the crosswalks near the Key Wester Hotel. Despite their arrival, though, the Beatles were managing to have some fun. John took a drive to Key Largo, the band ate a fried chicken dinner with the Exciters, they went swimming at the home of a local millionaire, and they retreated to their rooms for some genuine private time.

The next morning, there were rumors that Ringo was sick and needed to get his tonsils out. Keep in mind that every sniffle, sneeze or cough of any Beatle was recorded for posterity. The whole group had experienced sore throats on the Indianapolis-Chicago-Milwaukee run. I decided it was time to find out the real story.

KANE: A rumor going around is that you are going to have a throat operation.
STARR: Yes, well, everyone thinks any minute now I am going into a hospital to have my tonsils out, which isn't true. If you remember, when the boys went to Europe and Australia, I joined them later in Australia because I was in the hospital with tonsillitis. The doctor said, 'It would be a good idea if you had them out when you have time, when you have a holiday.' He says, 'You may go for five years, six months without them troubling you again, but they are not doing any good, so why don't you get them out.' So I said, 'So the next holiday we have in England, I will have them out to get rid of them,' you see.

In the land of the Beatles, this was a scoop. Sure enough, in December of that year, Ringo's tonsils were removed. Beatles fans slept easier.

With that bit of news uncovered, it was time to hit the road, or in this case, the air. Their trip to Jacksonville was to be another one-night stand, but this one was particularly important to me. The station was flying a hundred listeners in to see the concert at the Gator Bowl. You may remember that it was this WFUN promotion that had started my participation in the entire Beatles project. It would be a kick to greet the Miami listeners at the Gator Bowl.

As we took off from Key West, I asked John again about the controversy over potential racial segregation at the Gator Bowl. He told me that they had been assured there would be no seating by race. He was distracted as he spoke with me, because Lennon was obsessed with fear over the flight to Jacksonville. Hurricane Dora had battered the north Florida coast, with damage estimates reaching 1.5 billion dollars. And it wasn't entirely over yet. Remnants of the big storm were hanging on, hitting our plane with heavy winds as we made our ascent. Then, when we were ready to land in Jacksonville, there was an unexpected delay, one that the boys would talk about for days to come.

The Beatles had received the red-carpet treatment at every airport on the continent. But at Jacksonville, the American Flyer's Electra circled the city for quite a while, waiting for clearance. The band was taking a back seat to the president of the United States. Lyndon Johnson had come to Jacksonville to tour the hurricane disaster zone, and Beatles One was banned from landing until the wheels were up on Air Force One.

Finally, our plane got permission to land and did so without event. With the winds howling and a touch of hail hitting the cars, the Beatles and their traveling party arrived at the George Washington Hotel for a news conference, some freshening up and a quick meal before leaving for the Gator Bowl.

Once at the venue, I joined the WFUN crowd for a visit in the stands. The kids who had been flown in from Miami by the station were overwhelmed with excitement at being there, but they were also getting drenched by rain and wind, as was I. In other ways, too, this was an unusual Beatles concert. The stadium was almost one-third vacant, since the weather was keeping people away. And the concert was delayed because film cameramen refused to leave, forcing Derek Taylor to take the microphone and warn fans that unless the cinematographers left, the Beatles would not play. It was simple: Epstein wanted no film of the concerts, nothing that could be pirated for profit. That's why today there is little film or video available of actual Beatles performances. Eventually the cameramen left the front of the stage in Jacksonville, and the press secretary rallied the fans to welcome the band. I brought the topic up with Derek later.

KANE: Derek, why did you kick the newsreel guys out?
TAYLOR: Well, we've never let a concert be filmed—proprietary reasons—and they wouldn't leave. So the only way was for me to get on the microphone and let the fans know what was happening.

The concert itself had been conducted in winds of up to forty-five miles per hour. I asked the band how it felt to play under those circumstances.

KANE: You had thirty- or forty-mile-an-hour winds out there.
LENNON: It felt like a hundred-mile-an-hour one to me.
KANE: You still didn't have any trouble getting out the song—did it really bother you?
LENNON: Yeah, you know, we've never been through a thing like that. We were most sort of awkward with—all our hair was blowing up. We all looked like four Elvis Presleys or

something. We felt uncomfortable with all that wind. . . . Nice working with you, Larry—even in a hurricane.

The wind had been blowing so hard that Ringo's drums had to be secured to the stage. At times it appeared that he might become airborne at any second. I asked him to comment.

KANE: It looked like you might fly away.
STARR: Well, Larry, my hair was blowing, and I thought it was weird, but the drums were tied down, so we made it, you know.

In the stands, with winds howling and the Beatles' hair flying every which way, the fans, including Beverly Griffith, were electrified. Griffith remembers:

"I saw the Beatles in September 1964 in Jacksonville, Florida, at the old Gator Bowl. The concert was just a couple of days after Hurricane Dora hit Jacksonville, and the city was in turmoil. But that didn't keep us dedicated Beatles fans from getting downtown to the concert!

"I was just fourteen, and being female, too young, as I was told by my parents, to go with anyone other than my mother, who being the good sport she was, joined me graciously! Tickets were just five dollars, but a healthy sum back then. The Gator Bowl was packed with screaming kids and it was pretty difficult to even catch the words to the songs, and with everyone jumping up and down, there was no sitting there being quiet! If you wanted to see, you were on your feet, too!

"All in all, it was a wonderful, memorable night, and one that to this day I can still think of fondly and tell my kids about. I may be in my fifties now, but I'll always love the Beatles."

The weather that Florida fans endured to see the Beatles kept the crowds outside under control. And the motorcade to the airport was untouched by human hands or any form of blockade, which was a rarity. The Gator Bowl concert, which people had long assumed would become a simmering controversy over racial injustice, ended quietly by Beatles' standards. And the crowd was fully integrated. There was no official confirmation that the concert had been scheduled to be segregated in the first place, but the South was the South. In the end, blacks and whites sat side by side, sharing an experience. The Beatles had prevailed.

So, in a matter of five days, the Beatles had walked through a mugging in Toronto, endured threats in Montreal, enjoyed a few days in the sun, survived the winds and rain of a devastating hurricane and, before a long flight to Boston, wowed the crowd at the Gator Bowl, concurrently making a statement about the rights of human beings. If that wasn't exciting, what is?

CHAPTER 12:
North to Boston: Does Anyone Have a Compass?

The trip from Jacksonville to Boston was another example of the travel chaos the Beatles were constantly embroiled in. Following a normal, intelligent path from one geographical point to another was never a part of the Beatles extravaganza of 1964. Consider that we had started in the West, traveled east, then west again, then north to Canada, south to Florida and, lo and behold, we were now in Boston, the teeming, vibrant metropolis of the New England states. Boston, a city rich in history and known for citizens fiercely attached to their heritage and, of course, their sports teams. Despite the travel zaniness, there was at least a convenience factor in Boston. The Madison Hotel was attached to the Boston Gardens, home of the Boston Bruins and Celtics and, very shortly, the Beatles.

The hotel was eerily quiet on our arrival at 3:45 a.m. But the next day, thousands of fans arrived by subway, bus and rail to torment Boston police in a cat-and-mouse escapade that continued through the day as fans ran and hid and tried to penetrate the lobby area. They were aggressive and, in at least one case, very creative in their maneuvers.

An afternoon press conference for the Beatles was going to be held in a room just off the lobby. Two teenagers, a boy and a girl, infiltrated the room before the band got there and sat down, masquerading as newspeople. The boy, carrying a regulation reporter's notebook, gave himself away when he leaped at Ringo and tried to grab him. Malcolm Evans cheerily carried the boy out as though he were a baby in his arms. The girl followed them out on her own recognizance.

Other than that, the press conference went off well. And then the Beatles, following an afternoon rest, made their short commute to the concert via a pair of freight elevators. Inside the garden, a capacity crowd was sweating so much that no doubt pounds were melting off. The normal heat of a Beatles concert was exacerbated by the lack of air conditioning. For nearly fourteen thousand fans, that Beatles concert was the hottest scene in town.

One difference I noted in the Boston audience was the large number of boys. One of them was an eleven-year-old named Jim Morin, who today is the editorial cartoonist for the *Miami Herald*. Here's what he recalls:

"The atmosphere was electrifying. We took our seats on the side about center ice. When they bounded onto the stage, the place went mad. Hearing the screaming on video does not come near the feeling of being in the middle of it, enveloped in it. The sound was deafening.

"There was a flashbulb going off every millisecond; the sight of hundreds of flashbulbs going off constantly was the single most amazing "laser" experience I've ever seen. These guys were great live. Much is being made of not being able to hear them over the screaming, but I found out soon after the show started that if you were to cup your hands over your ears, the screams were filtered out to a great degree, and you could hear the Beatles quite well. During the chorus for "Boys," Ringo shook his head wildly while flailing away at the drums, causing an explosion of squealing. One audience member tossed a can of what looked like fruit salad, which hit the stage inches from George's head.

"Seeing the Beatles was far more than a musical experience. The throngs rushing the stage, clogging the aisles, the cops and security looking scared, the eventual moment they came on stage, giving way to an orgasm of joy and excitement. . . . It was an all-encompassing experience that went beyond the four Beatles themselves."

It was in Boston that I began to see a pattern in Paul McCartney's facial expressions. I began to call it the "wink factor." While John Lennon made weird, gyrating gestures with his face and body, sometimes mimicking the look of a wild-eyed crazy person, McCartney did his face talking with his eyebrows. When I looked up at him on the Boston Garden riser, I noticed that as his face wandered the crowd, he was in a nonstop winking-and-blinking mode, almost as if his eyes were responding to the backbeat of the music. Paul would look left and right, and wink to a face in the crowd. It was a sexy form of eye candy, tantalizing the crowd with his head gyrations. Paul was a world-class flirt when it came to the fans. And they loved him back.

From my vantage point, walking around the stage, the Boston concert was uniquely exhilarating. Maybe it was the heat, perhaps the closeness of the Boston Garden, but I felt closer to the fans there than I had at any other concert, so much so that I spent ten minutes chatting up the spectators.

My eagerness to speak to the fans led to what could have been my biggest mistake on tour. Fearing a riot, Boston police had escorted the Beatles immediately after the concert to waiting cars on a first-floor loading platform. But once I was ready to join the motorcade, it was difficult to make my way through the crowd exiting the concert. When I had finally made my way to the loading platform, the motorcade was beginning to move. Art Schreiber, good friend that he was, was flagging me down, holding the door open. I had just enough time to jump in the rear so I could continue with the rest of the crew to the plane.

On the plane, I took out my pad and noted, again, that our travel compass was pointed in yet another direction. After coming from Florida to Massachusetts, we were now heading south again, to Baltimore. As you've probably noticed by now, there was no directional rhythm to our travels.

And it would get worse. After Maryland, it was back to Pennsylvania, a second run through the Midwest, south to Louisiana, north to Kansas City, back south to Dallas, and returning up north to New York. The tour was, to that point, the most successful—and poorly planned—tour in contemporary music history.

But who could really complain? We had everything: food, cars, an airplane and hotel rooms. The only things missing were sleep and a compass.

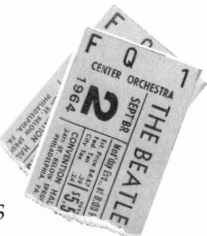

CHAPTER 13:
Memories from the Fans

"Other than the birth of my children, it was the single most important highlight of my life."

Debbie Taylor's experience at the Baltimore Civic Center on September 13, 1964, will stay with her forever. One of twenty-eight thousand people who watched one of the two Baltimore concerts, Debbie came well prepared and brought along her best friend, Margie. She recalls, "We were both thirteen at the time and crazy about the Beatles. We left for the concert three hours early so that we would be the first to get into the Civic Center. We took hatpins with us to keep from getting pushed away from the doors. We never had to use them. All we had to do was show them and we were left alone."

Hatpins! Two innocent teenagers, so determined to see their idols that they conjured up the threatening use of hatpins to make their point. In the fifty-one Beatles concerts that I covered over two summers, one thing was clear—Beatles fans, boys and girls, were unlike the followers of all other celebrities. Their dedication went beyond idolatry; a new degree of faithfulness was born. And, amazingly, forty years later, that dedication and love is still very much alive.

For many of those teenagers, now adults, the Beatles experience was a departure from otherwise normal lives. Nancy McFadden Lloyd was also at the Baltimore concert, where she learned how to scream.

"We are going to see the Beatles! Live! My sister is fourteen. I am twelve. We have never been to a concert, or anything like one, before. We are wearing our Beatle sweatshirts and Beatle boots.

"The two girls sitting in front of us are about our ages, so we talk a little. They don't know how to act, either. We don't know if we'll scream like the girls we've seen on TV and newsreels, but we certainly won't cry; we are all in agreement that crying is stupid.

"Then the moment comes. The Beatles are actually on stage right in front of us. They are breathing our air. They are smiling at us. They strike the familiar chords and sing the beloved songs. And we *can* hear them, despite all the news reports to the contrary. Oh, this is bliss. We clap and stomp and sing along and bounce up and down in our seats.

"The excitement is too much to bear. I want to scream, but I don't know how. My first two attempts fail miserably. On the third attempt, I take in a big breath and emit brief squeals. That's more like it! The next one is perfect: a long, eardrum-piercing shriek. The girls in front grin and nod their approval.

"Now that I've learned how, I scream again and again—but only when appropriate—never while they are singing. I don't want to drown them out with my new power.

"And then the show is over. We clamor for more, of course, but the lights come back on and we have to leave. Outside, it is still early evening. We are startled to meet up with classmates who are in line for the second show. 'Oh, yeah, we saw them. Yeah, they were great! Yeah, you're gonna love it, too.' And, oh yeah, I think to myself, you might even learn how to scream."

The screaming was contagious, as it always was at Beatles concerts. The scene I witnessed during the backstage break in Baltimore was also consistent with Beatles-concert behavior. At every stop, leaders of fan clubs were brought either to the hotel or the backstage dressing room to meet the Beatles. On the Baltimore visit, fan-club members from the mid-Atlantic region brought a variety of gifts and letters from members, and the Beatles treated them with food, photographs and autographs. The Beatles took their fan clubs seriously, even providing funding for promotion and organization of fan clubs in Britain and abroad. You might ask why a group as enormously popular as the Beatles would get involved with funding a fan club organization. It was simply, Brian Epstein told me, out of "loyalty to the fans." In the very early days, Epstein said, "fan clubs had been the basis of the strong early support." And even once they had achieved superstar status, the Beatles fomented and encouraged fan-club membership. If you could have seen the faces of the girls leaving their dressing room backstage in Baltimore, you would have understood how worthwhile spending that time with individual fans was to the Beatles.

Their backstage meetings with fan club members were sacred events, orchestrated as much for the fan's enjoyment as they were a direct connection for the boys. The girls, and sometimes boys, were escorted to the dressing rooms or trailers, usually with adults present. While John had episodes of limited patience, Paul was the master host, providing a welcome that made the extremely nervous fans at home and comfortable. In Baltimore, I watched three girls and a boy leave the dressing room and, in the hallway outside, break into tears. They were tears of relief and joy.

Our hotel for the Baltimore stop was the downtown Holiday Inn, so well secured that the Beatles hosted a post-concert meal in the restaurant on the top floor. The dinner there became the subject of some good-natured ribbing. When I arrived in the rooftop restaurant, I was not aware that it was slowly revolving. I had a few cocktails as the evening went along, and watching the Baltimore skyline change every few minutes, I thought the drinks were making me very drunk. I whispered to Art Schreiber, "Do you notice that the scene keeps changing?" He answered, "Are you okay? It's a damn revolving restaurant." I felt kind of silly, but it was always fun to get a little laugh on this hectic tour, even if it was at my own expense. Lennon heard about my conversation, and later he said to me with a grin, "Larry, I hear your whole world was spinning the other night."

The next stop was the Pittsburgh Civic Arena, which still stands today, home of the Pittsburgh Penguins hockey team. The single Beatles concert there drew twelve thousand people, including Joyce Feightner, who still has loving memories:

"I was from a small town ninety miles east of Pittsburgh, so it was so great to be able to go to the concert. I paid $5.90 for my ticket. There were three other girls with me from my hometown. While we were standing on a street corner we saw the Fab Four go by in a police paddy wagon, their means of escaping the crowds of screaming fans. After the performance I got back to my home by 3 a.m. My mom said I had stars in my eyes. I am now fifty-five years old and listen to oldies stations to get my needed dose of Beatles daily. Hearing their music makes me feel young again."

Feeling young again. It's the one constant in all the emails and letters from "fifty somethings" about their experiences at Beatles concerts.

As Joyce and her friends left for home, the Beatles and their entourage were heading back to the Pittsburgh airport to race off for the next event. Baltimore and Pittsburgh had been relaxed and joyful stops, but the next two stops would be anything but. Waiting for us in Cleveland was an ambitious police officer who almost started a riot. And New Orleans, the city known as the "Big Easy," would not be easy at all. There were also lessons to be learned about the Beatles' loyalty and the dangers of runaway fans.

CHAPTER 14:

Catfight in Cleveland, Wild Horses in New Orleans

Loyalty is a characteristic that John Lennon must have gained early in life. This noble quality appeared unfailingly on the 1964 tour and beyond, coming to the fore in particular during the Beatles' visit to Cleveland, home of Westinghouse news correspondent Art Schreiber, a frequent member of our official traveling press party.

After checking into the hotel, we made our way to Cleveland's Public Auditorium, where a familiar scene unfolded. In every city we had visited so far on the tour, radio stations had competed like warring armies to feature "exclusive" reports on or interviews with the Beatles. The competition got so intense that, quite often, competing stations that didn't subscribe to my WFUN-syndicated reports offered to buy taped interviews directly from me on the spot. Naturally, I turned them down.

Cleveland was the site of a classic catfight between local radio stations, and Art Schrieber ended up in the middle of it. Art had joined the tour in New York City, representing KYW Radio in Cleveland and other Westinghouse-owned stations around the country. He was a respected newsman who had covered the White House and the Capitol for Westinghouse, a company so impressed with his work that he was chosen to report on the Beatles tour to its entire network.

At the Public Auditorium in Cleveland, the rivalry became clear immediately. As usual, upon arrival in the city, the Beatles sat for a press conference to appease the local media's curiosity and hype. It was at these regularly scheduled news conferences that radio personalities had a chance to stand out. WHK Radio, the rival of KYW and

Schreiber's Westinghouse Group, was sponsoring the Cleveland concert with the local promoter, and the station's executives were trying
to prevent KYW reporters and deejays from attending the press conference. This infuriated Schreiber and deejay Jim Staggs, who had
traveled with us in the early part of the tour but was now back at his
regular deejay job at the Cleveland station.

Eventually, the warring stations arrived at a compromise, and personalities from both stations showed up for the news conference prior
to the concert. During the conference, when a WHK radio personality
asked John Lennon a question, Lennon looked over at Art Schreiber
and said, "Art, is it okay if I answer the question?" Schreiber said,
"Sure, John." That was Lennon's way of expressing his admiration for
and loyalty to Schreiber, for whom he had great respect after several
weeks of touring. John's little aside must have really irritated Art's
competitors, and no doubt Schreiber appreciated it.

I recall another Cleveland episode, too, that demonstrated John's
loyalty to the traveling press party. The concert was becoming quite
unruly, but this was not out of the ordinary. Still, when fans tried to
storm the stage, a high-ranking police officer ran to the microphone,
physically pushed the Beatles off the stage and stopped the concert.
The stoppage infuriated Lennon, who was still angry the next day in
New Orleans.

KANE: When the concert was stopped, what was the first
thing that ran through your mind?
LENNON: I felt like kicking him off, because it's so annoying
when they come marching up on stage the way they did, just
came in and pushed George and I off the microphone, but they
didn't say why. Apparently somebody was getting hurt, but,
nothing was really happening wild. He comes on, shoving us
off and shouting, "Get off the stage." I felt like kicking him.

Lennon initially ignored the policeman's command to leave the
stage; he did a little dance to sidestep the officer's hands while making faces at him. Soon enough, though, the Beatles left the stage, and
as they did John yelled out to Art Schreiber, "Art, come with us. Come
with us right now!"

Schreiber quickly followed them to a small dressing room, where
he scored a Cleveland radio exclusive. Much to the chagrin of the competition at WHK, Art got his station on the telephone and interviewed

the Beatles on-air during the stoppage, with thousands of people listening to the drama on their transistor radios. Score one for KYW in the Cleveland radio war. With the Beatles, loyalty reigned supreme.

As far as the concert went, the Beatles, angry at the police department's response, did return to the stage and complete the show. The fans, urged to stay in their seats by Derek Taylor's sterling public address, complied, but compensated while they waited with the highest-decibel screaming that I had yet experienced. That was their way of letting the grandstanding police officials have it.

Not ironically perhaps, after all the theatrics by Cleveland officials, the casualty count in the city was one of the lowest in Beatles' concert history. That claim can't be made about the city of New Orleans, which was the scene of the tour's most dangerous concert since the slugfest in Vancouver.

The flight from Cleveland to New Orleans featured a magnificent pillow fight, with Lennon and Jackie DeShannon leading the combatants. It was fascinating to watch John Lennon leaping up and down the aisle and—with that eager smile and those penetrating eyes—toying with the pillows and his targets like a five-year-old in a playground. Practically everyone aboard got involved until a flight attendant, giggling uncontrollably, broke it up.

When we landed in the Crescent City, limos took us to the Congress Inn Hotel, a low-rise affair off a remote highway that wasn't far from the City Park Stadium. The hotel was surrounded by trees and high weeds, a rather swamp-like environment, and the sound of crickets and other insects filled the air. It was dark and damp as we headed to our rooms in the middle of the night, unaware that, in the city of New Orleans, the stage was being set for a rock-and-roll rebellion.

The next day, the Beatles received a welcome from the mayor, conducted a brief news conference and were transported to City Park Stadium. The facility resembled a high-school football stadium. It was compact, with seats on both sides of a regulation-sized football field. There were no field seats. About 250 police were on hand when the Beatles arrived behind the stadium and entered a small trailer. I stood outside the trailer, which was anchored in a muddy area, and watched the comings and goings. One coming was especially exciting: The man who "found his thrill on Blueberry Hill" showed up to pay his respects.

This visit had special meaning for me, because the music of Fats Domino had accompanied me on many of my high-school dates. His voice on the car radio would punctuate the night air at remote locations in southwest Miami as I tried, most times unsuccessfully, to kiss my dates. Fats Domino was one of my favorite singers, and it was a thrill to meet him. I shook his hand before he entered the trailer to pay his respects. I learned later that the Beatles, reluctant sometimes to meet celebrities, shared my enthusiasm for the man and his music. Later, George told me that he and the other Beatles had jammed and joked with Fats inside that little trailer.

An hour after Fats Domino's visit, the Beatles were escorted to a makeshift stage inside the stadium. John walked the steps first, and a howl went up in the stadium, followed by a pincer-like movement in the crowd on both sides of the stage. Suddenly, four hundred fans began storming the stage, trying to break through the police barriers. They emptied the bleachers and spread onto the turf like soldiers running, swerving, seeking their targets. With each advance of the crowd, police officers added reinforcements to their front lines, but the front line kept inching closer to the stage. It was not looking good.

Here are some of the notes I scribbled while observing the goings-on:

"Ringo banging the drums hard, looking left and right. Paul lifting guitar up and down. John looks screwed up, like he doesn't know what's on or not. In front of me, two girls in big wide dresses take a lunge at cops, who push them back. But another girl makes it through to stage. Neil and Mal grab her and she runs back through police line. Cops look frustrated, sweaty, kind of angry. Waves and waves keep hitting them. Nightsticks come out and they wave them over heads as if to threaten. Paul's microphone seems dead. I think it's out but he doesn't know it. Now the horses come in, and some of them are agitated. What a scene—horses' hooves flying, children hurling themselves at police. Kids fainting. It's pandemonium or worse. Private security guards. They are not armed. Trying to keep kids back. Incredible."

I would describe the scene in my broadcast reports as a riot. After all, it took police wielding nightsticks and mounted patrolmen to put it down.

One can always measure the severity of a riot by the number of casualties. There were many. It was a regular MASH unit on the outside of the stadium. When I approached a nurse to get a sense of the tally, she told me that over a hundred fans had fainted. The next day, John Lennon compared the pandemonium to a sporting event.

KANE: Last night in New Orleans, fans were running around on the field and you kept playing. Does it ever affect you?

LENNON: Last night I was beginning to have hysterics because it got more and more like a football match or a polo match. It was just a scream. I even said into the microphone, "Who's winning now?"

Winning wasn't the issue for the Beatles in New Orleans. It all came down to getting out alive. On the plane, the press party knew little about what was coming next, but Brian Epstein and the Beatles were prepping for a memorable encounter with an American showman in Kansas City, Missouri. This episode would show us that pride mattered more than money to the Beatles.

The Beatles arrive in America for the first time ever, landing at JFK airport in New York City on February 7, 1964.

The Beatles face the media on arrival at JFK. Moments earlier, they were greeted by 5,000 delirious fans as they deplaned.

Beatlemaniacs scream their hearts out outside the Plaza Hotel in New York City, February, 1964.

The Beatles wave to fans from their Plaza Hotel room on February 7, 1964. Local authorities in most cities they visited did not allow the boys to greet their frenzied fans in person.

The Beatles make their first American appearance, February 9, 1964, on the *Ed Sullivan Show* on CBS-TV in New York City.

The Beatles perform in their first concert in America, February 11, 1964, at the Coliseum in Washington, D.C.

The Beatles goof off in a Miami swimming pool during their first visit to the United States in February, 1964.

Throngs of young, shrieking fans welcome the Beatles to San Francisco on the first day of their historic first tour of North America, August 19, 1964.

The Beatles, often confined to their hotel due to the constant threat of fan and media mayhem, get in a little fishing out of their hotel room window in Seattle, August 21, 1964.

The Beatles' first concert at the Hollywood Bowl, August 23, 1964, was remarkable for a couple of reasons. It was the first venue in which the sound system actually overpowered the screaming crowd; and it was the first event where I noticed a number of non-teenage admirers.

George Harrison, movie star Jayne Mansfield, and John Lennon (l-r) hang out at the Whisky-a-Go-Go in Hollywood, August 26, 1964.

George throws his drink at an encroaching photographer inside the Whisky-a-Go-Go, shocking Ringo and the others at their table and stealing the next day's headlines. In the commotion, no one seemed to notice the sexual energy brewing between John and Jayne Mansfield.

Ringo (center) holds his beloved St. Christopher medal which was infamously ripped from his neck (and later returned) by a crazed fan in front of the Plaza Hotel in New York City, August 28, 1964.

To beat the relentless pursuit of fans and media, the Beatles often traveled to concerts in decoy vehicles like fish trucks and this Loomis armored car.

Paul and I fill out press credentials while John relaxes on the Beatles' Electra charter airplane on the 1964 tour.

My job on the tour was to get as many daily interviews as
possible—forty-five radio stations in the United States
and Canada depended on my reports. . .

. . .the Beatles were always accommodating.

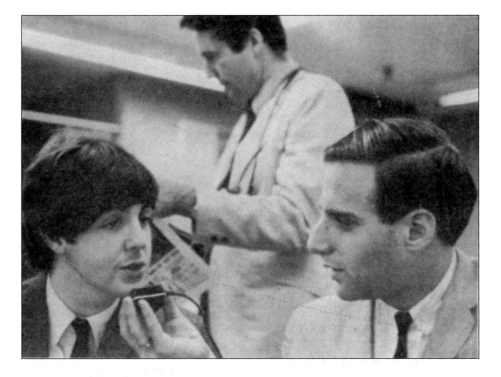

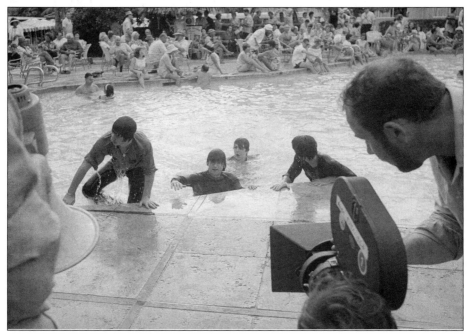

Ringo, John, Paul, and George
(l–r) climb out of a pool in
Nassau, Bahamas, while filming
Help! in February, 1965.

Me and the Beatles on the 1965 tour. John (left,
holding up the August '65 issue of *Ebony* magazine
with a cover story on race relations) and the rest of
the Beatles were remarkably informed and vocal
about the serious issues of the day.

City policemen fend off a raging swarm of teenage Beatles fans in front of the Warwick Hotel, New York City, on August 12, 1965.

The Beatles play in front of 55,000 screaming fans at Shea Stadium, New York City, on August 15, 1965. At the time, it was the largest audience ever assembled at a musical performance of any kind.

Two very young Beatles fans sob with joy at Comiskey Park on the '65 tour. Images like this played out wherever and whenever the Beatles appeared.

The Beatles' brilliant, troubled manager, Brian Epstein.

George, Paul, John, and Ringo (center row, l-r) are photographed between shows in the locker room at Chicago's Comiskey Park with a group of visiting deejays on the 1965 tour. Chicago deejay Jim Stagg (top row, far right) and I (next to Stagg), along with Neil Aspinall (the Beatles' road manager, center row, far right), Mal Evans (the Beatles' personal assistant, front row, right), and Tony Barrow (the Beatles' press secretary, front row, center) were at the core of the Beatles' entourage.

142

WFUN News Director Larry Kane has spent more time with the Beatles than any other radio reporter in America! Larry returns to Miami this week from a 16 day tour across America with John, Paul, George and Ringo. Last summer Kane traveled for 30 days with the boys from Britain. Here is Larry Kane's own story of what it's like to be part of the exclusive Beatle party.

Days after returning to Miami after the conclusion of the 1965 tour, WFUN ran this piece in their *Boss Beat* fan newsletter. Little did I know then that my experience with the Beatles would be a topic of great interest to others for the rest of my life.

LARRY KANE
Beatle Exclusive

LARRY KANE

Again the mobs came. Again the crowds cheered, and again that wonderful, wild world known as "Beatlemania" thoroughly enveloped the United States of America.

Several years ago, the word "Beatles" meant nothing to me. Who would ever have known that I would be one of the only American reporters allowed to travel with what some have termed, the most electrifying act in show business.

It happened last year when the four Beatles played before more than 250,000 fans in America and Canada. And it happened again this past month when I started on one of those experiences that only occurs once in a lifetime. In my case it was twice.

I thought that on this second-time-around, it would be somewhat of an anti-climax but, no, it happened all over again.

That sense of the unbelievable started in New York City when John, Paul, George and Ringo arrived to one of the most breathtaking scenes I've ever witnessed. A human wave of emotion and hysteria, followed by a never-before-seen automobile motorcade through the big city.

And then there were the Beatles themselves, showing that sincere frankness at their press conferences that have made them, not only musical favorites, but personal favorites.

And who will ever forget the Hollywood Bowl? Streams of human beings in the most beautiful outdoor theater in the world. Thousands of others waited outside, pining for one rapid glance, one shocked, one bullet-fast look at four heads of hair.

These were the visual, the physical experiences that one remembers and always will remember, but, most of all, forgetting the surface experiences, I will remember the Beatles at their best, in the quiet of the charter air craft, or the sullenness of the hotel rooms.

John Lennon is probably the wittiest person in the world. I sat with him numerous times, tried to out-talk him, out-joke him, but failed everytime. Throughout the trip, John consistently rapped reporters of gossip columns, who intimated that he had a child on the way. His favorite quip in connection with that statement is, "I would know about it, wouldn't I?"

And then there was Ringo. Ringo has a lot more depth than most people would believe. His consistently publicized lack of formal education never shows. He's perceptive and intelligent and since last year, has developed a profound wit. From all I could gather, married life has done him no harm.

The single Beatles, Paul McCartney and George Harrison are still as carefree and pleasant. It amazes me what a tremendous sense of humor they both have. When the unusual antics are pulled-off, you can expect it's McCartney or Harrison behind the wheel.

My days, my nights and my very existence were filled with conversations and discussions with the Beatles. Whether on tape or off, it was always interesting. It was always interesting to hear Paul McCartney talk about his marriage plans (latest word is that he's not married) and George Harrison speak out about his profound dislike of rumors.

With John Lennon, it was more a matter of laughing first and then trying to understand what he said. The Lennon world is a mish-mash of personal anecdotes, such as the now famous "Hello Larry, 12345794, how . . . 34869 are you . . . 2, 5 . . ." or his self styled words that have become world famous.

Ringo is still the most serious of the bunch, although he can laugh quite a lot when he's winning at poker.

And so it was. Reflections, reflections and more reflections:

. . . A girl pushing herself against a chained fence to get to her loved ones . . . A policeman yelling at the top of his lungs . . . Ringo beating on the drums and getting hit by jellybeans tossed on the stage . . . A detective who doesn't believe I'm really a reporter but thinks I'm a furious fan . . .

. . . A John Lennon statement shocks a reporter and a reporter shocks John Lennon . . . Policemen seeking autographs . . . Boys seeking autographs . . . Girls seeking autographs . . . Mothers seeking autographs . . Alleyways of escape for John, Paul, George and Ringo . . . A meeting with fan club officers where the Beatles are almost torn apart . . .

These are my reflections about my experiences with the Beatles. Believe me, as long as I live, I'll never forget them.

When John visited Philadelphia in 1975 to host a radio marathon fundraiser, he ended up filling in for the weatherman on the 6 o'clock news on WPVI-TV, for which I was anchor. John was hilarious, as usual, summing up the forecast by saying, "So the outlook is sunny, but the weather is funny, and you should find a yellow submarine."

Catching up with Ringo in Milwaukee, Wisconsin during his "Ringo and the All Starrs" 1989 tour. Our interview aired on "Reunion with Ringo" on WCAU-TV in Philadelphia.

CHAPTER 15:
Word War in Kansas City, Fear in Dallas

At every Beatles concert on the 1964 tour, the band played virtually the same song list, except in Kansas City. There, they added the song "Kansas City," Wilbert Harrison's top-forty hit from 1959. The crowd at Municipal Stadium roared with delight. The background story behind the Beatles' performing this extra number is also a devilish delight.

Kansas City was and is a gorgeous American metropolis, with breathtaking fountains, gentle people, and the quiet Midwest values of cleanliness and courtesy. But behind the scenes of the Beatles' visit there, it was anything but quiet and courteous.

The concert in Kansas City was important for two reasons. First, the appearance was a financial record setter. The 150 thousand dollars paid to the Beatles was at that time the largest amount ever paid for a single performance in the history of entertainment. More importantly, it was there, with characteristic defiance and outright distrust of the establishment, that John Lennon stared down a controversial American icon and accelerated his role as the outspoken, untitled leader of the Beatles.

Originally, a stop in Kansas City had not even been on the tour's schedule. But Charles O. Finley, the flamboyant owner of the Kansas City Athletics, had urged Brian Epstein to add his city to the itinerary, offering a larger sum for the detour each time Epstein turned him down. Epstein eventually agreed to the 150-thousand-dollar fee. Not a bad deal for one night's work.

When the Beatles arrived in the Muehlebach Hotel, Charles O. Finley was waiting outside of their suite for a direct conference with them. Art Schreiber and I were there as Brian Epstein brought Finley to the door. Finley had a request: He wanted the Beatles to play for longer than their usual thirty to thirty-five minutes. After all, he was paying an awful lot for eleven songs. And he was willing to go higher.

John Lennon was willing to make him go higher, too, though the least of his reasons was money. Lennon simply enjoyed sparring with and calling the shots at this establishment honcho who was used to getting his way. It was a heavyweight showdown, and Lennon got the best of it.

Finley tried to negotiate the extended set with Epstein, but Lennon did all the talking. When Finley first realized that his request was turning into a negotiation, he offered more money. John said no. He raised the price again, and Lennon shook his head. Each time the baseball magnate upped the ante, Lennon would stare at him and say no. The drama continued to build, and finally Finley, his face flushed with anger, called them a bunch of boys and stormed out.

This entire scene was played out in front of Epstein, who stayed silent. Every time Finley asked, Epstein deferred with his eyes to Lennon, who promptly shook his head or said no. It appeared that Epstein was ceding control to Lennon.

But Finley wasn't through. Just before the concert, he entered the Beatles' dressing room to ask one more time and was told by Lennon, "Chuck, you shouldn't have spent so much money on us." Finley stormed out again. Acrimony was the order of the day.

The concert was not sold out. Just over twenty thousand of the forty thousand seats at Kansas City Municipal Stadium were filled. And although it was estimated that Finley lost a fair sum of money, he himself considered the concert an enormous success and a great point of civic pride. To top it all off, the Beatles did end up playing an extra song, "Kansas City." That song brought the house to its feet.

The confrontation between Lennon and Finley was symbolic of John's changing public role. At each stop, he was becoming more brazen and a little angrier at symbols of authority, including the media. Looking back, Art Schreiber, who, like this reporter, was extremely fond of John, feels that the man was motivated by the need to assert himself. "He simply didn't want to be pushed around by anybody," Art explained, "especially some rich guy, an American with balls."

This mini-war with Finley, along with a woman who tried to sneak into the Beatles' room through the air conditioning duct (she was rescued by firefighters), provided enough fireworks for Kansas City. And what the big shots couldn't create in private—an air of joy and respect—was accomplished in public by the fans. On their feet, cheering wildly, the Kansas City fans were among the most respectful and well-behaved in the country. The Beatles, in the end, were content with the event but anxious about the next stop. When we left Kansas City, a feeling of gloom on the plane was palpable; it was a gloom similar to what I'd observed the night astrologer Jeane Dixon had predicted our demise by airplane crash.

Shortly after takeoff, John and Paul wandered over to the press area, looking a little fidgety. John asked me, "Ever been in Dallas?" I said, "Once, briefly." "A lot of guns, huh?" he asked. It was apparent that the boys, especially Lennon, were freaked out about playing in Dallas, the scene of the Kennedy assassination. To many Europeans, Dallas exemplified an America run by lawless cowboys who roamed the West looking for easy money and victims to murder. As I prepared my reports for the next morning, I noted that the Beatles seemed genuinely afraid of what was to come in Dallas. Their fears, as it turns out, were unfounded, but considering the state of America on September 18, 1964, who could blame them?

Less than one year before the Beatles arrived in America, President John F. Kennedy had been assassinated while traveling in a presidential parade through the streets of Dallas. It was a seminal moment in the history of our country; some say it essentially marked the loss of our innocence as a nation. Undoubtedly, this event seeped into the core of America's disposition in those times, and spoke to the way we were in the almost mid-sixties.

Four years earlier, at my high-school graduation, the educators and pontificators had talked of a decade of promise and prosperity, energized by the race to space and other advances in science and technology. Riches were just around the corner, they said. World peace was within our grasp. It was a hope for our lives that was never realized. No one on the podium could have visualized then how powerfully racial divisions would erupt in America, or the struggle for equal rights that would accompany them. Certainly, the forecasters of happiness could never have envisioned the shooting and killing that changed America in Dallas on the afternoon of November 22, 1963. How could they have predicted that, or the war that would kill fifty-four thousand Americans and split the country in a brutal divide of dove and hawk, peacemaker and warrior?

Against that backdrop, with the Kennedy assassination still fresh in their minds and the Cold War as icy as ever, Americans lived with fear and stress in 1964. And the city of Dallas was still living in the shadow of the infamous day at Dealey Plaza. As our plane touched down in Dallas, we heard names and saw places that were familiar from the roles they'd played in recent events.

Love Field. Yes, the Electra had arrived in Dallas at the same airport where Air Force One had waited for take-off on November 22, its passengers including the nation's new president and the body of the murdered former president. Our expressway ride to the Cabana Motor Inn mirrored the drive the mortally wounded president took to Parkland Memorial Hospital, where he was pronounced dead. The hotel itself was located a mile from the Texas Book Depository Building, from where the fatal shots had allegedly been fired.

One needs to understand the way we felt in America at that time in order to comprehend the anxieties associated with the Beatles' trip to Dallas. The subject of the assassination came up often during our time there and even before our arrival, as you can see from this section of an interview I did with Paul on the plane:

> KANE: When you were in England and heard the first news
> of the assassination of President Kennedy, what were your
> first thoughts as far as a British person looking at America?
> McCARTNEY: I just thought the whole thing was idiotic,
> y'know, 'cause anyone who wanted to shoot Kennedy, 'cause,
> y'know, from my point of view, and from a lot of people in
> England's point of view, he was the best president that
> America had had for an awful long time, y'know. And he was
> creating a great image for America, and he seemed to be
> doing great things, y'know. He seemed to have a good head
> on his shoulders, y'know, sensible. And it was good for every-
> one. The fact that someone bumped him off was a big, terrible
> big drag, y'know. Idiots, I thought.

The thought of going to Dallas was a terrible big drag, as Paul said, for the Beatles. Our late-night arrival in Dallas only enhanced their anxiety. The motorcade was engineered by the Dallas police to get the band safely to the Cabana Motor Inn, a glass-enclosed structure just off the city's main expressway. Everything was going smoothly, for the Beatles at least. But one of the press cars, the one I was in, had a brief upside-down experience. Overzealous fans mobbed our vehicle, began to shake it wildly, and ended up rolling it over onto its side. We remained stuck inside for several minutes before the highway patrol were able to right us.

We eventually arrived safely, and within a half hour I had gotten two contrasting impressions of how this stop was going to be, security-wise. The Dallas police brandished their rifles openly; this was the first time in America that the Beatles had seen rifles at the ready. I got the impression that we would be well protected on this leg of the tour, but the raising of rifles only reinforced the anxiety that the Beatles were feeling. The expressions on their faces, their eyes wandering around, gave me the feeling that they were concerned about their safety.

When we traveled to the top floor to get settled in, my reporter's intuition that something was happening started to settle in, too, with its usual surge of adrenaline. It was the noise of the crowd gathered outside that was setting the bells off in my head. I decided to go check out the scene from the safety of the lobby. From a reporting standpoint, my timing was perfect. On a personal level, the scenario that developed would haunt me for several days afterward.

I saw through the lobby's large glass windows a menacing crowd pressing against the Dallas police, who had formed a ring around the front of the hotel. In a few minutes' time, the fans were pressed hard against the plate-glass windows. Suddenly I heard the smashing of glass and watched the people inside the lobby rushing toward the windows. When I arrived by the windows myself, the scene was ghastly. Three girls were lying on the floor, bleeding profusely from head and facial injuries. A fourth was up on her feet and trying to stop the blood flowing from her knees. The force of the crowd had pushed these kids through the glass. The first three were treated for serious injuries. They were treated to something far more pleasant the next morning.

Later in that long night, several of us in the press corps informed John and Ringo of the accident. They were disturbed. And George and Paul were shocked to see still pictures of the accident scene in the morning papers. Derek Taylor told us later that day that all four placed calls to the hospital rooms of the victims and said that flowers would be sent. Once again, the Beatles were not content to look the other way when their fans were in trouble.

Dallas also brought other menaces, including two phoned-in bomb threats—one aimed at the Dallas Coliseum, the other at the

Beatles' airplane. The threats were taken seriously but turned out to be fake. Searches were made, and the all-clear signal was given. There was another potential hazard, too, but not a violent one. This was the hazard that Beatle handlers feared the most: the wrong kind of social interaction, or, as we would say in the twenty-first century, the dangers of sex with strangers.

The hotel itself was quite a scene. Aside from the panorama of plate glass, the Cabana was home to a private club hosted by cotton-tailed bunnies of the cocktail-waitress variety. The nightclub was adjacent to the lobby. Paul kept yelling out, "Bring up the bunnies." Meanwhile, Derek Taylor and his wise assistant, Bess Coleman, tried to keep the bunnies away for fear of scandal in the puritanical Bible-belt of Texas. But a delegation of the cocktail waitresses was brought in to greet the Beatles and take pictures. One of them caught Paul's eye. As the group was leaving, Art Schreiber, who was walking down the hall, heard a yell from Paul. He said, "Art, stop that girl. Can you get her to come back here?" Art, with his usual bluntness, answered, "You get her, Paul. I'm no pimp!" As far as Art could tell, the unidentified bunny woman never returned. The bunny threat was averted.

The concert itself was sparkling, with a surprisingly orderly audience of ten thousand and no known injuries. I was impressed by the clarity of the sound in the Dallas Coliseum. So was Stephen C. Hall of Tulsa, who had won his Beatles' tickets in a radio-station contest. He was fourteen on September 18, 1964, and this is how he remembers that night:

"The scene was exactly like those I'd seen in pictures and news-reels, with large banners hanging from the balcony sections declaring "We Love Ringo." Once the group took the stage in their dark blue suits and velvet collars, the screaming was constant; it never let up. I've never witnessed anything like it for any other group. However, contrary to the reports I'd read in the newspapers, you could actually hear the music and understand the lyrics. I was amazed I could hear them all. I was relatively close, within the first fifteen rows on the floor in front of the stage. People stood up the entire time. If the girls weren't screaming, they were crying."

Like Stephen, I watched the Dallas concert as a spectator, sitting on the floor adjacent to a row in the rear. Poor Jackie DeShannon, a spirited and energetic entertainer and the opening act that night, was as usual mainly ignored. I've thought over the years that she was so good, yet she was hardly appreciated in 1964. When the Beatles emerged, the clarity of sound, although not perfect, surprised the screamers. For the first time, I could actually hear the words to "Hard Day's Night" and "Can't Buy Me Love," which was becoming a personal favorite. A young girl sitting near my perch on the floor seemed to be in dreamland, her head rocking back and forth, as she appreciated the melody and words of "If I Fell."

The boys seemed relieved after the event, and why not? They were ready for a great escape. No fans. No dumb questions at press conferences. They were going on a vacation. Within a half-hour of the Coliseum concert, they were off for a few days of private rest in the Ozark Mountains of Missouri, guests at the ranch of Reed Pigman, owner of American Flyers Airline.

We in the press stayed behind in Dallas for thirty-six hours. That break gave me a chance to take a breath, prepare my final reports and absorb a little piece of morbid U.S. history. The gift shop in the hotel was selling postcards that sadly depicted the way local entrepreneurs were viewing the Kennedy murder. Each card featured a map on which key locations were highlighted: the places where the first and second shots occurred, what path the president's car took on its trip to the hospital, where the flight of Air Force One took off from. The card also bore a timeline of key events. To me, at the time, the touristy postcards looked more like a sign of celebration than a suitable commemoration of the tragedy. As the years passed, we would comprehend the deep wounds absorbed by the people of Dallas, but in that gift shop, I felt none of that.

The next day I cabbed over to the Texas School Book Depository and, playing amateur sleuth, checked the line of fire from the window of the building to where Kennedy had been felled. It looked like an almost impossible angle. In September 1964, conspiracy theories were just in the developmental stage, and I suppose I was hatching my own, or at least questioning the official explanation of events. I also walked through the plaza and visited the grassy knoll, where theorists placed another gunman. It was all so fresh then, and being at those Dallas sites in the flesh reminded me that we were still a nation torn apart by the murder. This second brief break from Beatlemania reminded me again that we were a nation troubled and still recovering from the trauma of a year before. The news of the day was coming back to my mind, and there was a lot of it: civil rights marches in the South, a tense election campaign, and serious questions about our intentions in Vietnam.

We had just two days remaining once we rejoined the Beatles on our way to New York City. The journey on which I had been reluctant to embark was beginning to look like what it would become to me years later—an historic trip through the heart of America, a cultural phenomenon and, inadvertently, a chance to assess the way we were.

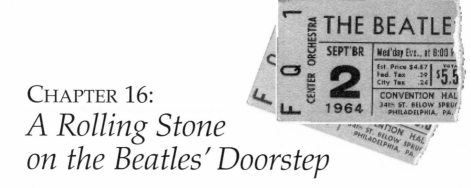

CHAPTER 16:
A Rolling Stone
on the Beatles' Doorstep

One day and one night. That's all that was left. The Electra, which had been our flying apartment for over a month, taxied down the runway at Love Field and soared into a northern flight path, headed for Walnut Ridge, Arkansas. There, the boys, buoyant from a few days on the farm in Missouri, looked tanned and rested as they walked down the aisle. Even Epstein was smiling and had a bounce about his walk.

I was beginning to get those jitters you endure when something special is coming to an end. I knew that, whatever happened in my career, nothing could even come close to this experience for its sheer excitement and unpredictability. Reporters are trained to keep emotions out of a story. So this moment, the final flight with the Beatles, was difficult to handle.

The Electra landed in New York in the late afternoon, the low September sun starting to fade into the west, the colors of the sky looking radiant as the band, the technicians and the last remnants of the press corps walked down the stairs of that plane one final time. A cavalcade of cars took us to midtown Manhattan, while the Beatles flew by helicopter to an East Side landing pad and a brief ride to the Paramount Theater in Times Square. The Beatles had a few hours to prepare for a much smaller appearance than usual, the kind they were used to from their early days in England. But it was an important event nonetheless.

The Paramount Theater was, after all, the place from which Frank Sinatra had ruled the forties, the landmark theater to which Duke Ellington and others of his generation had brought memorable silky sounds and heartfelt moments. This concert was to be a benefit, its proceeds earmarked for United Cerebral Palsy. The Beatles would join Steve Lawrence and Edie Gorme and many other musical stars. The Paramount had less than four thousand seats, and once the concert had begun, I found the contrast with the other concerts I'd witnessed on the tour striking. From the rear I saw the usual teenagers in their mod, fab attire, but they were seated next to men and women in tuxedoes and gowns. Despite differences in style and attire, as far as the attitude toward the Beatles was concerned, there seemed to be a united front of cheering and enthusiasm. The big change that night was in the Beatles themselves. They were far more relaxed than I'd seen them to date.

After all, this venue was far more like their stock-in-trade, the little theaters throughout the British Isles that brought them close to the fans. John Lennon soaked it up, smiling, winking to the crowd and doing a lot of waving. Paul McCartney, the heartthrob of Beatles' fans, displayed more body language than ever. Another amazing sight was McCartney almost kissing the metal of the microphone as he sang into it. McCartney fit the central-casting stereotype for "cute," and he knew how to play the role. At the Paramount, he could see the faces up close, and the people could see *him*. George, enveloped in his guitar, seemed right on top of the crowd as he pranced back and forth. Even Ringo, from his vantage point on the drums, was closer than usual to the fans, less than twenty yards from the adoring audience. It was too bad, I thought, that all the concerts couldn't have offered such an intimate connection between band and audience.

For this reporter, the interviews were done. I stayed that final night and day in New York mainly to observe, to be a part of it till the end. When the concert was over, I awaited my final travel instructions. Brian Epstein and Derek Taylor approached, careful to give me and Art Schreiber the location of the "secret" hotel where the Beatles would spend their final night in America. Our luggage was already being transported there from Kennedy Airport. I could have flown home to Miami that night, but I wanted to spend a final few hours with the Beatles, Derek, Bess and the others.

The hotel was called the Riviera Idlewild. Idlewild had been the name of New York's international airport before the facility was renamed for John F. Kennedy after his assassination late in 1963. I arrived by cab at the airport hotel, a perfect spot for a send-off party, since it was isolated by perimeter roads and far from the city's population centers. In fact, when I arrived to register, the lobby and front desk area were almost bare. Adjacent to the airport and far from Manhattan, the Riviera was quiet, and after the last month, quiet was a strange feeling. I took the elevator to the top floor, where I checked into a room not far from the suite where Derek Taylor had arranged refreshments for a farewell party.

It was an open house, and the house was open to some mysterious people. A very aggressive reporter from *Cosmopolitan*, for instance, was trying hard to get a one-on-one interview with John Lennon She was young, attractive, soft-spoken but determined. Years later, I learned her name: Gloria Steinem, soon to become an icon of the campaign to promote justice and opportunity for women. She got the interview.

The room was filled with others, too—technicians from the tour, a small group of young women, Art Schreiber, Long John Wade and some British reporters. Derek Taylor and Bess Coleman were perfect hosts, offering drinks and food and nonstop thank-yous for our reporting on the tour. The Beatles walked in and out of the room, except for John, who stayed most of the night, reminiscing about the tour.

After midnight, the phone rang and John took it. "Hello," he said. "Uh, okay . . . I'll send someone down right away." John looked over at me and said, "Larry, would you do me a favor? There's a friend in the lobby. He's with his business partner right at the front desk. Could you bring him up?"

"Sure," I replied. I took the elevator down. At the front desk, a short man wearing rumpled jeans and carrying a guitar case was leaning against the desk front, chatting with another man.

"I came to get you," I said. "My name is Larry Kane."

"Hello," the guitar man said. "I'm Bob Dylan."

So this was Dylan, I thought. Mr. Marijuana, as the legend went. He looked kind of ordinary, but he was making an extraordinary mark on the subculture in New York. I never had confirmed the report that he'd turned the Beatles on to drugs earlier in the tour during our first stop at the Delmonico Hotel in New York, though years later each band member would freely admit to being turned on by Dylan. As Paul put it, "We had a crazy party the night we met [Dylan]. I thought I got the meaning to life that night."

I led Dylan and friend up a back stairway and brought him to John, whose face lit up when Dylan entered the room. John took them into another room, where Ringo was waiting. There was no sign of George all night, but Paul was busy chatting up the crowd, with a beautiful brunette woman standing beside him. They, too, later disappeared, and the only people left were the traveling press and Derek and Bess. We spent the rest of the night smoking cigarettes, getting drunk and telling combat stories from the tour. By 4 a.m., the party was over.

All in all, it was a tepid climax to a month that included more dynamic nights than most human beings would see in a lifetime. I made it back to my room in the same hotel and faded off to sleep, confident of the job I had done, nervous about getting back to real life and sad that the tour was over.

The next morning, all of us boarded a small bus that would take the Beatles directly to a commercial airliner bound for London. To avoid the crowds, the bus took the boys right to the steps of the plane. On the way to the airport, Ringo complained that he was "sore" from his overnight recreation. He wasn't in a health club, so we all presumed it was sex he meant. I thanked John, Paul, George and Ringo for being so helpful with all of my news needs for the entire month. In a salutation that would become a routine part of my taped interviews with the Beatles, all of them called out, in near perfect tandem and harmony, "Nice working with you, Larry."

When the Beatles traveled up the steps and into the aircraft, I thought that I would never see them again. After all, no one knew if they would even come back to America. It was an emotional moment for me. The bus took the press people back to the hotel, and as I packed up in my hotel room, I realized that I had been a part of something special and that my life would now seem routine. The tour was over. I didn't know on that morning of September 21, 1964, that this thrilling month was really just a beginning for me—that many, many more surprises, culture shocks and unpredictable moments of joy and agony were still ahead in my traveling career with the Beatles.

I would wind up on the shores of the Bahamas, hear the inhuman roars at Shea Stadium, witness the boys' meeting with the King of Rock-and-Roll and experience an emergency landing and a flight of fancy in Hollywood. Yes, there would be reunion with the Beatles, and it was only a year away.

PART TWO:
Life on Tour

CHAPTER 17:
A Plane Life

In an airplane, you really learn about people—what they eat, drink and take pleasure in, the things that irritate them and those that provoke. In the cylinder-driven atmosphere of an airplane, night after night, our time became filled with close and spirited conversation, incredible music and serious high jinks. There was no place to run and no place to hide, except in the bathroom, and you know what that's like on a commercial airliner.

Travel can be enervating in the best of circumstances. But just consider our timetable. On modern tours, performers will allow three or four days between concerts. The 1964 tour had a few rest periods, but it was mostly a daily whirlwind. And the day-after-day travel on both the 1964 and 1965 summer tours added up to some impressive numbers. We traveled a total of thirty-one thousand miles in approximately sixty airborne hours and crossed the continent four times. We went to thirty-six separate destinations and traveled on two different models of airplane, both flown by a Texas-based charter service, American Flyers Airlines. One was a Lockheed Electra, the aircraft of choice of many charter airlines in those days, a turboprop that was steady but noisy. The second aircraft, a Lockheed Super Constellation, finished the tour in 1965. The Constellation was called into service when the Electra, a workhorse on the 1964 tour, had a bit of a mishap that scared the living daylights out of the Beatles.

Even without that mishap, it was abundantly clear that the Beatles didn't enjoy flying. None of us did, really; it was tedious and draining. And the whole tour experience sapped the strength out of you.

People reading about superstars on tour typically picture a life of excitement, glamour and endless possibilities. There is a little of that, but mostly the tours were grinding and debilitating. I spoke with Ringo about this on the 1965 tour.

> KANE: You look tired at times.
> STARR: Well, the traveling knocks you out in the end. You sort of get fed up with planes and cars. You wanna sit down for a year.
> KANE: Last year, after the tour, I found it hard to get back to normal.
> STARR: It took me about three months to get back to normal in Britain—sorta sleeping and waking up at all the wrong times—I just didn't know what was happening.

That much plane travel took its toll, and to compensate for the boredom and anxiety, members of the traveling party—usually led by John Lennon—invented ways to pass the time, ways that in some instances turned our flights into a flying circus.

The first time mashed potatoes covered my face was as part of a John Lennon plot to wake me up. It has been common knowledge throughout my career that I am far from a party animal. Derek Taylor, the suave and hard-living press boss, and his buddy Lennon knew right away that I was a target for mischief. In the confines of an airplane and within the limits of safety, a favorite weapon became edible ammo.

Case in point: I was taking a light nap on the flight from Denver to Cincinnati on the '64 tour, and I woke up when my breathing was suddenly interrupted. Why? Because mashed potatoes with gravy and peas had been pasted over my face by an icon of world peace. I opened my eyes to see John Lennon just across the way, giggling and looking just like the cat that caught the canary.

"A direct hit," said Mr. Lennon. "Smoosh, whoosh and whack."

John had the marvelous talent of creating his own vocabulary to fit the moment. As I wiped the food off my face, I was stunned, not realizing at first that the sneak attack was part of a larger pattern of combat that would soon become familiar. This common airbound activity would cause me problems later, when my expense account for hotel dry cleaning came due at the station.

Yet the activity was a necessary part of coping with being on tour. Tired from the ordeal of traveling, bored by the grinding sound of the engines, and looking for action, the tour rider seeks relief. Therein lies the motivation for the food fight.

John Lennon was a master of the sneak attack, and the chief strategist of most food fights. The food fights, launched with gusto, were always perpetrated shortly after meals had been delivered and before the worthy flight attendants had been able to make their rounds to pick up the trays. Lennon usually went on the attack against media representatives, notably the senior George Harrison (no relation), correspondent for the *Liverpool Gazette,* the boys' hometown newspaper. And when the food started flying, there was no stopping the likes of usually demure Jackie DeShannon, Beatle George Harrison and even Bill Medley of the Righteous Brothers, who seemed more pissed off than playful as he flung his grub.

The favorite selections were Jello and pudding, both of which made a real mess, which was the general idea. The flight attendants who had to clean up this mess handled it with great humor, even with pillow fights taking place at the same time, which were also launched by chief instigator Lennon. The combination of messy food and burst pillows, their feathers flying into the food, was a double whammy. Having been both a perpetrator and a victim, I can tell you that it was silly, juvenile and harebrained fun.

As the tours progressed, both in 1964 and 1965, fatigue would set in, almost forcing the imaginative among us to find creative ways to pass the time. Lennon spent his down time from on-board mischief getting a small but valuable education. Westinghouse correspondent Art Schreiber, who spent three weeks on the 1964 marathon, regaled John Lennon for hours with stories of his own travels. Art, a retired radio executive and now director of the New Mexico Federation of the Blind, remembers:

"John was the most intellectual of the group. We would sit together near the rear of the plane. He was especially fascinated about my coverage of John Kennedy's campaign in 1960 and his funeral in 1963, and my coverage of Martin Luther King, James Meredith and the Selma and Montgomery marches. The other Beatles were strumming guitars, joking around a lot. John wanted to know every detail of the rights struggle. I joined the tour in New York, coming fresh from the Democratic Convention in Atlantic City that had just nominated Johnson and Humphrey. John soaked it all up. He was already forming opinions about the war in Vietnam. There was the soul of an activist building up in him."

As for me, when I wasn't fending off food and pillows, I spent my time reading, talking, playing cards and occasionally joining in the drinking of an official Beatles cocktail: rum and Coke.

Board games and card games were another staple of plane travel. Art Schreiber pursued his seemingly never-ending Monopoly contests with George on the airplane. And photographer Curt Gunther claimed that he was paying his way on the tour by taking the Beatles at poker.

We talked a lot, too, and the talk was cheap and good among such an interesting group of people. British reporter Ivor Davis, assigned to Hollywood, was a master storyteller. Davis, in his mid twenties, unusually young for print reporters of the day, was an animated Englishman who was a favorite of George Harrison and Derek Taylor. Today he covers the entertainment beat in Hollywood. Ivor remembers the time on the aircraft in 1964 with unbridled glee:

"The time on the plane was fascinating. We are all, you know, in this isolated cabin, far from the maddening crowds. When people can't escape from each other, you really discover things. I was ghostwriting George's daily column for my newspaper. There were times when he was complaining to me about the columns. I said, 'You know, if you gave me more of your valuable time instead of vegetating in the back of the plane, the column would be more interesting.' After that, he was always available. I found him to be the most sensitive of the Beatles. The airplane rides brought a closer bond. There's no place to run, is there?"

Jackie DeShannon was friendly with the Beatles, making her way up and down the aisles with regularity. Clarence Frogman Henry was a regular aisle walker, and so was Brenda Holloway on the second tour. Of the Beatles, John and Ringo were the ones who regularly left the rear and walked the plane, often sitting down in a vacant seat and chatting with reporters and opening-act musicians.

I found Ringo the most surprising Beatle. The so-called quiet Beatle would ask questions about everyone's families and jobs. It was with Ringo that I first brought up my mother's recent death. He seemed genuinely concerned and wanted to know the whole story. Ringo was also very open on the '65 tour in talking about his new wife, Maureen. And it was from Ringo that I learned about life in Liverpool, which wasn't so good. The boys had grown up in a blue-collar, working class neighborhood with few of the fifties-style luxuries of life. There was little attention paid to their band until the early sixties. Now, just a few years later, they were overwhelmed by the spotlight of fame and the accompanying perks. Despite this quick transition, the boys rarely displayed the side effects of stardom—ego, temper and neglect of others' feelings. They talked, but they also listened.

John was an especially great listener, especially on the airplane. He was full of questions—about growing up in America, broadcast journalism, deejays, social mores and, most of all, politics. In contrast, Paul and George mostly stayed to themselves, taking a casual walk through the aisles on occasion.

But it wasn't all food fights and conversation for the Beatles; they also worked on the Electra. On a flight from Dallas to New York, I managed to overhear a bit of musical history. As three of the Beatles worked on guitar, Ringo tapped his knees and all four sang as they tested the tune for a song that would later become "Eight Days a Week." On the plane, they were just humming the song and jamming with each other. The final version was even more catchy. When I've heard it over the years, I've always been reminded of that moment.

Of course, there was also alcohol on the plane, but despite the close quarters, it rarely led to any problems. Well, at least most of the time. As I was the so-called "straight man" among the journalists, there were frequent attempts to get me lost in the sauce. I escaped most nights, but on the 1964 flight from Montreal to Key West in the midst of Hurricane Dora, George had the flight attendant put small portions of rum into my Coca Cola, as I learned later. At the time, I was so tired, I couldn't tell the difference. But when we arrived in Key West in the predawn hours, I was so affected by the drinks that Mal Evans had to hold my arm as I walked down the steps off the plane for fear that I would fall on the pavement. Thanks to Mal, I arrived back in Florida in one piece.

Liquor, airborne food and flying pillows, good conversation, great music, apprehension about the next stop—these were all part of the remarkable plane life with the Beatles. And even through all those miles, there was hardly a close call, except for one night in 1965, when I saw the Beatles as mere mortals, hoping for survival like the rest of us.

CHAPTER 18:
Flirtatious Mothers and Candy Kisses

Getting close to the Beatles was priority number one for thousands of people—mostly young women and girls. Most fans, of course, were content to see them from a row inside a concert hall. But others' determination to get closer—much closer—inspired them to make attempts that were clever, controversial and almost unbelievable.

And for these rabid fans, if they couldn't meet the Beatles themselves at any given moment, they would gladly grab a piece of—or make an offer to—someone who had. That meant all of the Beatles' staff as well as the press crew that traveled with them. Second-hand Beatlemania, it turns out, is almost as wild as the real thing.

In their desire to meet the Beatles, not only young fans but also their mothers would go to great lengths to find a way. For a young reporter who was naïve in some respects, this "let's make a deal" mentality was both shocking and hilarious. These fans' logic was simple: If you can't get to them, get to the people who can get to them. I first realized the determination of Beatle-seekers when I discovered the flight attendant in my San Francisco hotel room. That was on the first day of the first tour, and the action just mushroomed from there. Children, parents, young women and even other reporters played this game. The children were fabulously funny and creative in their exhibitions of affection and desire. The adults were generally seductive and potentially dangerous, although most were also charming.

After the San Francisco incident, the next frontal assault I experienced, no pun intended, happened in the Brown Palace Hotel, the lodging legend in the heart of Denver. A heavy woman with a massive chest and a deep cleavage visible above the front of her sundress approached me to ask the time. Since there were huge clocks in the lobby, I was immediately curious about her motive. I gave her the time. She said, "Can I talk to you?" I replied, "Look, I've got to file a report. What's up?" The woman pointed to a sofa in the rear of the wood-paneled lobby, where three girls were sitting and laughing.

"One of those is mine," she said. "It would mean a whole bunch to me if you could get them to meet John and Paul." She grinned widely, her body leaning closer to me, which was obviously a distraction, if not an attraction.

"I'm a reporter," I answered. "I can't make that happen."

"Why not, honey?"

"Because I can't."

What she did next was incredibly seductive and funny. Right there in the lobby, she placed a finger on the inside of my hand and moved the finger slowly up to my wrist and all the way up to my shoulder. It was cozy and hardly noticeable to others in the lobby. She whispered in a Western twang, using language from the fabulous fifties, "Honeybunch, I can make you feel better than that."

Awkwardly, I dropped my tape recorder to the floor and reached out to shake her hand, saying, "It was nice meeting you." I would be a total liar if I said I wasn't rattled, but I was also convinced that she was just being seductive and teasing me to charm her way into a meeting with the Beatles. I wasn't sure, nor did I ever find out, if her dare was the real thing.

I would be caught in far more intricate traps in the next weeks and during the 1965 tour. And the types of offers people made can tell us something about the social revolution going on in America during the sixties. While free love sixties-style had not yet made its complete arrival, it was clearly just around the corner.

In Denver's Red Rocks Amphitheater on the '64 tour, I learned that another seduction technique was also fair game—bribery.

Those of us in the press party were roaming backstage before the show. I needed some extra tape, but my spare reel (we used reel-to-reel tape in the good old days) was back in the van. I ran back, retrieved it and returned to the backstage area. Red Rocks was just that—a theater carved in the rock. It held about six thousand people. To penetrate the security, you'd have to have sturdy boots and great legs—exactly what the two women had who confronted me on the gravel path behind the stage. Their skirts hardly fit the conservative western fashions of the day but instead gave a preview of the mini-skirt wave then rocking Britain that would soon surface in the America. The driver of the van, a funny fellow, later asked me, "Who were those women with the skirts up to their navels?"

The women's exact words are hard to forget. One of them said, "You with the Beatles?" I said shyly, "No, just a radio reporter traveling with them." The second woman said, "Can you get us to meet them?" I replied, "No, I can't do that."

"Well, it could be worth your while," one said.

"Could be what?"

"Worth your while."

She opened up her purse and handed me two neatly pressed, fresh-smelling fifty-dollar bills. I handed them back, but she pushed them into my palm. Finally, entertained but not impressed, I stuffed the bills into the purse slung over her arm.

She wasn't finished. The woman, who looked thirty-something, said, "If you're looking for a good time, we can meet you later." I smiled and said, "Gotta go," which in fact I did. I headed to the men's room, and that's the last I saw of the bribing mini-skirters, who I later learned had been chased out of the property by eagle-eyed sheriff's deputies.

So, in just one night in Denver, I was flirted with by an overzealous mother and turned away cold cash and possibly hot romance. It is with great humility that I say those advances had nothing to do with my charm and youthful good looks. I was but a vessel, a conduit by which people sought access to the Beatles.

When I told these stories to the other reporters on the tour, several warned me that what I had seen so far was just the beginning. They claimed that mothers would offer their bodies to get their kids to meet the Beatles. I hadn't ever seen anything like that before the visit to Denver.

Long John Wade, the deejay from Hartford, told me that he was astounded by the number of people who would recite those immortal words: "I will do anything to meet the Beatles." And he'd had his own experiences to back that up. Landing with the Beatles in Key West in the early morning on the '64 tour, Wade noticed a young woman in dungarees so tight that they looked like a second skin, leaning against the baggage truck and striking a pose as the Beatles came down the plank. Wade says, "Words were not needed. Her face relayed the message so well that Paul said to me, 'John, find out who that is.'" Wade discovered that she was the daughter of a local politician. Paul was no longer interested, but her "look" had been worth a thousand propositions.

The bids to meet the Beatles sometimes reached the point of hilarity, at least in retrospect. At the time, you couldn't be sure where these ploys were headed or what their provocateurs were ultimately capable of. At the Whittier Hotel in Detroit, a housekeeper kept knocking on my door in the early morning, despite the Do Not Disturb sign on the doorknob. Finally, I went to the door, opened it and asked her to go away. She insisted on coming in, and in a flash of a second or two, she had plopped herself on the twin bed beside mine and said, "Are you with the Beatles?" I replied in the negative. She got up and resigned to start making my bed.

But that wasn't the end of it. This woman had chutzpah. As she was flattening the sheets, she said, "You lie, big boy. What is that tape recorder—that's not for music? You lie and I know it. What rooms are they in? Just give me the numbers."

I replied, "Get lost."

She said, "You want something?" as she began to fluff up the pillows.

"Yeah, I want sleep," I said. "Can you go now?"

"Not until you sign my skirt."

"Are you kidding?"

She said, "I want your autograph."

So, in a desperate bid to get her out, I took a pen and signed her skirt with the words, "Best wishes, Larry Kane." Content that she had gotten *someone's* autograph, she left the room and wandered off into her fantasy world.

Perhaps the most dramatic proposition I heard about came in the lobby of the Lafayette Motor Inn in Atlantic City. A mature and attractive woman approached a member of the traveling party who shall forever remain anonymous. According to his account, she pointed to two other, younger women across the way and said, "You see them? You can have me and them for as long as you want if we can get to meet the guys."

Well, we didn't see much of him for two nights and three days, but legend has it that his companions never met the boys. Unfortunately, I am sworn to secrecy and cannot disclose the name of this opportunist.

There was also kid stuff that was wholesome and wonderful, a tribute to the creativity of young people. Across from the Delmonico Hotel on New York's Park Avenue, for example, thousands of kids stood beyond yellow police barricades, screaming for several days for the Beatles. They were energetic but orderly, and I decided to cross the lines to seek some interviews and some laughs. I got both.

The fans were happy to see somebody, and almost every reporter who ventured behind the barricades was surrounded by eager fans. One girl, who said she was from Queens, said, "Can you get something to Ringo?" I answered her: "I'll try." Excitedly, she reached into a little purse and handed me a bagel with the words, "Luv you Ringo. Debby" scrawled in black ink on the side. I was impressed. I figured that a bagel would certainly get Ringo's attention, and it did when I presented it to him during a tape session later in the day.

KANE: Ringo, I have one of the more unusual gifts for you. [I handed it to him.]
RINGO: I love this. [laughter] Well, y'know Larry, most of the fans are so sweet. I mean, c'mon. Without them, there would be no Beatles. If you see her, thank her.

Of course I never did see her again. And I never brought anyone to meet the Beatles. That would have been inappropriate. But, whenever I could, I collected notes and souvenirs to bring to them, and sometimes I accepted a sweet treat for myself, such as a pastry or chocolate. This was the least I could do for all those loyal, waiting teenagers.

The gifts from fans took all sorts of forms. Aside from the expected jellybeans, candy kisses were a favorite, along with marshmallows. There was also no shortage of small lockets with messages, simple notes of affection, coloring books, sandwiches, homemade cookies, magazines, personal snapshots, friendship rings, playing cards, soaps, toothbrushes, and assorted makeup, especially lipstick.

In Cincinnati, where we stayed just long enough for the concert, a cute little girl slipped her school report card into my hand. Before I could give it back, she ran away, screaming, "Give it to Paul!" Feeling the tremendous weight of responsibility, I showed the straight-A report card to Paul in the backstage area. He shook his head and moved on. From New York, I put the report card in the mail and addressed it to the Cincinnati school system. I hope she got it back.

The fans' pursuit of the band made fantastic stories for the radio announcers at WFUN to share with our listeners. While the stories of the adult capers were much too hot for sixties radio, the zeal and artistry of the young fans made great stories then and remain as price-less memories today.

Forty years later, many of those young fans are mothers and even grandmothers. Wherever they are, I want them to know that I felt this way then and still feel it now: Although the flirtatious mothers got my attention, it was the candy kisses that received my affection.

CHAPTER 19:
What Were They Really Like?

The present story shows the Beatles as the "boys," not as the individual artists and activists they became in later years. The Beatles of 1964 and 1965 were not the men of 1970 who broke up their band to pursue their individual destinies. The John Lennon of the seventies was different in mood and maturity than the Lennon of the sixties. Similarly, Ringo Starr was a more serious individual when I interviewed him in 2000 than when I interviewed him back in 1964 and 1965. Paul McCartney, the embodiment of the entertaining extrovert on the tours, went on to lead an adult life marked by almost total privacy. And George Harrison, struck during the nineties by illness and violence, also lived a very different lifestyle on the tours than he did later on, when he was rarely interviewed and also very private. But what they were like to be with and watch during almost two months of tours and filming does provide interesting clues to who they later became.

They were always excited and eager to talk during our interviews. While that behavior signals most of all that an interviewee is comfortable with the questioner, it also speaks volumes about the kind of people they were. They were, in a phrase, "nice guys." And as a group, they had a genuine and delightful sense of humor. Here's Paul ribbing me in Houston in 1965:

KANE: John, I'd like to ask you about reporters.
McCARTNEY: Is that so, Harry?
KANE: Oh. Paul.
McCARTNEY: Remember me?

KANE: I'm sorry, I'm sorry.
McCARTNEY: It's okay, Harry.

Lennon, too, had a lot to do with creating this humor-filled atmosphere, as he was forever finding ways to make jokes. Ringo behaved like a man with no cares. And George was one of the most unaffected people I've ever met, in show business or out.

Q: George, some in the press say your music is bad.
HARRISON: It is, don't you think?
Q: Will you get married?
HARRISON: Do you think anybody will have me?

"Real" is the key word here. Unlike the big stars of the era, the Beatles were not afraid to let their hair down. Their casual everyman's view of life, coupled with their soulful music, endeared them to a whole generation of young people who followed their lead and let their hair down in a big and protest-filled way in the late sixties. The music and lyrics forged a connection to a generation looking for answers and staring down the truth. Songs as varied as "Revolution," "I'm a Loser" and "Help!" gave support for the youthful challenges of protest, disenchantment and reaching out.

Real and connected to their generation, and sensitive to the joys and frustrations of growing up—these were qualities of the Beatles that continued to unfold. Though they were separated from their fans by security and privacy, they were connected to those same people by their style and their music, a connection few other artists were able to make to that degree.

One of the untold stories of the early Beatles years was their outright appreciation for their fans, demonstrated by their attempts to guarantee them access when security said otherwise. In hindsight, there is a tendency to view the Beatles' fans as crazed, delirious, possessed and determined—which they were. But the fans' story is also one of dedication, admiration and love. And the feelings went both ways.

Perhaps the biggest frustration that John, Paul, George and Ringo experienced on the first American tours was the inability to meet their fans. In some cases, they were prevented from even looking at the fans from a distance; in other cases, they were prohibited from waving out of hotel windows. The Beatles were perplexed, and they tried to get closer even when conditions dictated they could not. Their humble beginnings, overnight success and sense of compassion left them feeling guilty on many occasions about their inability to have direct contact with their fans, most of whom they were separated from by less than ten years in age.

Even the simple act of saying hello was a daunting task. So the fans who propelled the Beatles to worldwide fame would have to settle mostly for the shared experience of watching them, with joy and passion, from a distance. But not always.

The Beatles' road manager Neil Aspinall and press secretaries Derek Taylor (1964) and Tony Barrow (1965) were often asked to pick out a few fans from the early-gathering concert crowds and bring them to the dressing room. Taylor, with his usual aplomb and wisdom, tried hard to find young ladies who were sweet but not necessarily candidates for Miss America. Aspinall and co-road manager Mal Evans made no such distinction. But let one thing be clear: Fans at the concerts were brought back for conversation, autographs and nothing else. What happened in the hotels was another story, and from my limited perspective it involved young women, not teenagers.

I watched a few of those dressing-room meetings. In Baltimore, after the traditional fan club meeting, the Beatles broke the ice with three teenage girls and a boy by asking them about their own lives. Sitting down in the dressing room, the girls were entranced, especially when John and Paul asked them if they wanted to pose for a picture. The boy who accompanied them was actually shaking. I left the room for awhile. When I returned to the dressing room door, the four teenagers were leaving, walking down the corridor, looking at each other, immersed in shared shock and disbelief.

During these special fan meetings, the Beatles made a significant departure from their usual lifestyle. All four of them were rabid cigarette smokers; it was rare for them not to have cigarettes in their hands. But when the kids came around to talk and take pictures, they stopped smoking. Despite all the episodes of pleasure-seeking and backroom intrigue, the Beatles were genuinely concerned about the image they conveyed to their fans.

There was also commitment to family in evidence. John Lennon, in 1964, was the only married Beatle (Ringo got married before the '65 tour). Broadcaster Art Schreiber speaks fondly of John's phone calls home, and he was touched by John's need for family. Schreiber says, "Lennon seemed to have a very traditional love for Cynthia [his first wife] and would call her nightly to check in and talk, in baby talk, to his son Julian. It was exciting to watch. Here was a Beatle, the idol of millions, savoring a few minutes on the phone with his wife."

The Beatles also revealed their individual personalities in different ways to the press people traveling with them, and each member of the press has his own memories of them. Art Schreiber especially remembers the quiet times, shooting the breeze with the boys on topics ranging from the frivolous to the serious.

Art says, "They were lonely, isolated from the world, both on tour and at home. They couldn't go anywhere. Remember, aside from all the fame and glory, they were young men, barely out of boyhood. I've always been a pretty tough reporter when it came to the people I covered, but let me tell you, they were terrific. I actually started feeling close to them. They really opened up. I was also impressed with how bright they were. They knew how to treat people. They were terrific."

Ivor Davis, reporter for the *Daily Express* of London, had a special rapport with George Harrison. Davis was ghostwriting George's column for that paper, and he had a deep fondness for both George and John. He recalls, "George was, in truth, unaffected by his success. You could talk to him as an individual. John grew with his success and was not afraid to tackle the tough issues of his time. I really enjoyed being with all of them. They had their moments, but most of all, they made the difficult journey a delightful experience."

Tony Barrow, press secretary on the '65 tour, had perhaps the most focused insight on the Beatles of anyone who knew them. Decades later, we compared notes. When speaking of John Lennon's role, Tony describes a man who seemed controversial because he took on the group's responsibility for dealing with serious issues, like the Beatles' quiet efforts to wrest control from their controlling manager, Brian Epstein.

Barrow says, "John made the most noise, especially with Epstein. But it was Paul who let John do the heavy lifting when there was a dispute with Brian. Then Paul would finish the persuasion. John would make Brian cry at times, but Paul, more of a politician, would use a quiet influence to get his way. John's bark was worse than his bite. He used the bark to cover up low self-esteem. You could really get to John when you talked about real things, like family and kids. But his attention span was limited. He was in front with his 'noise,' but he was much more sensitive than people realized."

Barrow's view of McCartney shows a man eager to be seen as the good guy. "He promised people everything, tickets, gifts, then left it to people like me to fulfill the promises," Barrow recalls. "He wanted to look like a good benefactor, [and he was] long on promises, short on performance. He was a charmer who was a public relations delight, a man who was a master of image making. He is and was a sheer showman, from his bone marrow to his fingertips. He feeds [on] the approval of his public. He did then. He does today."

Ringo Starr, so easy to get along with, was conscious of all the times he'd missed school because of childhood illness, according to Barrow. Barrow notes that, at times, Ringo felt unable to keep up with the others in terms of knowledge. "Ringo was content to stay in the background," Barrow says, "but he fit in very well. He may have a sad face, but he was a very happy and content person."

The story of George Harrison is more complex, according to the former press chief. "George was the friendliest of the Beatles. He always spoke close to your face—was interested in being a good listener. George was very affectionate. He did not have an ego in the normal range of a music superstar, and he was the most serious musician of the group. Ironically, because he was such an inward, creative person, he was most affected by the hysteria of Beatlemania. Occasionally, he let his disenchantment with celebrity show." Like, for instance, the glass-throwing incident in Hollywood.

My own positive relationship with the Beatles was formed early on. Despite my cynical skepticism at the beginning, I became a fan, not only of their professional personas and their music, but also of the individuals they were. What impressed me most about all of them was their indisputable naturalness and, to varying degrees, the depth of their humanity and their lack of phoniness. Even McCartney, with his suspect superficiality, was generous with his thoughts and caring about other people's feelings. Ringo, especially, was a man without hang-ups who lived up to his everyman image by practicing a code of treating people equally. He appeared to abhor the frailties of show business, realizing that when you began to believe your own press notices you could begin to become superficial and unreal, in the stereotyped Hollywood sense.

KANE: You are so relaxed and so frank.
STARR: In England they are so used to people always saying, "I'm so happy to be here" and "It's very nice of you" and all that. Well, you know I don't think we can say that, I mean it is nice to be in different cities but we don't put it on as such as

we call "showbiz" people, which we are not. You know what
showbiz people are?
KANE: Stars?
STARR: Acting like stars.

Doing without niceties didn't always serve the band well; being
real and honest could be damaging. If there was ever a man who said
in public what he thought in private, it was John Lennon. The following quote, while endearing to fans, infuriated some police officers:

KANE: John, in a lot of newspapers around the country there
are headlines like "Beatles Dodge Their Fans." There's another
story behind that?
LENNON: It's usually someone comes up and says the police
chief of so and so won't let you go. . . . And we don't even
know the fans are there 'cause they drag us off so quickly.
There is no time at all when we say let's go over there and
wave. They are always preventing us one way or other. Even
when they allow us to wave, they give us about half a second.
They just sort of shove us and drag us out . . . and that's it.

It's not that hard to understand why the security forces protecting
the band from potentially dangerous fans might be upset to hear
those sentiments. And some members of the band also spoke openly
about media coverage. Show business stars of today rarely criticize
the media that cover them, in public at least. What George Harrison
said in 1964, for instance, would never be heard from mainstream
stars now:

KANE: There are a lot of magazines around America that
print rumors. Does that ever bug you?
HARRISON: It drives you up the walls sometimes. Well, you
know, since we've been over here they've been asking, "Is
John leaving?" Well, the new one today is it's me; I'm leaving.
That's because some idiot in Hollywood has written in the
papers that I'm leaving, so now for weeks I will have people
coming up to me and asking, "Is it true you are leaving?"

Of the four boys from Liverpool, Lennon was the most philosoph-
ically and politically oriented. However, because he often said what he

felt, he learned that sometimes the public inflicts great pain on extremely honest people.

In early March 1966, John was interviewed by the *London Evening Standard.* He told reporter Maureen Cleave, "Christianity will go. It will vanish and shrink. I needn't argue with that; I'm right and will be proved right. We're more popular than Jesus now; I don't know which will go first—rock-and-roll or Christianity. Jesus was all right, but his disciples were thick and ordinary. It's them twisting it that ruins it for me."

The worldwide reaction to that was fast, furious and punitive. In addition to giving the group horribly bad press, some broadcasters in America boycotted Beatles records. While that ban was short lived, the controversy wasn't. It took John Lennon months to live down the comment, months spent explaining in earnest that he was trying to describe his generation's declining interest in spirituality.

It was typical of Lennon to speak his mind. His candor was revolting to some, refreshing to others and ammunition for those jealous and fearful of the Beatles' growing influence on the young.

And while history remembers Lennon as the leading Beatle of conscience, the allegedly quiet man in the background, Ringo Starr, was also a profoundly interested antiwar spokesman. Late in the 1965 tour, Ringo began to talk to me about escalating conflicts in Africa, the Middle East and Southeast Asia:

KANE: Are you angry about the war drums beating now? What would be your method or way to go about ending war? RINGO: I think it's unfair that you get a leader of a country— then they force so many people to fight each other, and they don't get touched hardly. It is all the young men of the world who get shot, and bombed, and blown to bits. It's unfair. I know it sounds silly but they should let *them* fight it out, instead of fetching all those innocent bystanders.

Was that a simplistic answer to a profound question? Perhaps, but it would become a typical sentiment among a growing number of youths who faced disenchantment in the midst of widespread change.

Speaking of change, it is hard to state what the Beatles were really like as individuals without acknowledging that, to a man, they kept changing themselves. In one short year, from the summer tour of 1964 into the winter of 1965 in the Bahamas and then through the second national tour in 1965, I witnessed a transformation in each band member that was unmistakable. Each Beatle was more self-confident. The four acted less as a group and more as individuals, stating their minds, speaking their piece and belying the mop-top, fab-four cultural stereotyping that had accompanied their early rise to fame.

Like lawyers, doctors, carpenters and journalists, they were growing into their jobs. But despite the enormous fame, power and financial trappings of life in the spotlight, they remained remarkably normal human beings.

Another unaffected aspect of their behavior that was special to watch and be around was their relationship to each other. Much has been said about the static between Paul McCartney and John Lennon after the breakup. But on our tours, we saw nothing but a sensitive closeness between all of them. They masked each other's bad moments with laughter. After the great escape from Vancouver in '64, they were humorously congratulating each other in the airplane cabin. Following the famous flying cocktail at the Whisky a Go-Go nightclub in Los Angeles, the band stood behind George Harrison and defended his actions. It was truly all for one and one for all. To let them tell it, I asked whether there were troubles behind the scenes:

> KANE: Do you ever have any problems between the Beatles, the four guys? You're bound to have differences. I know it's a tough question.
> LENNON: No, it really isn't. We have plenty of arguments. We're also attuned to each other. We know each other so well through the years, an argument never reaches a climax. We know each other so well. Let's say an argument is building up between Ringo and I—let's say, we just know what's going to come next and everybody packs in. We have ordinary arguments like most people, but no conflicts.
> KANE: Ringo?
> STARR: In America, there's always a group, then someone gets too big for the group and leaves. I would hate to leave the other three. If it did happen, I just wouldn't know what to do.

Oftentimes during both tours, there was practically nothing to do but sit around, on airplanes or in hotel rooms, and wait. It's in these times, when energy can become stagnant and feelings can become boxed up, that we are all susceptible to snippiness or worse. Not so with the Beatles. They were truly interested in each other, and also interested in many of the same things. One day I asked Ringo and Paul what they do when they're killing time together in a hotel suite:

> KANE: What do you do, tell jokes when you're in there?
> McCARTNEY: No, we just had hysterics.
> STARR: Just one of them nights where . . . just one little thing starts one laughing, then we all end up curling up.
> KANE: Do you do a lot of reading in your spare time?
> STARR: Uh, sometimes, all depends how I feel, y'know. We have phases where we read like lunatics.
> McCARTNEY: Last tour, it was in Australia, we just read every James Bond book out. Y'know, all of us did. And we were just talking James Bond for the whole tour, y'know.

Another pastime was reading some of the thousands of letters collected by fan clubs across the country and delivered at each stop by fan-club officers. The Beatles took their fan mail seriously. "Owing the fans" was a feeling shared by all the Beatles, who adored their fans, even the ones who could only reach them through the mail. Many late-night hours would find them curled up on sofas, opening fan mail.

It was the fans, the music, and the genuine affection for each other that kept John, Paul, George and Ringo together during the crazy, hazy days and nights on tour through America in 1964 and '65.

Eventually, the Beatles would go in different directions, but throughout their lives they cared for and respected each other. So when people ask, "What were they really like?" I have an easy answer. They were decent, caring, nice people who were even richer in character than they ever would be in financial success.

CHAPTER 20:
The Late Show: Free Love and Free Parking

The nocturnal scene on a continuous trip, whether it be a political campaign or a rock tour, can be uniquely exciting or insanely boring. The great Beatles tours, especially 1964, saw a mixture of both. Some nights, after endless days filled with traveling and activity, boredom itself became appealing. But other nights, parties, girls and casual drugs were what the boys craved. In general, staying up late was a fixed feature of the tour for the Beatles.

> KANE: Are you really sleeping all day long when you tell us you are?
> STARR: No, we get up at about three in the afternoon.
> McCARTNEY: Well, we're up now, aren't we, y'know. . . .
> STARR: What time is it now?
> McCARTNEY: It's half past three! And here we are. We're up. Well, we didn't go to bed until four.

The guys rarely retired for the night just following a concert. Imagine, if you will, a nine-to-five worker heading off to sleep at six o'clock. The band, too, needed time to kick back after they finished their work. The night was truly their recreation time.

Those with lively imaginations might conjure up night after night of being attended by attractive servants and exotic women, nights of sensual pleasures galore. Well, there were plenty of women, but there were also nights when the company of others on the tour and playing a family-oriented board game were just fine for the young superstars. Monopoly was their favorite.

At the Brown Palace Hotel in Denver, hours after the beautiful concert at the Red Rocks Amphitheater, I took a walk outside to get some air and get away from my insomnia. Wading through the ever-present crowd, I noticed a fan with a sign that said "Park Place for Sale." I didn't get it at first. But after a few minutes I realized that this clever young woman was appealing to the Beatles' fascination with the board game Monopoly.

Art Schreiber probably played the most rounds with the boys. "I played Monopoly so late with them, that I barely had time for an hour or two of sleep before getting to work in the morning. It was fun. They really enjoyed being land moguls, and rich, which I guess they already were."

I only once played Monopoly with George and Ringo; it was a two-part competition that was brief but rewarding. In both games, I walked away with the lot of cash. They were the experts, but I must have got lucky and landed on the Free Parking jackpot. Unfortunately, of course, it was all Monopoly money.

Another game the band engaged in with enthusiasm was poker. Curt Gunther, a serious and intense photojournalist who traveled with the group for almost the entire 1964 tour, was known for his poker face. Apparently, it came in handy: he claimed major wins in poker games with the Beatles. Fortunately for him, though I cannot confirm it, I would guess they were playing for *real* cash.

So, in the wee hours of the morning while on tour, Monopoly, poker, late-night television, reading and just sitting around and sharing the company of people were the Beatles' favorite pastimes. Well, *almost* their favorite pastimes.

Women came and went from the Beatles' floor in most hotels, but with rare exception, the boys were discreet. They did prefer young adult women to teeny-boppers, and they objected to professionals. The few teenagers who showed up late at night were fan-club leaders delivering gifts and mail, and they were given soda and a chance to take pictures with the band, nothing more.

As for the rest of the late-night female visitors, the system was pretty simple. Getting women into the hotels required somebody with the power to do so. The Beatles couldn't just wait in the lobby for someone to show up! So Mal Evans and Neil Aspinall would arrange for access and transit. For the most part, Neil or Mal would select the women who would have access to the band, with some obvious benefits attached. Tony Barrow recalls the process: "Neil would usually 'audition' potential partners, assuming that it was part of his job. Sometimes it was Mal, but mostly it was Neil."

Mal, for one, was a suave and smooth procurer, able to spot a target with incredible intuition. It was as though he could pick up on the scent of women who were willing. Only rarely did I see him alone in a hotel corridor. At least his flair for recruiting included an understanding of the difficulties the Beatles could face if any female companion was underage or wronged in any way. If one could get an Oscar for safely procuring women, Mal Evans would have received the lifetime achievement award.

While the Beatles did entertain women on the 1964 tour, what was absent—at least on the surface—was overt drug use. Although I was not witness to illegal drug usage for the most part, it has since become common knowledge that the Beatles had discovered marijuana in 1964, and other things by 1965.

Legend has it that Bob Dylan introduced the Beatles to marijuana at the Delmonico Hotel in New York City during the '64 tour. It probably happened the first time we were in New York. Ironically, and unwittingly, during our second stop in the Big Apple I played a small part in this legend by escorting Dylan from the front desk to the Beatles' hotel room. But the first time I actually saw a Beatle with a marijuana cigarette was in Nassau during the filming of *Help!* in February 1965. I noticed, upon arriving in the Bahamas, that their behavior was a little more peculiar than it had been at any time throughout the 1964 tour. I knew then that the 1965 tour would be different.

Throughout '65, Malcolm Evans made no secret of the fact that he was the stasher who dispensed the goods when requested. But the morality of the day required judicious, prudent behavior. Discretion was the watchword. The Beatles, Epstein insisted, would always nurture their image. As the drug use increased, Epstein and others in the party took great pains to hide it. Epstein was especially sensitive. He was, after all, the boss. But he was also, as we would learn after his death, enchanted with the world of drugs himself.

I remember one night in particular that exemplified this approach. Hours after the final concert of 1965 in San Francisco, the promoter held a small cocktail party at our hotel in Palo Alto. It was a lively affair, with the Beatles upbeat about the tour's end, waiters roaming the room with finger food, and some glamorous young women setting their eyes on the boys. In a corner, John sat quietly and reached into his jacket for his cigarettes. He pulled out a thinner cigarette from his pack, a marijuana joint, and thumbed his lighter to start it. But before he was able to light the joint, Brian Epstein took a quick detour away from chatting with me and a few others, walked over to John, and glowered at him, shaking his head. John slipped the object of his desire back into his jacket pocket, pulled out a legal smoke from his pack and lit up.

It was a telling moment, showcasing the protected and his protector dancing on the edge of danger. Marijuana possession, in an age of protest and outrage, would have landed Lennon in hot water then. It eventually did in the seventies. Ironically, his battle with the U.S. government over the ramifications of drug use would bring him on a special mission to my new hometown of Philadelphia ten years later. But in San Francisco, on the eve of Labor Day 1965, Lennon and the Beatles were saved from embarrassment. Propriety ruled, as it did most nights. Which is why there were no major repercussions—legal or in the media—due to the Beatles' late-night diversions.

CHAPTER 21:
The Beatles' Inner Circle

One of the genuine treats of traveling with the Beatles was meeting the people who played pivotal but mostly hidden roles, background players who made things work and sometimes in the process brought a few laughs in the middle of the chaos.

The inner circle was formed by two groups—Liverpool insiders and traveling press. The Liverpool gang was a group of six people devoted to their charges, and touched by the glory. From a historical perspective, they were the very first rock entourage in what was, at the time, the first real rock-and-roll concert tour. Each had his job to do, but along the way, we were able to work together in the eye of the storm, sharing the experience of a lifetime.

The most unlikely member of the inner sanctum was a tall man named Malcolm Evans. The personal assistant to the Beatles never stood in the spotlight, but his contributions to a happier environment on the tours were immeasurable. Whenever I think of the Beatles, I think of Mal Evans, the joy of the man, and the surprise twist his life story took after he and the band parted ways.

Mal was tall and rangy, with a bushy head of hair and eyes that shone from behind plain spectacles, conveying a sense of wonder that you would find in the eyes of an eager child. In fact, Evans had a childlike quality about him. At times, he would be laughing so hard, it would make you laugh just to listen to him. When it came time to bite the bullet, he would become serious in an instant, but you knew he was faking. This was a man whose smile and cheerful demeanor were contagious.

Professionally, he would have done anything to protect and serve the Beatles. He covered for them when their social activities required the need for secrecy, and he willingly used his body to guarantee their safety when security provisions were insufficient. And when it came to protecting the Beatles, Mal's height, six feet two inches, was a plus. In our harrowing escape from Empire Stadium in Vancouver, Evans shielded John Lennon from onrushing fans, at one point stiff-arming a boy who tried to get to the Beatles' car. That move would have made an NFL running back proud. On the plane later, I laughingly complimented him on his prowess. He replied, "Just wait for me next act."

Ultimately, Mal was a man who smiled cheerfully while accompanying the Beatles but who also lived on the edge of the dark side, drinking heavily and indulging in illicit pleasures. During the filming of *Help!* in Nassau, Mal Evans joined me and Long John Wade at a local bar for a late-night drink that turned into a nightmare. Evans got so drunk that Wade and I had to carry him back to my hotel room. That was no small task, considering that he was huge. The next morning, cheerfully and genuinely, Mr. Evans told us over coffee, "Had a great time last night. Thanks for joining me."

You can tell that I really liked the guy. That's why it was so sad for me to read the account of his death on the news wires on January 4, 1976. Evans had left the Beatles' Apple organization years earlier. There is no question that life after the limelight and the excitement of touring was difficult for him. Separated from his wife and children, he moved to Los Angeles, where he was working on a book about his life with the Beatles. According to the woman he was living with, he had been suffering from depression. On the night of January 4, fearing his suicide, she called the police. They came to the couple's home and confronted Mal in the bedroom, and he reportedly aimed a shotgun at the police. The police fired at least four shots at him. Malcolm Evans was dead.

Today, Malcolm Evans is but a footnote to the history of the group, but to the Beatles and those who traveled with them, when we were flying from place to place, rushing through crowds, running for safety and living the frenzied life of touring North America, he was much more than that.

Neil Aspinall was the most essential and powerful of the Beatles' assistants, so much so that he ran the Beatles Apple Corps empire for decades after they broke up. Aspinall was handsome, self assured, and a vigorous gatekeeper. He was the boys' age, and actually first met up with Paul and George while in school at the Liverpool Institute. Soon John joined the trio of pals and together they indulged in teenage joviality. When the Beatles were born, Neil lent a hand as a temporary roadie. As they grew and needed full time assistance, they turned to Neil and made him their official road manager in 1960. The Beatles always trusted him greatly with their safety and their secrets.

There was more skepticism about the role of Derek Taylor. The traveling press secretary embraced his insider role with joy, but was often at odds with Brian Epstein. Taylor was the best-dressed person on the tour, showing off tri-colored dress shirts with those thin ties that were the rage of 1964. Debonair and dashing, Taylor seemed to fancy himself as almost a fifth Beatle. He was, in fact, a fabulous spokesman for the group. Derek Taylor was a magnificent orator, and his words flowed like journalistic poetry. I admired and respected Taylor, but was aware of the underlying tension between him and Epstein.

Derek's assistant, Bess Coleman, was a delightful person who was able to ease tensions between reporters and Taylor. Bess and I became friends, and in 1966, I hired her to do reports for WFUN Radio. My time on the 1966 was limited because of military obligations.

The traveling press chief in 1965 and beyond was Tony Barrow, a man of great honor and integrity, who used his prior skills as a journalist to deal exquisitely with press pressures facing the Beatles. Barrow, who was a great help with this book, had the demeanor of an English gentlemen, coupled with the eye of a tiger. Barrow had a scent for trouble, and a delightful nose for good news. He was, and is, a friend.

The most intriguing member of the team was its leader, Beatles' manager Brian Epstein. Formal to a fault, moody and pensive, Epstein was the first real rock-group mogul. Just a couple of years older than the boys, he relished the role of Beatles' booster, promoter, confidante and decision-maker. But there was always an edge to him. He expressed great compassion for my challenges as a reporter, and as it became clear on our second visit to Hollywood, wanted a more intimate relationship. His homosexuality (which was actually illegal in Britain in those days) and accompanying depression led him to lean on drugs and alcohol for support and solace. And his lust for dangerous sexual experiences, coupled with the drugs, contributed to his early demise. But he was at bottom a smart person who cared greatly for the Beatles, and whose contribution to their success cannot be measured.

This team of insiders made life for the Beatles palatable. They also upheld an incredible energy level and created significant opportunities for another group of insiders—the traveling press, an elite group that I was proud to be a part of.

While every city featured at least one staged press conference and an endless swarm of reporters looking for even more coverage than that afforded, the Beatles' organization also decided to assemble a traveling press party to accompany them. During the 1965 jaunt, a variety of radio personalities flew a leg or two of the journey. But in 1964, it was an elite and constant crew, including several disk jockeys, a few British journalists, and two American reporters. I was the only American newsman to travel to every stop. The second American, who joined us in New York, was a great veteran journalist.

"It was the most difficult assignment I ever had." This line was spoken by a man who has covered the White House, the Capitol, the grueling pace of John F. Kennedy's campaign for president, the grim aftermath of his assassination, and race riots in American cities. The same man, radio correspondent Art Schreiber, ran radio news operations, stewarded entire stations as general manager and became a legend as a rugged individualist in a business dominated by fragile egos and hard-nosed moguls. And now, retired from the business, Schreiber says of traveling with the Beatles, "No doubt, it was the toughest damn assignment I ever had."

It was especially difficult for us radio guys. The sheer weight of the stuff we had to carry was an occupational hazard. Running for a car, limo or bus at full throttle with a heavyweight tape recorder over a shoulder and pockets crammed with other tools of the trade is excruciating work. Art carried a fifteen-pound Grundig tape machine everywhere he went, along with a portable typewriter and his briefcase. He remembers our task fondly, saying, "We were like a bunch of pack mules."

Joining our ragtag group of "mules" was young Ivor Davis of the *London Daily Express*. Ivor was a jolly good guy with an eye for news, and a sense of great camaraderie. Davis and Art Schreiber were great companions, along with two popular deejays. Jim Staggs, from Cleveland, was a great interviewer with a golden voice. Long John Wade, from Hartford, was tall, rangy, and although one of the "jocks," often asked tough questions of the boys.

For all of us, it was an exciting job, with great pleasure and great pain. The impact on one's body was enormous. In addition to carrying a bulky tape recorder, I endured the banging of people against me in the crowds, which eventually took its toll. Bruises and welts were not uncommon. And the print guys carried typewriters with them. They were bulky and could crush against you in a big crowd. The worst injury that I suffered was when a pencil in my pocket cut into my thigh during a crowd scene. Considering the proximity of the cut to another part of my anatomy, I stopped putting pencils in my pockets.

Technical difficulties aside, I faced the constant pressure of needing direct access to the Beatles to get the interviews that would make my reports special. Derek Taylor and Bess Coleman (and later Tony Barrow) were dealing with the worldwide press swirling around them and other insane pressures, but still they were wonderful to me, and to the rest of the traveling press party. Epstein also encouraged this accessibility.

Still, the Beatles' support team had its own problems to deal with to be sure, and the press men often had to fend for ourselves. The anxiety of not being sure if we would be able to penetrate the security barriers, for instance—even with our identification—was another grating reality we faced from city to city. Imagine having to talk yourself through every checkpoint, and sometimes losing the battle. Long John Wade actually missed the flight from Kansas City to Dallas because police wouldn't let him through to the airplane. He managed to catch up with us in Dallas on his own.

The security challenges were tougher than they might have been at another time because the first tour took place just nine months after the murder of John Kennedy. Police were edgy. Some were overbearing. But that was, for the most part, a very good thing, since security breakdowns occurred all too often. Security actually toughened up as the first tour progressed, which was a real pain in the neck, and the back, and especially the ribs.

The pace of the daily routine was another challenge. Wake-up was early, especially for me, since I needed time to write and file my reports and "feed sound" to the guys at my station. My reports usually had to last about a minute and fifteen seconds each, and I had to file seven every day. That meant writing stories and picking out the best "sound bites" from my tape of the Beatles. After filing as much as I could and eating breakfast, I would call Derek Taylor to check the day's schedule. Usually he would report that an interview session was planned for the afternoon and would outline the day's events. Then I would record a spot for the affiliated station in the town I was in. In some cases, I would go "live" by phone or even pay a visit to these stations. As you might imagine, I was very popular at each of these stops.

In fact, each of us press men also became, quite unexpectedly, overnight "celebrities" and targets of fans' obsession. When rabid Beatles fans couldn't get close to the objects of their desire, they often settled for harassing the Beatles' management, the crew, and even the press party. This attention took many forms, from simple touching and asking for autographs to more physical grabbing and clothes-ripping. Or worse.

Such incidental violence was always waiting in the wings as a sideshow to Beatles events. At the hotel in Milwaukee on the 1964 tour, Art Schreiber had his tie cut off by a souvenir-hunting fan. If you couldn't get close to the Beatles, then you got close to someone who could. This sort of rationalization affected me outside Kansas City's Muelenbach Hotel, where a teenage boy grabbed my seventeen-pound tape recorder and tried to wrest it away. I grabbed him back, instinctively. He laid his hand around my wrist and almost ripped my arm from its socket. I fought back, swinging at the young man with unmistakable intent. That was the first time I had ever thrown a punch at anyone on the job. Incidentally, I won the fight. As a member of the traveling Beatles entourage, you never knew what fans were going to do to you next.

Another member of the inner press circle, George Harrison (no relation), a reporter for the *Liverpool Gazette* whose famous name was a lively talk item on the tour, got into a lively scrum himself in Atlantic City. Because of a mix-up, he was forced to spend a night at another hotel away from the entourage. When his cab pulled up to that hotel, some delirious fans saw the name George Harrison stenciled on his luggage and went berserk. They grabbed his suitcase, which split wide open, revealing his most private garments. Harrison wrestled the fans to the ground, winning the battle but losing portions of his pants to the overzealous fans.

For each of us, this spillover fame actually spilled over into our lives away from the tour. When Art Schreiber returned home to Cleveland, for instance, he was flabbergasted by the attention paid to him. "Kids came to my house to kiss my door. In restaurants, young people would fight over my cigarette butts. I was invited to give speeches at birthday parties, and the parents were as interested as the kids. Universities called for lectures. I, a radio newsman, was a certifiable celebrity, and the deejays at my station were green with envy."

As for me, when I returned to Miami, the sales department at WFUN Radio sent me out on tour. I appeared in rallies at five Miami malls, including the huge Dadeland Mall in Southwest Miami. The ads said, "Meet the Man Who Met the Beatles!" The crowds were so large, a small army of security guards had to be brought in. High schools and colleges offered invitations to speak, and my mail never stopped. In all, I answered a thousand letters from around the nation.

In subsequent years, at college campuses, churches, synagogues and even political forums, I have been confronted by questions about the Beatles. Whenever my bio is read at personal appearances, my experience of covering the Beatles draws more oohs and ahs than my interviews with presidents. In fact, one president, briefed by staff on my full resume prior to our one-on-one interviews, offered his own question. In November, 1980, before a live pre-election interview in Philadelphia, presidential candidate Jimmy Carter said to me, "So I heard you toured with the Beatles. What were they like?" As I gave him a brief description of the Beatles on tour, he smiled. He seemed eager for more information when the cue came to start the actual political interview. Even the thirty-ninth president wanted the scoop on the Beatles. Everybody does.

From my perspective, both then and now, traveling with the Beatles was an adventure that I would never want to have missed. But I won't say it wasn't tough. In the ensuing years, I have covered riots, inaugurations, eighteen political conventions, urban combat, earthquake disasters and the like. But I will say, without qualification, as Art Schreiber says: "It was the toughest assignment I ever had."

PART THREE:
1965

CHAPTER 22:

Help! *in the Bahamas*

The letter arrived on March 17, 1965.

Dear Larry,

Thank you for your letter of March 11. It was good to hear from you and I appreciate your comments.

Of course, the boys and I will be delighted to have you traveling with us once again as news correspondent on the next Beatles tour, and under separate cover, I am sending you an unconfirmed schedule.

In the meantime, we will certainly put your name down amongst a limited number of reporters who will be traveling with us.

Best wishes and many thanks for your help with the unfavourable articles arising from the Nassau visit.

Yours sincerely,
Brian Epstein

Once again, I would be able to join the Beatles on their cross-country tour. I was thrilled. And I was touched that Epstein remembered my help with the aftermath of the Nassau visit. He was referring to the Beatles' trip to Nassau earlier in 1965, when certain "scandalous" events incited the international press to heap torrents of rain on the Beatles' parade. My reporting helped to calm the storm.

The story unfolds in a mysterious little cove on the shores of Nassau, Bahamas. It was Sunday, February 22, 1965, shortly after the Beatles had arrived to begin filming their second movie, *Help!* Since they were filming so close to Miami, I had been encouraged by the Boss Jocks (that's what the deejays were now calling themselves at WFUN Radio) to fly over and get some more interviews. So I called and got permission to do so. Brian Epstein's assistant gave me all the details via telephone, and I showed up at a winding road adjacent to the Balmoral Golf Club on the outskirts of Nassau, also known as New Providence Island.

When the taxi dropped me off, I stood alone on the gravel road. It was eerily silent. I walked toward the beach, tape recorder in one hand, overnight luggage in the other. The sun was setting over the ocean in the west, and darkness was overcoming light as I approached a small cottage propped up on the top of a small hill overlooking the turquoise Bahamian waters. After a persuasive talk with a solitary security guard, I started walking toward the door of the cottage. Two giant hands touched my shoulders from behind. Turning around, I saw tall, wiry and happy-faced Malcolm Evans, who greeted me with a bear hug. "Great to see you, Larry my boy, just great," he said. "Let's go see the boys."

When the door to the cottage opened, the scene I saw surprised me. The living room was unkempt, very much lived in and strewn with soda bottles, napkins and laundry. Malcolm asked me to take a seat, and I surveyed the big room. Jalousie windows that opened to large screens allowed the ocean breeze to cool the room, and an overhead fan whirled round and round. The room was dimly lit and depressing. There were no Beatles to be seen, so Mal and I sat down and he began talking nonstop about the upcoming tour and the five days we would spend in Hollywood.

In a few minutes, a door opened and George Harrison walked into the room. "Good t'see ya, Larry," he said. When George sat down on the sofa, I realized that he was not in a good state of mind. George always looked pale, but this time his face was even whiter, and his eyeballs looked like they were going to pop from his sockets. Either George was sick or in a serious trance provoked by a substance. This was a different George Harrison than the man to whom I had bid farewell at the airport in New York just five months before.

I soon determined that George wasn't sick; he was high. So was Mal. Paul and John walked in a few minutes later, sandals in hand, fresh from the beach and very excited to see a familiar face. My first interviews with the group were off the wall.

KANE: Hey Paul?
McCARTNEY: Yeah?
KANE: How ya doin'?

McCARTNEY: Hello, Larry . . . lovely to see you.
KANE: John?
LENNON: What's that, Larry?
KANE: How are you doing?
LENNON: Well, look, all I can say, Larry, is, this thing's wide open. Anything can happen, man.
KANE: Well.
LENNON: It's the new phrase—have you got it?
KANE: What is this 'everything can happen' business?
McCARTNEY: Listen—everything is wide open, anything can happen, man. It's a new phrase which sums everything up.
LENNON: Now look, Larry, all I can say is, this thing is wide open—anything can happen, man.
McCARTNEY: That's it.
LENNON: Anything.
McCARTNEY: See the way he said it?
KANE: What was the highlight of the '64 tour?
McCARTNEY: Um, meeting Larry Ellis.
KANE: That's Larry Kane.
McCARTNEY: No, I didn't like him. Larry Ellis was the one. Larry Kane. Remember him. Couldn't stand him. Hello, Larry.
KANE: Thanks a lot.
McCARTNEY: Mr. Kane, for you, okay.

The Beatles always played me as straight man, didn't they? It was good to see them again, even if McCartney and Lennon loved putting me on. The conversation I had with Ringo and George later was a little more lucid.

KANE: George, welcome to Nassau.
HARRISON: Hello, Larry. And welcome you to Nassau, too.
KANE: Looking forward to another tour?
HARRISON: First the film, Larry. That's what we're thinking of.
KANE: Ringo, welcome to the Bahamas.
STARR: Thank you, Larry. It's good to see you again, and give my regards to everyone in Miami, and all over America. And I haven't changed 'cause I'm married. I'm still nice.

The Beatles had an early film call, so I dismissed myself and took off with Malcolm for dinner in a restaurant on Bay Street, Nassau's main shopping area. The evening out with Evans and Long John Wade allowed me to observe the depths of Evans' newfound love of marijuana combined with drink, a love that sent us off to several nightclubs and climaxed with Long John and me dragging Malcolm by his arms back to my hotel room.

The real news would come the next morning at the Nassau Beach Hotel. There, the Beatles were filmed fully clothed in the hotel's main swimming pool. Shooting the scene was a security nightmare, a dreadful and frustrating experience for the director, crew and actors. Scores of people, both locals and tourists, kept crowding into the filming area, and several news people, origins unknown, tried to interview the boys during their breaks. Filming movies is a hard business; the security guards and the Beatles had little patience. At one point, Lennon yelled to a photographer, "Get the fuck out of here!" But the press pursuers rarely paid attention to how their prey felt about them. This battle of wills continued on the beaches and streets of Nassau for the several weeks of filming.

What followed that battle was an international media attack on the Beatles, with strong suggestions that the Beatles were rude and nasty to ordinary people and members of the press. Since I was there, and partial, I took great pains in my own reports and dispatches to the wire services to explain what was really happening. And I gave the boys a chance to tell people in their own words. That was the reason for Epstein's gratitude in his letter. The interviews that I recorded received widespread distribution.

KANE: Describe exactly what happened in Nassau.
McCARTNEY: We were doing a film and we were trying to learn the script. A couple of pressmen kept taking pictures and things so we asked them if they would sort of go away while we were learning it because we hadn't really learned it well enough. I think a couple of them got ratty and started writing things about us being rude to everyone. I don't think it was true, you know. But what can we do about it?

Ringo Starr was more direct about the uproar.

KANE: All those reports. . . .
STARR: Well, the thing is, this was in an English newspaper that we sort of insulted everybody. The thing is, in Nassau there were a lot of tourists having a good time. They didn't

seem to realize that we were in the middle of a shot [and] sometimes someone would leap across with a piece of paper saying, 'Sign this.' And we didn't mind signing things as a rule, but if it ruins a shot and we have to start over again, then I think it is a bit much. So I think maybe we were to blame and maybe the people were partly to blame.

And then this English reporter said, 'How about an interview?' Then [one of the guys] said okay. Then he said, 'What can you say?' [Ringo is suggesting that the reporter didn't set them up with specific questions about the incidents.] We just ignored him, and so this article came out. Really it was a lot of rubbish, 'cause if we were insulting, I would tell you.

The filming on set that I viewed showed me no rudeness or callousness toward fans or tourists. And so I reported that. But it was obvious that the Beatles I visited in Nassau were both more confident and a bit more impatient and cocky in their relationships with strangers than they had been in '64.

KANE: A lot of people approaching you at times do not use proper manners. How do they treat you as human beings?
STARR: A lot of people don't. We go in restaurants sometimes and you can have your fork full of food halfways to your mouth and someone will smash you on the hand and say 'Sign this!' Without a please, thank you or anything, and this annoys you, naturally. I don't want anyone to think of me as a piece of furniture. I'm not a piece of furniture; I'm a human being. I have feelings same as anyone else.

Those were telling comments from the drummer. The Beatles, in 1965, were beginning to feel the impact of superstardom and to show the maladies that can accompany it: impatience with public life and frustration at the almost total lack of privacy. But the press attack in Nassau was further proof that the media, still skeptical and doubting, was waiting for the Beatles' bubble to burst. The 1965 tour would prove, however, that the bubble was just getting bigger.

After returning to Miami, I began to plan for the second tour, which was scheduled to start in August with their arrival in New York City. The day of their arrival, August 13, 1965, would mark another milestone in the history of the Beatles, as well as a foreboding moment in the history of the United States.

CHAPTER 23:
The Beatles Have Landed!

The Beatles ended the 1964 tour in New York City, and they returned there to begin their second North American adventure on Friday, August 13, 1965. Almost at the same hour of their touchdown in New York, Los Angeles exploded in a wave of racial violence and terror that would rock the foundations of urban America. The Watts riots were so intense and costly that Americans were forced to search for the roots of the desperation, the hunger for justice, that led to them. Suddenly, those who believed in the possibility of peaceful racial coexistence in America found their ideals shattered.

Another myth—that the Beatles were but a fleeting craze based on the whims of teenagers who were victims of temporary insanity—was also put to rest. By August 1965, a reality had sunk in across the world: The Beatles were truly superstars. No longer were critics forecasting an early demise or suggesting that their music belonged in the waste bin of history. Critics who had insisted that "this too shall pass" were suddenly silent, or converted.

The band's new traveling press secretary, Tony Barrow, set the tone for the second great American tour by creating an upbeat atmosphere from the beginning. For this second time around, Barrow offered a cheerfulness that reflected the Beatles' own confidence for the 1965 adventure. Reminiscing, Barrow tells me:

"They were suddenly playing at being superstars. The boys were all smiles, less the tension of the 1964 tour, which was uncharted territory. Looking back, in their only four years of touring, 1963 to 1966, they were happiest in 1965. Their high spirits were felt throughout the tour. Nineteen-sixty-four was tough, 1966 was forgettable because they were ready to stop touring, but 1965 was the best for them, I would guess."

Barrow was born in the Liverpool area, and he had carved out an unusual career path for a young man in the fifties—pop journalist, album critic and music columnist for the *Liverpool Echo*. That column caught the attention of Brian Epstein, who hired him in 1961 to handle publicity for the fledgling Beatles on a part-time basis. By 1963, he was indispensable and signed on full time as their personal press secretary, though he didn't go on the 1964 tour. In 1965 he began traveling with the band, developing a reputation as a tough but sensitive press boss.

So Tony Barrow and his Beatles, so superstitious about traveling in airplanes, landed at Kennedy Airport on that Friday, the 13th of August. Much to their dismay, the plane touched down on a remote runway. Once again, they were denied the chance to at least wave to fans waiting to greet them. Moments after arrival, the Beatles were whisked off to the Warwick Hotel on New York's Sixth Avenue, where Bob Dylan greeted them on the thirty-third floor, which was fully booked for their touring party. They settled in and greeted old friends, confidently looking forward to another jaunt through North America, this time on a more leisurely schedule. When I was reunited with them in a press reception arranged by Barrow, they seemed excited. They also were happy to razz me over the unusual events that took place outside the Warwick moments before I arrived.

I was anxious as I tried to get into the hotel. Several thousand vocal and excited fans had surrounded the place, and a thin blue line of New York's finest, protected by yellow barricades, was all that stood between the crowds and the lobby. I stepped up to the police line, hoping for the best. Since the tour had not commenced, I didn't yet have my credentials, and I knew I would have to cajole my way in.

I first approached a tall, wide police officer. "Hello," I said. "I've got to get inside to interview the guys. I'm going on tour with them." He replied, "Sorry. No credential, no admission. That's what I gotta do." I knew it was time for direct action. I leaped across the barrier and yelled out, "Where's your superior?" It was typical reporter bravado. Before he could answer, a voice rang out, "I'm his boss." Suddenly I felt arms around me. Spinning me around, a police officer embraced me and laid heavy kisses on both cheeks. The crowd roared with laughter. The kissing cop said, "It's so great to see you, Larry."

The commanding police officer on the scene was Lieutenant Felicia Shpritzer, who was as famous in the NYPD as the Beatles were to their fans. Felicia was a pioneer—the person most responsible for breaking the gender barrier for promotions in that police department. She was also an aunt to me by marriage. Naturally, I got into the hotel. Somehow, word spread quickly of my unusual arrival. When I walked into the Beatles' suite, Lennon had that eyes-popping, ear-to-ear, devilish grin that needed no words to accompany it. But that didn't stop him. He said, "Great to see you again, Larry. Did you really go after a lady cop?" George grinned, Paul laughed and even the usually reserved Brian Epstein managed a radiant smile.

After our greetings I shifted into reporter mode and asked the Beatles to comment on a special moment they recently shared. Since our last visit in the Bahamas that February, royal honors had been bestowed upon the Beatles by Queen Elizabeth. But some Britons objected to music superstars receiving the accolades.

KANE: Concerning your honors from the Queen. When others voiced their protest, did this bother you in some way?
McCARTNEY: We thought there would be some kind of protest because anything, most things anyway that young people do or get given or anything that happens to them that are successful, there is always a load of people who are jealous, just plain jealous, and they say it should never have happened.
KANE: The royal honors you received this year . . . was one of the greatest rewards of your life.
STARR: I think it means a lot more to us, it means a lot more when you are English than it could to an American, really. To be made a member of the British Empire and all things like that is a great thing, 'cause all of these people who have done great things have been nominated and accepted for this great thing. Me personally, I thought it was fantastic.

"Fantastic" was one of Ringo's favorite words.

As the Beatles embarked on their tour of America, Part Two, they had to be wondering if it could get any better for them in New York. In a short time, we would find that it could. New York City was the apex of America for John Lennon, who marveled at the buildings, the energy and the people. In New York, he reflected on his love for the magnitude of America.

KANE: What do you think of America as a country—the cities, the land, the people?
LENNON: I think it's marvelous, you know. I like it, and especially places like New York and Hollywood. I like the big places. And it's amazing to me, a place like Las Vegas. Who ever thought of building a place in the middle of the desert? Things like that are marvelous. I like cities, preferably big ones.

When I saw George Harrison again, the usually quiet Beatle broke out in a big smile and gave me a warm handshake.

KANE: I have with me George Harrison. How ya doin', George?
HARRISON: I'm very well, Larry, and how are you?
KANE: Fine. Are you glad to be back in America?
HARRISON: Yeah, it's great.
KANE: Don't you think a lot of times you'd like to spend more time here?
HARRISON: In the States?
KANE: Yeah.
HARRISON: Uh, yeah, definitely, y'know. I mean, in fact, one of my ambitions before we became well known over here was to bring a car over here and just drive 'round, y'know. It'd take a lot of time.
KANE: Have you been happy with the response to the movie, and are you happy with the movie yourself?
HARRISON: Yeah. Um, the only trouble is, that it's like a hit record, it's so hard to follow. And *Hard Day's Night* was a hard one to follow, and it was obvious that some people were gonna dislike it. But, y'know, we're very pleased with it.
KANE: George, it was great talking to you, and we'll be talking to you throughout the tour.
HARRISON: Okay, Larry.

If New York in 1964 was a home run for the Beatles, in 1965 it was a grand slam. And the game began once again where it had all started for the band in America: Studio Fifty at West Fifty-third Street and Broadway, the home of the *Ed Sullivan Show*.

The side entrance to what is now the Ed Sullivan Theater looked like most Broadway theaters in 1965. A steel-bolted stage door adorned the side of the building, which was lined with old-fashioned fire-escape ladders. This was where the stars entered to begin the rehearsal and taping for the show that owned Sunday night in American television.

The Beatles were excited about their August 14 taping for the *Ed Sullivan Show*. After all, it would be a signature moment in the second year of their relationship with America. Once again, Sullivan was playing a big role in their New York visit. But this time, in addition to giving them the prime-time spotlight, Sullivan's production company was preparing to film the upcoming landmark concert at Shea Stadium. His company, on the recommendation of the Beatles and Brian Epstein, had hired me to tape the audio interviews for a TV special surrounding that event. I was honored and pleased. The interview sessions also gave me backstage access to the *Sullivan Show* performance.

To begin the interviews, I made my first visit to Studio Fifty for a rehearsal at 2 p.m. that lasted almost three hours, with the Beatles insisting again and again on sound checks. The band's fine-tuning of the sound and their insistence on making it better and better was a hallmark of their demand for excellence. But the Sullivan producers were getting edgy as the afternoon wore on.

The main event—taping the program that would air as Sullivan's fall premiere show on September 12—was scheduled for 7 p.m. I left briefly, then returned to the theater ahead of schedule to wait inside a vestibule area for the entourage to show up. The technicians were putting the finishing touches on the lighting and the sets. Soupy Sales, the famous slapstick comedian, was pacing back and forth, rehearsing. The comedy team of Allen and Rossi was getting ready, along with a magician named Fantasio. Ed Sullivan loved magicians.

Flanked by Tony Barrow and Brian Epstein, the Beatles arrived on the east side of Fifty-third Street, which was blocked off by New York police on both ends. CBS pages, the people who served as ushers for the performance, carefully watched the side doors and other entrances. Ed Sullivan came over to greet the party. That was about the time when I noticed a rare happening. John was fidgeting with his hair, he looked grim and nervous, beads of sweat were forming on his forehead, and his pace quickened toward the small dressing room in the back. Was something wrong? I'd been watching the Beatles arrive for shows for a while now. I had never seen the confident John Lennon look so unsure, so obviously perturbed. I asked Malcolm Evans what was wrong. "Don't really know," he said.

Minutes later, I peered through the curtain to see the audience of a little more than seven hundred people eagerly awaiting the start of the program. It was an interesting crowd—lots of young Beatles fans accompanied by mothers and fathers who looked just as eager. They didn't know it yet, but they were in for a real concert—six songs in nineteen minutes: "Ticket to Ride," "Act Naturally," "Help!," "Yesterday," "I'm Down" and "I Feel Fine."

I was still wondering which song title—"I'm Down" or "I Feel Fine"—John Lennon was feeling like when the announcer gave the time signal: "Five minutes till air!" Although the program was being taped, the format was called "live on tape," because they would be recording with no interruption, as though the program were live. Makeup artists were walking in and out of the various green rooms, including the dressing room where the Beatles were getting ready. I was still concerned about John. Was he down or feeling fine? Maybe it was just my imagination, but I had spent some valuable interview time with the group since their arrival, and he just didn't look right. I thought about 1964 and what Derek Taylor, the press chief on that tour, had said then about nerves.

KANE: Do the boys ever get uptight, tense?
TAYLOR: Well, they are always nervous before a show, but that's part of their routine. Especially when they start getting dressed, the laughing ends and the seriousness begins. But when they go on, the nerves disappear quickly, you know. Quickly.

I hoped that would be the case this time.

Soon, the wait was over. The door to their dressing room opened, and lanky Malcolm Evans emerged with a worried look on his face. Evans almost never looked worried, even during those miraculous great escapes and close calls. I said, "What's going on?" He answered, "He's sweating, shaking, looks like too many pills and shit." I said, "Pills?" He said, "Yeah, uppers, downers, pain stuff, I think, y'know."

Up until that point, I had never heard of any pills—over-the-counter, prescription or illegal—associated with the Beatles. So I was genuinely shocked. There had been some marijuana cigarettes around, but as far as I was concerned, the pills were something new. But they weren't really, apparently. Later, John Lennon would talk about having taken pills of some sort since he was a young teenager.

"How bad is he?" I asked Mal.

"Don't say anything. The other boys are cool, they think he's just nervous," Mal said. "The boys are always nervous. They get nervous just before, you know."

On that evening, nerves also seemed to be a problem for Paul, who was usually calm and cool. Later, Tony Barrow would shed light on the McCartney mood. At the sound check, and before the show, Barrow said, Paul was fidgety about singing "Yesterday." The pressure was on him. It was his song, a hard song to perform, and he was a nervous wreck about it.

Meanwhile, the evening was getting underway. The floor lights were shut off. Sullivan, with that hunched-over posture and unique walk, sauntered over to the area behind the big curtain. The orchestra fired up, Sullivan walked through the opening in the curtain and the show was on the air (or at least "live on tape").

The boys quickly emerged from their dressing room, McCartney holding his guitar high, checking out the strings, pacing back and forth. Trying not to appear nosey, I walked over to the area, nodded at George Harrison and Tony Barrow and leaned against a wall. John brushed by me. Much to my surprise, he looked great, with color in his face, a twinkle in his eyes and the boyish grin that made him so appealing.

In a few minutes, Ed Sullivan proudly announced, "And now, ladies and gentlemen, the Beatles!" Within seconds, the performance was underway. I wanted to see it as the audience did, so with the help of a CBS page, I wound my way to the standing-room area behind the orchestra section and watched. The concert was even better than the rehearsal, with Lennon standing out on "Help!" and McCartney at the top of his game with his wonderful version of "Yesterday." In fact, Paul's performance on his signature song was flawless and stunning to watch. Also, this was the first time I had seen and heard "Help!" performed. "Help!" is a difficult song, with its complex harmonies and arrangements. The Beatles' live performance of "Help!" on August 14, 1965, was a masterpiece, the high point of the show.

Viewers would have to wait a month to see it, but I had witnessed it firsthand, and when I walked back to the hotel on that hot summer night, I was getting chills thinking about it. I couldn't get the song out of my head, or the look of Lennon, all bright-eyed and energetic, emerging from whatever his troubles had been that night to give the performance of his life.

This "newsie" was continuing his music education, learning how to enjoy it more and even getting a little rhythm. The Beatles magic was picking up where it had left off after the last tour, continuing to work its powers on me. That, as my friends will tell you, was a cultural miracle. The Beatles are back, I thought, as I strolled through New York on the way back to our hotel. And once again, I was in the middle of it. Every day with them would bring something new and adventurous.

The genius who was Brian Epstein had determined in 1964 that the Beatles would not play in large outdoor stadiums. Epstein was concerned that there might be empty seats, an image not conducive to polishing the reputation of rapidly emerging superstars. There had been one exception that year, the hastily arranged concert at Kansas City, where the house wasn't filled. But that was 1964. Realizing the potential to make profits and history, Epstein took a big gamble in 1965 by booking the Beatles into a huge new facility in New York City, Shea Stadium, for their first live event. The concert was promoted by legendary music entrepreneur Sid Bernstein. Years later I asked Bernstein, "Were you afraid of filling it up?" He replied, "I'm never afraid of anything, but I knew there would be a capacity crowd. They were great. They were hot. They were exciting."

The concert date was August 15, 1965. The preparations had been exhaustive, supervised by the band's new traveling press secretary, Tony Barrow. Barrow arranged the careful travel route, a dramatic entrance and the necessary press access to the stadium. He was a man with a plan. The Beatles and Barrow were taken by car to an East-Side heliport. As the big helicopter moved over Manhattan and the East River, Barrow was watching the Beatles stare at the lights of the city and the glow from the lights of Shea Stadium. He recalled that moment years later:

"Paul was looking out the window with wonder at the lights of New York. But for George and John, it was a white-knuckle flight. George couldn't understand why the flight was necessary. They were both frightened to death of flying. To add to it, the pilot circled around Manhattan several times for a little sightseeing. George was a very nervous flyer, and to him, he could see absolutely no good reason why this bloody great helicopter should be suspended up in the air like that. But the fear turned to absolute wonderment when we arrived over Shea Stadium. The popping of flashbulbs simultaneously created a truly amazing effect. It was like an oval Christmas tree. And this was just for the helicopter. The boys were stunned by the thousands of flashes and the size of the crowd. So was I."

If the sensation of all those flashbulbs was stunning for the flying Beatles, the feeling on the ground was electric. Jim Staggs, a veteran of the helicopter trip a year before at Forest Hills, watched the crowd erupt from inside the stadium. "It was phenomenal," he says. "We were waiting for the guys to land. I looked around and realized they would be here any minute. In my career, I had never seen a crowd this large for music. I wondered how they felt up there, hovering around this huge gathering. It must have been exciting and fascinating. For this era, it was a first, and I wondered, could it ever get bigger than this?"

I surveyed the situation from the on-deck circle outside the Mets' dugout. Try to imagine why it all seemed so huge and grand. Although crowds in our current era often exceed the crowd at Shea that night, this was the largest crowd ever assembled in show-business history, and few of those present were sitting in their seats. The security was visibly concerned. While nervous ushers paced up and down the aisles and exit ramps, a sea of blue uniforms surrounded the field, down the right-field foul line and around the home plate area to the left-field line. The New York police, despite being sophisticated in the fine art of crowd control, looked nervous.

My senses overwhelmed me. The visual effect alone of this enormous crowd was powerful. I was standing on a patch of grass, my head turning in different directions, my eyes catching the inescapable sight of young boys and girls lunging forward in their places like an army ready to attack. The truth is that no one could have stopped that sea of humanity. And the sound that crowd generated, its sheer volume and intensity, was enough to make you dizzy, or numb.

But somehow, above the roar, just above me on the dugout's roof, I could hear footsteps. Ed Sullivan heard them, too; he looked over from his position just off the field, and his head cocked toward the ceiling of the dugout. An eager New York cop was brushing back a group of fans trying to climb onto the dugout roof.

Within seconds, all eyes looked to the sky and listened to the sound of whirling rotor blades. The big helicopter circled once, then once again, over Shea Stadium. It hovered over center field, the pilot rounding the big stadium from a safe distance, tantalizing the fans. With each fly-over, the screaming intensified to a point where I had to wonder how long a voice could scream that high without causing complete vocal failure. In the helicopter, Tony Barrow recalled, "The boys just kept staring in disbelief at every fly by. Even George, flight sensitive as he was, was smiling broadly."

At my level, the shouting continued. Then came a pause as the chopper flew away from the stadium and toward its landing pad at the New York World's Fair, just a mile away. There, a Wells Fargo truck picked up the boys and drove to the rear of Shea, where they entered the gates from the centerfield area. The truck moved around the stadium and let the Beatles out near second base, where the stage was set up. The sellout crowd jumped to its feet, bursting the night air with a primal scream of desire and adoration.

Ed Sullivan looked around and said to the group around him, including me, "I've never seen anything like it." Years later, Ringo would remember the moment.

KANE: Wasn't that something?
STARR: Those were fun days. Just a blast. No one had ever been there. Amazing, you know.

Amazing, you know, but that was just the beginning. The shouts and screaming continued as the Beatles sprang across the infield, waving and waving, looking stunned by the enormity of the crowd and stepping into the dugout, from which they headed to a dressing room. There was a small debate about the suits they would wear, and a half-hour later, dressed in a khaki, military-style ensemble, they emerged from the dressing room, shook hands with Ed Sullivan, glanced over at Epstein and trotted out to the stage to begin a thirty-five-minute concert.

They played twelve songs—"Twist and Shout," "She's a Woman," "I Feel Fine," "Dizzy Miss Lizzie," "Ticket to Ride," "Everybody's Trying to Be My Baby," "Can't Buy Me Love," "Baby's in Black," "Act Naturally," "A Hard Day's Night," "Help!" and "I'm Down."

Twelve songs and one strange interruption. During the middle of the performance, Lennon stopped singing. He stopped—just like that—while the music continued around him. For the first time while performing, he could hear the words of his own song, "Help!" He was stunned by the fact that, over the din around them, the Beatles could actually hear some of the music in an outdoor concert. Accustomed to performing indoors very close to the screaming fans, perhaps he found their distance from the crowd unnerving. There were no field seats at Shea Stadium. They couldn't gauge the crowd's reaction from such a distance, but they knew the moment was special.

> KANE: I noticed you stopped singing briefly at one point.
> LENNON: Well, yeah. Y'know, the acoustics are always so godawful. And it was strange. I could hear my voice. Odd, though.

Tony Barrow watched them from close up. "They were playing so hard they were sweating profusely. Cascades of sweat were pouring down them. Then John rocked the place by playing the electric piano with his elbows. The crowd went wild again. Every time John moved up and down the keyboard, boys and girls screamed louder and louder."

From the steps of the dugout, I looked around the stands. In addition to the high-pitched screaming, fans were mouthing the words and swaying with the music. I realized that some of the fans could actually hear the music clear enough to pick up some of the lyrics. The acoustics at Shea were improved, but still far from the special sound that would come in the next few days.

Later, the New York tabloids would report that fans were disappointed. If that was the case, the kids they referred to must have been hiding in the toilet. The reception to the concert was ecstatic. June Champion, a Beatles fan forever, remembers it well:

"I went both times that they played at Shea. The first time I went with friends but didn't sit with them because I bought my ticket later. I had a field seat. We got there real early and walked around and talked to other Beatles fans. It was quite an experience. It was hard to believe that it was them out there on stage. It seemed unreal. I am not a screamer and actually was annoyed at those that did because I wanted to hear the music. After the concert I got caught up in a crowd that had surrounded a car. I ended up losing my wallet with my train ticket home inside. My father had to come to a Queens police station to pick me up. I even lost my shoes with all the pushing and shoving."

Mary Troumouhis, who still lives in the New York area, also made it a doubleheader:

"I had attended both Beatles concerts at Shea Stadium in 1965 and 1966. I was fifteen years old and my aunt took me and my two cousins. I can still feel the excitement I felt and the mania that surrounded everybody there. The Beatles did it all themselves. They didn't have all the hype and technology that the new bands have. It was just them. Seeing the Beatles is something I still talk about, and feel very honored to have been part of these times in music history. I still have the tissue I used when I cried at the concerts."

The fans loved Shea. So did the Beatles.

KANE: It appeared that Shea was a hit?
STARR: Oh, I remember one New York paper saying that all the kids at Shea Stadium weren't having a good time at all. That's not having a, a healthy laugh, y'know, shoutin' and runnin' 'round. But, y'know . . . what does he know about it? Because he's about ninety.
HARRISON: I dunno, y'know, I mean, depends entirely on the person, y'know. On the individual, y'know. I think most fans want to see us, and say sixty percent'll want to hear us as well as see us. But the ones who just want to see us are, are the ones who are influenced by each other, and who are the type if one person screams or shouts, then the one next to them'll follow suit.
LENNON: I, y'know, I'm just sorry for the people that can't see us live. Y'know, sometimes you haven't missed anything because you wouldn't have heard us, but sometimes I think you might have enjoyed it, and I'm sorry for them, y'know.

On a personal level, the Beatles never got over the spectacle, the grandeur, the chills they felt at Shea Stadium. At the end of the 1965 tour, sitting in a trailer at the Cow Palace in San Francisco, the sensation of Shea was still with them, and they reflected upon it.

KANE: What was the highlight of this tour?
STARR: Well, it was just great at Shea. Oh, it's just amazing.
LENNON: It's been fantastic.
HARRISON: Yeah, it just knocks you out, y'know, it makes you feel good inside.
STARR: Biggest thing ever.
McCARTNEY: Fift-six thousand, five hundred, someone said. That's fantastic.
HARRISON: Last year, at the Hollywood Bowl, it was the biggest show we've done. This tops that.

On top of the crowd, the sound was another amazing aspect of the Shea concert. There would be other valiant attempts by sound engineers to amplify the Beatles' music, especially in Atlanta, but the results achieved by that first effort at Shea, above that capacity crowd, were considered a minor miracle of technology.

The Beatles weren't the only people who were thrilled by the size and sound of the concert. The mood was celebratory back at the Warwick Hotel, where the Supremes, rocker Del Shannon and the Exciters (one of groups that had opened for the band in 1964) waited for the boys. Tony had arranged a reception in the living room of a suite, and the Beatles, all aglow from Shea, arrived there to join in the celebration after freshening up. Lennon was especially jubilant. He kept winking at me from a corner of the room. Sometimes he could be strangely goofy, childlike in temperament. Epstein was also particularly radiant, whispering to me that he should have booked them in stadiums in 1964. Epstein put his arm around my shoulder and reiterated the words of his March letter. "Now Larry," he said, "thanks again for telling the truth about what happened in Nassau. Means a lot, you know."

Brian Epstein was being publicly friendly. This was odd, considering that the man was more buttoned up and starched than anybody I'd ever met before. I wondered for an instant whether there was something behind this friendliness, but put that thought off till later. First came our jaunt to Toronto, the Beatles capital of Canada, and an interesting example of how long Beatles fans will wait to get close to their idols.

CHAPTER 24:
Mugs and Drugs in Maple Leaf Country

The Shea Stadium performance had left a glow on the Beatles, most notably on John Lennon, who while walking down the aisle of the Electra said to me, with high spirits, "How can you top that?"

Another joyous member of the team was Ira Sidell, company manager for the tour, also known as the King of the Road. Sidell was a hardened veteran who handled all business arrangements, travel and, most importantly, box-office receipts. Aside from the glories and fringe benefits of Beatlemania, on a megatour, money talks. Shea had brought in the biggest box-office take yet. I asked him a little about his work.

> KANE: What are your duties on the money side?
> SIDELL: We get a guarantee of the gross, less taxes. I have to be in the box office to check. Even if nobody shows up, we can't get under the guarantee. But if it's a bigger house, we get the percentage figure, so it always goes over.

Sidell was a fixture on the tour, a veteran of 1964 and a man who had traveled with plenty of entertainers, from Frank Sinatra to teen idols such as the Beatles. He was well versed in the egos of superstars, and for that reason he had deep respect for the Beatles.

"Truthfully, they're just wonderful kids," Sidell said. "I mean, success hasn't spoiled them. They've had this now three or four years. I shiver every time we get in a limousine, the kids run through the barricades, but to them it means nothing."

On the flight from New York to Toronto, even the usually moody Brian Epstein was in a state of what I can only describe as elegant exuberance, his face beaming with admiration and pride. After all, it was Epstein who had shunned big sports stadiums in 1964 for fear of looking at empty seats, but with the sell-out at Shea, his 1965 risk had paid off.

Epstein was notably changed in 1965. His temperament now seemed in the volatile range. One moment, his face was beaming; the next moment it bore a look of outright depression. Tony Barrow looked back with me recently at the reasons.

KANE: Where was Epstein coming from?
BARROW: He gradually lost control [over the Beatles], I think, as he got more and more into drugs.
KANE: Can you clarify that?
BARROW: The Beatles used drugs, but they were beginning to see that Brian Epstein was a different kind of drug taker alto- gether. He did it because he was unhappy, and he used to try and bring himself up. He would keep himself awake, put him- self to sleep and wake himself up again.
KANE: So you believe he was basically an unhappy person?
BARROW: He was a very unhappy person. He was gay at a time when being gay was frowned upon and even illegal in Britain, but he never had any kind of steady relationship. He liked some very weird things. He mixed with very rough peo- ple. He liked roughing it up sexually, and that often got him mixed up with bad people, something he couldn't talk about.

There was no question that, at the peak of the Beatles' touring experience, Epstein appeared to be on an emotional roller coaster. And I would unwittingly contribute to one of his low times later on the '65 tour.

Meanwhile, our wild ride from city to city continued with our arrival in Toronto. Because of all of the taped interviews I had done in New York, I decided to give the interviewing a rest for the day, but I did get an earful of Lennon humor as he mugged for the obligatory press conference of local media:

REPORTER: Ringo, how did you propose to your wife?
STARR: Same as anybody you know. Are you married? If

you're not married, find out.
REPORTER: I want to be married, but I want to do it right.
STARR: You want to do it right?
LENNON: Use both hands. [laughter]

The laughter at the news conference briefly drowned out the screaming outside the King Edward Hotel, which today holds the title as the most besieged Beatles hotel in the world, since it hosted the band and tolerated huge crowds outside in 1964, 1965 and 1966.

Fans were trying desperately to get inside. When I ventured into the crowd, a group of four girls from Ottawa presented me with four beautiful ceramic mugs, personalized for each of the Beatles. Of course, I couldn't get those fans inside the hotel, but I did deliver the mugs.

Some fans were so intent on reaching the Beatles' suite that they would wait years to make the visit. Lynn Angelo and her friends from the Buffalo area, for instance, would not be denied, as she recalls:

"It didn't matter that you couldn't hear John and Paul singing, we were there to see the Beatles, to be in the same room as them. That was the dream come true. John, Paul and George did a lot of talking and fooling around amongst themselves while on stage. I remember "I'm Down" and how we all went crazy when John did his bit on the electric piano.

"Since we were never able to get even close to the Beatles' hotel room, the same group of us went back in 1968, knocked on the door to the suite and were allowed in by the family staying there. We took lots of photos of the rooms."

Maple Leaf Gardens in Toronto hosted two shows, one at 4 p.m. and the other at 8:30 p.m. Thirty-six thousand people attended altogether, and both shows were sellouts. But as usual, something was missing: crystal-clear sound. But the pleasure of being able to hear the Beatles well enough to savor their music would soon be realized in the modern capital of the American South.

CHAPTER 25:
A Few Hours of Heaven

Nineteen sixty-five was a heady year for the city of Atlanta. It was achieving big-city status because of the expected move of the Braves baseball team to Atlanta from Milwaukee. The Braves' arrival had been delayed for a year because of a court order, so the Beatles had the distinction of playing the Fulton County Stadium before the Braves ever did. Despite the delay, Atlanta was still wild about the move.

While the city was considered the pride of the new South, however, Georgia was still facing down the demons of its history. A year before the Beatles arrived, restaurant owner Lester Maddox had made news by refusing to serve blacks and then shutting down his restaurant instead of complying with court orders to serve all. By August 18, the date the Beatles arrived in Georgia, Maddox was already hinting at a run for governor. He would in fact become elected in 1967, and served one term.

Clearly, race was still an issue in the South when the Beatles arrived in the dressing room at the magnificent new Fulton County Stadium. The Beatles, who became stronger advocates of activism on this second tour, were aware of America's national challenges and were more daring in their protests. John kept holding up a copy of a magazine bearing the headline, "The White Problem in America." And Paul was prepping for the Atlanta concert when I brought up the subject of race.

> KANE: Do you think it [race relations] is as bad as it has been reported?

McCARTNEY: You see things like the big race riots [in Los Angeles] now and it's a drag, you know. Obviously they are nowhere near integrated. And it's all a lot of bad feelings. I was thinking the same kinda thing about the South. Here in Atlanta, as we came in, somebody said this is an integrated place and it's very progressive. And I was just wondering, because when we were in New Orleans last year, we were driving along the road and the driver was talking to us and we were saying, 'We have heard there is a lot of colored prejudice down here and in the South of America generally.' And he said, 'No, it's okay.' He said, for instance, 'Look over there,' and there was a toilet, and it said 'White' and 'Colored.' It was as if they were saying, 'Look us at us, we are great, we allow white and coloreds into our towns.'

Paul and his friends understood early on that America had a problem of racial prejudice. The subject would continue to come up during the tour. And in response to such issues, a pattern was developing. In Atlanta and throughout the 1965 tour, the Beatles, discouraged by manager Brian Epstein in the early days from speaking on controversial issues, were beginning to take their message beyond music, to put their celebrity to good use by speaking out and stirring up debate.

I was having my own sensitive and continuous debate with John Lennon over my obligations as an American. There was no question that, as a healthy twenty-two year old, I would soon be on the top of the list at my draft board. In the Atlanta dressing room, Lennon and I went head to head on the subject of the Vietnam draft. I remember him saying, "Leave, Larry. Come with us to England. It's all bullshit. Why do it, man?" I replied, "Easy for you to say, John. You don't have to deal with it. It's easy to take shots, isn't it?" His exact reply escapes me all these years later, but I do remember his final words. How could I forget them? He said, "Fuck you."

I was touched by his passion but irritated at his ignorance of my responsibilities. When John became the "give peace a chance" activist in the early seventies, I remembered those moments in 1965 when the man from Liverpool was voicing his angst over our Vietnam involvement. By 1970, he would be a true nonviolent protester, with the world as his platform.

The stirrings of political interest I experienced on the tours are worth noting because of the trail the Beatles were blazing. Before them, it was unheard of for a rock group to get politically involved in any way. After the Beatles, and especially due to Lennon's public activism, scores of popular music icons followed the lead, and they continue to do so. The Beatles' role in this synergy of music and protest has been largely ignored by historians of the era. I saw it at its beginning, but I had no idea at that moment what significant ground had been broken.

Another standout feature of the Atlanta trip was the quality of sound achieved by sound engineers there. A sound barrier was smashed in that stadium, and the innovations there affected the future of music. The stadium itself was impressive. It was sparkling clean, with neat shrubbery surrounding its entrances and wide walkways surrounding the entire complex. And the sound system was supposed to be state-of-the-art, but those who traveled with the Beatles were highly suspect of such claims. On the second tour, I became the unofficial expert on judging sound, having been the only American correspondent who traveled to every stop on the first tour and came back for the entire second go-round. Claims of superior sound quality had been made at many venues, and just as many had fallen short of the expectations they raised. Like many of the fans, I was still waiting for truly great sound.

But in Atlanta, a man named Paul Drew, program director of a local radio station, made the difference. As a co-sponsor of the concert and a recently arrived member of the touring party, he promised pure sound. Drew and the stadium engineers designed a strategic plan to try to ensure that the voices and instruments would be heard above the screaming. But would it work?

I sat in the dugout facing third base. When Cannibal and the Headhunters, one of the opening acts, came onstage, listeners got the first hint that this situation was something special. The sound was loud but clear. I wanted to report the good news to the band. In this town, the Beatles spent a lot of time in their dressing room, since there was no overnight hotel in Atlanta. I arrived at the dressing room an hour before showtime and found John Lennon spitting into a garbage can. Someone had sent a food delivery to the boys to help them pass the time. In it was some plum juice, which John had tasted. It didn't make the cut. Once he had recovered from his taste test, I let him know that the sound seemed perfect. "Heard that before," he said.

I returned to my seat in the dugout. When John and the others took the stage in the stadium's infield, the first song, "Twist and Shout," which contained perhaps the highest pitches of the concert, was a bit distorted. But by the second song, "She's a Woman," attentive listeners knew that we were witnessing a musical miracle in Atlanta. We were hearing stereo before the age of stereo, plus precision and clarity that made the concert a joy to listen to. The music overwhelmed the crowd noise, and that in turn brought joy to the audience of thirty thousand, including Jill Sutton Finan, whose memory of the Atlantic concert has a special family ingredient:

"My parents assuredly were not fans and took a dim view of their daughter's obsession with this long-haired band. They didn't even want me to go to the concert, but my beloved older sister, Barbara, stepped in and bought the ticket for me. It cost $5.50.

"That small sum bought me a seat in an upper level of the stadium and a few hours in heaven. A group of girls in the latest-fashion miniskirts, long straight hair and knee-high boots (in Atlanta, in August, no less) filed into premium seats. Those in the know whispered that they were the Beatle Bobbies, girls who were sworn to protect the guys from onslaughts by less-disciplined fans.

"And then the moment came. John, Paul, George and Ringo, wearing their brown suits and brandishing guitars and drum sticks, bolted from the dugout to the stage set up in the middle of the field. Because of that moment, I can accurately describe pandemonium. From my vantage point they appeared only about an inch tall, and the only song I clearly remember is "Ticket to Ride." But they were the Beatles, and they were in my hometown. They had come to see me as much as I to see them.

"My sister Bobbye is gone now. She passed away seven years, almost to the day, after that August evening. I will always be grateful to her for defying my parents and spending that $5.50. It bought me a cherished lifelong memory. It truly was an investment in pure, everlasting joy."

That night in Atlanta, this everlasting joy was shared by the Beatles and press chief Tony Barrow, who remembered the concert as a pivotal event:

KANE: You liked the sound?
BARROW: Larry, for the first time in three years, I hear a complete Beatles performance because of a very fine loudspeaker system which lets every note and every word come over clearly and ring 'round this super stadium. The Beatles were talking about it to people around them for days, particularly comparing it to less adequate setups in places as we went on.

The sound was astonishing, so much so that Lennon, on the way to the cars, shouted at me, "You were right, baby, you were right, baby! Sounded great!"

The Atlanta concert took place on a beautiful summer night, with a happy crowd and even happier entertainers, who were convinced once and for all that, with the proper planning, they could indeed be heard. And being heard seemed to be a new priority for George Harrison on this 1965 tour. George was always the most polite Beatle, but it seemed to me during this 1965 tour that George had suddenly blossomed into a more public figure. On the way to Houston, I sat down and recorded a relaxed George Harrison.

> KANE: On your first U.S. visit, George, you were known as the quiet Beatle, the somber, thoughtful and pensive one, and suddenly here in 1965 you've kind of, according to most people's way of thinking, opened up. You're talking a lot at the press conferences, a lot of the questions are directed at you. What's the reason for all of that?
> HARRISON: Actually, I did talk about the same amount on the last tour. It's just that, you know, first of all, when we first came over here they didn't know us all that well. People, like, hang tags on you. Ringo was the cuddly one or something. Paul was the lovely one, and I was the quiet one, and John was the shouting one. I've been the same all along. I talk when I feel like it. I shut up when I don't feel like talking.

That last line tells you all you need to know about George Harrison: no pretense, no showboating, a strong sense of self and, for an entertainer in the glare of the spotlight, nary an ounce of superficiality. But he definitely was, on this second go-round of America, less shy and more willing to speak out.

In less than a week with the Beatles on this second tour, I was finding changes. The Beatles were already sowing the seeds of protest, they were enjoying the American visit in a more relaxed and cheerful way, and their mood was upbeat, especially in Atlanta. As the Electra soared west, who could know that the mood of the 1965 tour would change greatly in just a few hours, when some people in Texas would start playing with fire.

Chapter 26:
Mayhem and Music in Texas

T he unthinkable happened on the tour's arrival in Houston, Texas. As usual, the plane slowed down as it taxied toward the gate. I could see the lights of the terminal and hear the shouting outside. Shouting and yelling were a normal part of a Beatles arrival, but these sounds seemed awfully close. Suddenly, I heard George yell out, "What the hell is going on out there?" I looked over at Malcolm Evans, who rarely looked concerned. He wore a troubled expression. As soon as I had a look, too, I understood why.

I was sitting in a window seat on the left side of the plane, over the wing. When I heard the commotion and looked out the window, I saw swarms of fans on the tarmac, edging closer to the plane. The engines were still running. Many of the kids had their arms stretched high in the air, looking like they were hoping for some sort of deliverance. Airport employees were trying to stop them, but with no success. Some of them, with lit cigarettes in their hands, were even climbing onto the wings of the plane! After the engines stopped, a few of them made it onto the wings and were waving at those of us inside. It was a funny sight, but a potentially deadly situation. Tony Barrow later recalled that scary sight and the dangers that could have resulted.

KANE: Do you remember them sitting near the engines?
BARROW: Many of the older youths were climbing over the outside of the plane. Those cigarettes could have sparked off a tragic explosion.
KANE: Remember the lift they used?

BARROW: We were imprisoned on the plane until they could
get a forklift truck out to the plane to bring people off, to
bring Brian and the boys off. They were amused but scared.
The police had no control. The airport people didn't even have
the steps ready for us to climb down. Eventually, the rest of us
waited till the crowd dispersed, and then we reached the hotel
about three in the morning.

When I awakened the next morning, I had the story of another
great escape to tell. This one was bizarre and included an unusual
and new potential for danger. But my report focused on yet another
near-disaster, making me consider how I was approaching the
Beatles' tours as a reporter. These tours offered so much more than
the easy stories of imminent danger and close calls, and I realized I
had to take special care to report on other dimensions and not to let
these episodes blur the real essence. There were so many notable distractions that made it easy to forget that, to millions of people, the
Beatles were all about music. So, starting in Houston and continuing
through the remainder of 1965, I tried to find out more about how
they made their music.

At first I met with a reluctance to talk about the music-making.

KANE: Are you writing any songs on this tour?
LENNON: Well, actually, two.
KANE: What are they?
LENNON: They're good songs, but I can't tell you the names,
because in the music business, well, you can't give away what
you're doing.

Yet we got clues all the time during our long hours on the plane.
Lennon and McCartney, with the others present, would often take
their guitars out in the rear of the airplane and strum them. They were
listening closely to their own sounds and obviously preparing to compose. Occasionally, George would join them. I asked George how this
process worked.

KANE: We know that John and Paul write the songs. Do you
and Ringo ever contribute any ideas?
HARRISON: On every record . . . it's all our own arrangements, but Paul and John write a song, bring it into the studio

and usually, nine times out of ten, Ringo and I haven't heard the song before, and we get into the studio and try all different arrangements. We all stick little bits here and there, you know.

In those early years, George Harrison was not viewed, in the press and music industry, as a major force in music. But as the years progressed, there became increasing understanding and admiration of his enormous talent as a guitarist and as a songwriter. Even before he wrote "Something," on the 1965 tour, he humbly shared his thoughts about growing into those roles.

KANE: Do you have any individual plans for songwriting in the future?

HARRISON: Well, I am still trying to turn out a couple. My main problem is trying to write lyrics, and I don't think it is worth writing songs and getting someone else to write lyrics because you don't feel as if you have done it, really. So I have written a few more songs I've got taped at home, but if I get something going, then I'll tape it. I'll leave it for about five weeks, then I'll suddenly remember. Then I'll add a bit more to it, and so it will probably take me about three months before I finish one song. I'm so lazy it's ridiculous, but I'd like to write more.

How many public figures would admit to laziness? Once again, George Harrison exhibited that he was clearly and simply the most honest Beatle.

George displayed a wonderful humility on the tours, but he and the others were not reluctant to express their pride about events surrounding them. For instance, the Beatles were thrilled that, even by 1965, other musicians were playing their tunes. Big groups like the Boston Pops were playing Beatles songs, showing that these four young men had arrived in a new way and were leaving a permanent imprint on the American music scene. I talked about this with John.

KANE: There are a lot of people who have albums out with your music on it, like the Chipmunks and the Boston Pops. Do you find this a credit to you, or an abortion to your songs?

LENNON: No. We enjoy it. We always try and get a copy of these people that do our songs. The thing about the

Chipmunks and the Boston Pops, they do it so differently
from us and from each other—it's very interesting. And also
we, Paul and I, get a lot of money when they make these.
KANE: There is a cut in it for you when they do record.
LENNON: Yeah, 'cause we compose them, so we get a good
lot of money.

Other bands recording their songs was one thing, but copying
their style was another. John Lennon had little appreciation for the
numerous musicians who tried to do that.

KANE: Does it ever bother you that certain groups will copy
you completely, and whatever you do?
LENNON: No. Because everyone knows, only the dumbest
people don't know, that they are copying us. You just sort of
laugh when you just see imitation of you going around. They
are never really making it. They may have a hit, but nobody is
fooled for long.

McCartney, ever the diplomat, had a different take.

KANE: Do you have any feelings about other musical groups?
I know there are about four or five from England . . . that are
doing well . . . that completely copy your style and the personality to the T.
McCARTNEY: Yeah, well, sure. I can't think of anybody who
has completely copied us. Most of them who want to make it
are always trying to be a bit different, which is good.

Thus I began to report on a wider range of topics thanks to our
dramatic entry into Texas in 1965. In Texas, a place that is always
unruly and rarely predictable, as we had learned in Dallas the year
before, the boys played two shows at the Sam Houston Coliseum.
Capacity crowds of twelve thousand watched each show in a hot and
sticky auditorium. There was no dressing room at the coliseum, so
between shows the boys returned to the Sheraton Hotel for a little
relaxation.

I hung out on the floor where we were all staying and saw Mal
Evans roaming the halls. "What's up?" I asked the lanky road manager.
He said, "Just trying to keep some nasty reporters off the floor. They're

trying to crash the floor." I replied, "Well, let's not have a repeat of what happened in Paris!" I learned about the Paris episode in an interview I had done earlier with Evans about his work with the Beatles.

KANE: Ever find yourself in a personal confrontation with someone—a fight?
EVANS: We were in Paris a year ago last February, and the first night backstage at the Olympia, the press officer wouldn't let the press photographers in. Well, they burst into the Beatles' dressing room—about ten of them got in there. I had to throw them out physically, and there was a great big punch-out. It was nice.

Although he found his fistfight in Paris "nice," Mal Evans took no such pleasures in America. The top floor of the Houston hotel was secured, and the Beatles returned to the coliseum to play their second show, a successful affair with a minimum of riot.

Back at the Houston airport, fans with lit cigarettes were nowhere to be seen, at least not near the airplane. We headed to Chicago, where a different kind of confrontation was underway. The people who were spinning records on the air were trying to beat each other to the punch. It was an all-out war on the airwaves, with John, Paul, George and Ringo right in the middle of it.

Chapter 27:
Air Wars and the Beatles' Radio Daze

The summer of 1965 was unusually hot in Chicago. The windy city was sweltering when the Beatles arrived from Houston. And behind the scenes, a phenomenon was heating up the radio dial in Chicago.

WLS Radio, a fixture in Chicago since the early part of the century, had dominated popular music since 1960. In 1965, another legendary station, WCFL, whose call letters stood for Chicago Federation of Labor, changed its format and took on WLS in a radio war. At the heart of it was a battle over the Beatles.

The late fifties were the golden age of what was commonly called top-forty radio. Top forty was the popular format featuring a rotation of the top forty hits of the day. It was, in a sense, jukebox radio, a chance to hear the hits interspersed only with the voices of disc jockeys who kept up the pace with light yet spirited commentary, mostly about the time and the temperature. Unlike radio today, which is dominated by a variety of formats ranging from jazz, talk and news to urban music and hard rock, top-forty radio dominated the American radio scene in the late fifties and early sixties. And in Chicago, WLS was king.

When WCFL decided to challenge WLS's top status, it brought in deejay heavyweights from around the country. One of them was our old friend Jim Staggs, who had joined us for a portion of the '64 tour, representing KYW in Cleveland and the Westinghouse stations. (Jim used the name Stagg on the air, without the "s" at the end.) Jim was a premiere personality who had, in the parlance of the business, "deep pipes"—a smooth and deep voice. Because of the quality of his voice, mixed with his delightful personality, Staggs was always cast as the "afternoon drive man," usually broadcasting from 4 p.m. to 7 p.m. That was the most important and lucrative time period for a competitive radio station.

When Jim Staggs arrived in Chicago in May of 1965, he was thirty years old and ready to take on WLS. But WLS was ready for the challenge, as it was already deeply rooted in Chicago. Interestingly, the station's call letters stand for World's Largest Store, a reference to the early owner of the station—the Sears & Roebuck Company. But all popular radio stations were losing their momentum in America by the mid-sixties. Elvis Presley, the catalyst for the rock-and-roll revolution, was still enormously popular, but with a relative lack of new talent and creativity, the music scene was hardly pulsating. Many top-forty stations mixed "adult" music, the likes of Sinatra and Perry Como, with the youthful sound, in order to fill out the hours. The music business was depressed in 1963, and something had to give.

Enter the Beatles. Gary Stevens, one of the nation's most successful deejays in the sixties, told me: "The Beatles, with their arrival in 1964, jump-started the music industry and supercharged top-forty stations. Add to that the rest of the British groups, and radio listening was at an all-time high by 1965. It was fantastic, just spectacular."

Stevens, the evening personality at WMCA in New York, went on to explain the role the Beatles played in radio at that time. "They were the whole ball game. Identifying with them, being part of them, getting close to them, meant that listeners looked at you in a different light. In New York, it was madcap competition. My station was constantly competing with the other rock stations in New York. Interviews were at a premium. Inside information was crucial. Getting their singles on the air first was a big deal. They were so big and all consuming."

Stevens, who eventually become one of radio's leading brokers—buying and selling hundreds of stations for his clients—has a keen business sense. He said of those days: "If you could find a hook to connect to the Beatles, it could affect your ratings. That, of course, meant more advertising dollars."

All of these dynamics were in play in the fight between those two Chicago stations. Against that backdrop of fierce competition, the Beatles arrived for their second trip to Chicago. You may remember that, in 1964, we buzzed in and out of the windy city—no overnight stay. But in 1965, we planned to stay overnight, leaving more opportunity for local press to gain access to the group. More time usually meant more time for controversy and chaos.

Our arrival was marred by confusion. The plane was supposed to land at O'Hare Airport, but instead it arrived at Midway, leaving us with a far longer drive to the motel, which was adjacent to O'Hare! Still, the Sahara O'Hare Motor Inn was presumed to have the perfect location—a suburban setting away from the city center. But the place was teeming with potential invaders who had been alerted to the Beatles' location by WLS, although the people at WLS later blamed the broadcasters at WCFL for releasing the Beatles' whereabouts. Whatever the case, both stations had marked-cars camped outside the hotel—cars that incurred heavy body damage from the influx of fans.

The war between the stations began even before the concert. Ron Riley, a broadcaster on WLS, was playing over and over what he was calling "an exclusive interview" with the Beatles. It was an interview conducted over the phone. Ron Riley even started calling himself Ron "Ringo" Riley to increase the station's association with the group.

Jim Staggs was the heavy hitter for WCFL, and he had an obvious head start on the other station. He still possessed on tape all those interviews he had done on the 1964 tour, plus he was traveling with us on the tour plane as we arrived in Chicago. Staggs already had a relationship with the Beatles, and as a result of all these connections, WCFL was advertising itself as "your Beatles station."

Sometimes radio stations went too far in their attempts to associate themselves with the group. New Yorker Gary Stevens remembers that some of the competitive instincts could backfire. "We had to be careful not to appear to be too cozy when we really weren't. After all, we didn't really know the Beatles," Gary explained. "You did," he told me, "and we took advantage of that." Gary's station, WMCA, was part of the syndication network established for these tours by the Miami station I worked for, and received my reports every day.

These radio wars—and my role on the tour—came to play a role in my home city of Miami as well. My station, WFUN, was in a ratings war with WQAM Radio. My reports helped lock in listeners and ratings, and WQAM had no way to compete with us. Yet the programming people at WFUN still wanted more, asking me to urge the Beatles to record promotional announcements like this one that John did: "Hello, I'm John Lennon, and you're listening to Boss Radio, WFUN in Miami, home of the Boss Jocks."

In general, I never pressured the Beatles to record these announcements. My relationship with them was enough, and I wasn't going to cross the boundary between familiarity and contempt. But John did voluntarily record that one announcement for my station.

The radio wars were happening everywhere. Scott Regan, a popular deejay in Detroit at WKNR Radio, was a good buddy from Miami radio. He came to visit me during the 1965 tour in Chicago, and I introduced him to the Beatles. Regan, whose real name is Robert Bernstein and who is currently an advertising executive, remembers the heat of the competition. "You got me an interview with them," he says. "From that moment on, I was called the 'Beatle Deejay' in Detroit. It was also critical to get Beatles songs first. I was good friends with the Capitol Records rep in Detroit. So he gave me the first copy of the song 'Hello, Goodbye.' I played the song nine times in a row! My listeners never forgot. It made me a hero in Detroit."

Stations in Detroit, Miami, New York and points in between had their own versions of the Battle of the Beatles. But the Chicago competition was the most intense I had witnessed, primarily because WCFL had just begun its assault against WLS. Staggs remembers the battle for the minds and hearts of Beatles fans: "It was a minute-by-minute war of words. We listened to them. They listened to us. We had people staked out at the hotel, but they couldn't get near me at Comiskey."

Comiskey Park was the home of the Chicago White Sox baseball team, and our motorcade arrived there at two in the afternoon on the day of the two concerts. The Beatles headed to the White Sox clubhouse. I wanted a look at the field. John came into the dugout wearing a baseball cap, checking out the stadium and the stage, hoping to get a feel for the environment. Both of us noticed a temporary sign on the electric tote board that read, "Welcome. Have a good time. Make as much noise as you wish, but for safety's sake, stay in your seats."

At both the 3 p.m. and the 8 p.m. concerts, the spirited fans of Chicago ignored the advice. Some audience members got onto the field and dug up pieces of turf for souvenirs, and a few seats were missing at the old stadium after the melee was over. A total of sixty-two thousand people watched the two concerts, many of them from Detroit, St. Louis, Milwaukee and other Midwest sites.

The crowd was buoyant, but the jubilant atmosphere was marred by a disorganized security mechanism. I spoke with Tony Barrow about it years later. He said, "The security seemed . . . I won't say inadequate, but certainly sort of mild and passive. It seemed to consist of some attendants patrolling the stands. They're lightweight guys with flat white caps. Their main job seems to be to ask individual kids to sit down, a request that was almost totally ignored."

Another notable feature at Comiskey was an amazing solo act: a fan streaking naked across the field in a solitary flash of passion. I saw her coming out of the seats along the leftfield line and racing like an Olympian for the rear of the platform, running with sheer abandon. This fan's hundred-yard dash was witnessed by thousands, including fan and spectator Judy Kline, who recalls:

"I was a wide-eyed thirteen-year-old Iowa girl who was one of the friends chosen to see the August 20, 1965, second performance of the Beatles in Chicago at Comiskey Park. I didn't scream much. I wanted to hear the music and was too much in awe. The things I remember . . . the stage was on second base, a girl jumped over all the barricades and ran towards the back of the stage. It took two or so guards to tackle her and carry her off. I don't think the Beatles even saw her gallant efforts because she ran towards the back of the stage. [I remember] John putting his leg on the piano during "I'm Down" [and that] they wore the same tan jackets as they wore at Shea Stadium. It was . . . one happy time for me."

This streaking episode was so typical of fan passion that I felt compelled to seek a reaction from the band, which I did in the clubhouse in between the two shows at Comiskey.

KANE: Do the fans go too far?
LENNON: If they weren't doing things or connected to us, it would be something else. I don't really think it is going too far. People are slightly nutcases. I had one girl that thought she had a message from above to meet Paul. He talked to her for about two hours, trying to tell her that he never heard no message, which she insisted he had the flash, too. She would be having messages about other things if it wasn't about us.

When I spoke with him, John was sitting next to a locker, chain-smoking. Paul was entertaining some fan-club members, and Ringo and George were chatting. And in that casual, dressing-room atmosphere, Jim Staggs' friendship with the Beatles allowed WCFL to leave WLS in the dust, at least for that night. Staggs' one-on-one interview with all the Beatles was broadcast after the concert to hundreds of thousands in Chicago. The Beatles' greetings of "Hi, Jim," "Hello, Jim,"

"Good to see you, Jim," and the like convinced listeners that WCFL was the Beatles station.

Despite that temporary victory, the competition between WCFL and WLS continued for eleven years. Each station scored their victories in the ratings, and both survived. But on August 20, 1965, in Comiskey Park, WCFL was the winner for a night. It must have been a hard day's night for Ron "Ringo" Riley.

CHAPTER 28:
Engine on Fire:
John! Don't Jump!

We hit Minnesota in the summer of 1965: on August 20 and 21, to be exact. Memories linger of larger-than-life mosquitoes—humorously known as the Minnesota state bird. I was itching, and so were thousands of young Minnesotans. But their itch was to see the Beatles, and it wouldn't go away.

Our visit was short, and at its climax it presented the Beatles and their traveling party with one of the most dangerous nights in our tour lives. But, for a change, this risky business was not related to any concert or fan frenzy.

This was the Beatles' first trip to the twin cities of Minneapolis and St. Paul, and their presence drew thousands of fanatics from throughout the upper Midwest to downtown Minneapolis, where the streets were Midwest-style spotless and the police were hardly ready. I will always remember the friendliness of Minneapolis, but I will never forget the sleeplessness and craziness inside our downtown hotel, the Leamington Motor Court.

If there was ever a free-for-all on a Beatles tour, Minneapolis was the place. Our flight from Chicago to the city's airport was routine, but after that, the trip was anything but. The old hotel was overrun by fans and parents, with courteous and friendly police trying to handle the crowds with a wonderful charm. Charm and patience were desirable virtues for this scene, given that the fans managed to make their way into every crevice of the hotel. Here's a play-by-play account of the most menacing stay-over of both tours.

After check-in and registration, I called my radio station, fed some tape and walked up a short flight of stairs to the Beatles' floor. In their suite, the boys were catching a snack, watching TV and entertaining a small group of visitors, including fan-club members, a promoter and several housekeepers, who were ever-so-slowly picking up drink glasses and tidying up the big room. It was the housekeepers and what they were wearing that attracted my attention. Wouldn't you be suspicious of a hotel housekeeper wearing a black-and-white uniform that hung so low the hemline was almost touching the floor? Apparently, I was the only one who noticed, because life was going on quite merrily at Beatles Central in the Leamington.

After grabbing a banana, I stepped out of the room and headed into the stairwell, where I came face to face with about ten teenagers, boys and girls, walking up the steps unescorted and smiling broadly. They ran past me and headed into the Beatles' hallway. I chased after them but couldn't reach the door to the suite before they opened it. The next thing I heard was screaming outside the door, where police were struggling with the kids. Amazingly, the young marauders got away and started scrambling down the stairs on the other side of the hallway. The good news: The first skirmish was over. The bad news: The cat-and-mouse game continued until well after seven the next morning.

After that first tangle, I headed back to the stairwell, exited at my floor and walked back to my room. The shower felt good. The water running down my body relaxed me for the first time that night. It was peace at last. Or so I thought. I was drying off when I heard the turn of the lock. Quickly collecting my shorts and shirt, I ran into the bedroom and straight into an embarrassing situation. I encountered the "housekeeper" in the oversized uniform, but this time, she wasn't wearing the concealing uniform. She was clothed in jeans and was crouching behind the TV set in the corner of my room, her hands holding her shoulders, her face buried in her arms. The position was definitely protective, defensive. She was trembling. "Don't let them take me away," she said. I asked, "To where?" She replied, "To jail."

I gently coaxed the girl to come to the door. She and I took the elevator to the lobby, where she told me her story of daring and risk. The girl and a friend had arrived at the hotel hours before the Beatles had. Somehow, like a couple of fans in Toronto in '64, they managed to steal housekeepers' uniforms. The two simply walked into the Beatles' suite in the middle of the reception and started playing house, if you will. When the teenagers from the stairwell had rushed the door, both of the would-be housekeepers panicked and fled in separate directions. The friend disappeared. The woman staring me down had used her key to enter my room to hide. It was as simple as that.

I deposited her safely on the street. She seemed happy, her memories of the events intact. After all, she did manage to see the Beatles. That situation was resolved fairly simply, but the rest of the morning was a nightmare: screaming in the hallways, cops chasing kids, kids playing hide-and-seek and noise outside the hotel that seemed louder even than the big crowds of Manhattan.

Thankfully, just about the time the sun came up on August 21, I fell asleep. Awakening just after 1 p.m., I readied for the concert at Metropolitan Stadium. But first, I had to do more work, writing down notes on the events of the previous night. As I recounted the events, I found myself astounded at the lengths that fans would go to in order to get close to the Beatles. I also knew they would undergo unusual trials and tribulation just to get a concert ticket. Take the case of Kathryn Osmondsen, who was eleven years old on the night she saw her first Beatles concert, August 21, 1965:

"I drove my friends and family nuts, I am sure. I was allowed to spend allowance and babysitting money on the records of my choice and play them at reasonable hours with friends over, but Mom and Dad drew the line at going to a live concert. I was way too young.

"I begged and reasoned, but no, I was not going. I had received as gifts from time to time silver dollars, and had saved them rather than spent them on my music passion. Well, now was the time to dig those out! The ticket price was $5.50, so I put five silver dollars and a fifty-cent piece in an envelope, mailed it off and, somehow, an honest person sent me my ticket for the Minneapolis concert at Met Stadium. Just a few days after the famous Shea Stadium concert.

"My parents were angry, and my punishment was not being allowed to eat with the family for a week. I had to sit out at the picnic table by myself. Funny, but that gave me a chance to have my little transistor radio by my side and listen to the Twin Cities rev up for my favorite group.

"I remember sitting out there the night of the concert, eating spaghetti, wearing a red cotton dress with little white sailboats on it, awaiting my ride (a girlfriend's mother drove the two of us) and not really knowing what else to expect. The concert was great, and I get to relive it any time I see footage of Shea and hear the song "Help!" My parents got over their anger, and we talk and laugh about it to this day. First and only time I ever really disobeyed them."

Kathryn's description of her red cotton dress with little white sailboats is a reminder of just how young and innocent so many Beatles fans were.

The Minneapolis concert was typically magical. The exit from the stadium, though, was marred by groups of kids climbing on the cars in the motorcade. The Minnesota highway police had a hard time clearing the way. When we finally reached the airport, John and Ringo especially seemed to appreciate the safety of the Electra's airplane cabin. Little did they know that this would be their final flight in that aircraft, and almost the final night of their lives.

On the 1965 tour, reporters would constantly ask the question, "When will the bubble burst?" This was a less-than-subtle reference to the insinuation that the Beatles' string of startling successes could not last forever. Of course, we know now that their success has endured forty years and will endure for countless more. That, in show business, is as close to forever as you can get. Even with breakup and death, the Beatles' bubble really never burst. But it almost did on the night of August 21, 1965.

On that windy and wet evening, the efficient Electra took us from Minneapolis to Portland, Oregon, pulling its wheels up at 10 p.m., an hour after the Metropolitan Stadium concert. As the plane followed the sun west, there was an air of relief on board. Minneapolis, especially at the hotel, had been nonstop mental and physical combat. The Beatles, especially Paul, laughed about the night and sought refuge in food and drink.

After dinner was served, I pushed the recline button and tried to sleep. With all the excitement around me, sleep was hard, but I dozed off. My seat was on the right side of the Electra, and my head was leaning against the window. It was in that position, several hours later, that my eyelids popped open in reaction to what appeared to be a bright light off the wing.

Was I dreaming? I looked and looked again. My adrenaline surged. I swallowed hard. There, in front of my eyes, was a fire, racing out of the right engine on the wing. Smoke was pouring out of the engine and trailing the aircraft. I got up, stepped on and over the person sitting next to me, quickly ran to the front of the plane and slammed my fist into the door of the flight deck. No response. Much to my disappointment and shock, I discovered that the pilot and copilot were in the back of the plane, chatting up John and Paul. The plane, with an engine fire in progress, was on some sort of automatic pilot!

I rushed to the back, where I motioned to the pilot and, in a moment of fear and panic, yelled out, "There's a fire in the right engine."

That would turn out to be a gross mistake in judgment. The Beatles, after all, were real people with no supernatural ability to ignore fear. What I saw in the next few minutes can only be described as fright night on the Beatles tour. John, for all his macho bluster and confidence, glanced outside, and after a few "Oh shits," ran to the rear emergency door, where he began to grasp the handle with both hands. I pulled his hands off and pushed him away. Almost yelling, I said, "Are you crazy? You'll get killed."

There was never a truer statement. At twenty-two thousand feet, there was no place to go. But he charged back at the door, where by now Mal Evans, grinning and bearing it, stood in his way. Ringo just stared at the fire, and Paul was the cool man all the way, trying to ignore the excitement but biting his lip and thus subtly giving away his fear. I was scared to death, and George and I looked at each other with that thousand-mile stare of dread. No words were needed. It was as bad as it gets.

The next day, George let it all out, even managing a bit of humor.

KANE: How did you react inside?
HARRISON: Well, the first reaction was, What smoke? When I looked and saw it, and we all ran to the back where we were far away from the flames—cowards as we are, you know—all sat around the emergency door and even tested the emergency door, ready to jump out. Of course, I said, "Beatles and children first."

Upon a return to the controls, the pilot advised us that we were close enough to Portland that the other engines would be sufficient. Lennon blurted, "What a bunch of rubbish." He sat down in a rear seat, closed his eyes and kept the rest of his apprehension between his ears.

A half-hour later, smoke still pouring from the engine, the plane landed in a sea of foam and an army of firefighters, along with a chorus of "Oh God's" and the expected chorus of "I'll never fly again." The Electra never did fly again, at least not with the Beatles inside. The next night, a plane called the Constellation arrived to fly us through the rest of the tour. Ringo jokingly said, "Let's stay alive in sixty-five."

There were no other safety problems in 1965, but American Flyers Airlines and the Electra would make some other news before long. An Electra operated by the same charter service crashed into the foothills of Ardmore, Oklahoma, on April 22, 1966. Five crew members and seventy-eight soldiers on their way home from basic training perished in the crash. It was the sixteenth crash of an Electra, and today that crash stands as the worst air tragedy in Oklahoma history. That downed plane had been one of the two Electras used to fly the Beatles. If that isn't chilling enough, three of the Beatles' flight-crew members, pilot Bill Mar and flight engineers Charlie Gray and Anthony Pica, were killed in the Oklahoma crash.

The entire next night and day in Portland was overshadowed by our precautionary landing on the foam-covered Portland runway. The two concerts at the Portland Memorial Coliseum, a brassy, glass-enclosed structure, drew twenty thousand people and some surprise visitors backstage—Carl Wilson and Mike Love of the Beach Boys. Ringo, the ultimate Beach Boys fan among the Beatles, was dazzled by Wilson and Love. "A thrill to meet them," he told me later. But for Ringo and the others, the biggest meeting was yet to happen. The King, Elvis, was waiting for them in Hollywood. To get there, we had to brave the dreaded flight from Portland to Los Angeles in a new airplane.

When we boarded the Constellation at the Portland Airport just one night after our frightening emergency landing, Brian Epstein looked like a man who had developed airsickness before takeoff. I whispered, "You all right?" He mumbled, "Out of sorts, you know." Before I sat down, I looked back at the Beatles, who were seated in the rear seats of the new aircraft. They looked tense.

After the interminable wait for permission to take off, the safety instructions and the race down the runway, the Constellation became airborne, the sound of its landing gear folding into the bottom of the plane drowned out by an ovation of hand-clapping and cheering. Even Brenda Holloway, the young vocalist who opened for the Beatles on that tour and usually a shy woman offstage, put her hands over her head and clapped wildly. The astute Tony Barrow screamed out, "Cheers!" We were all relieved. We had cheated death and lived to fly again.

Hollywood was next, and with it, a negotiated meeting with Elvis Presley, a surprise bedroom guest, and my own personal encounter with Brian Epstein inside a bungalow at one of the world's most exclusive hotels.

CHAPTER 29:
Back to Hollywood: Famous Faces in the Bedroom

The sunshine was seductive, and so were the mountains. And for a change of pace, we suddenly had a valuable commodity—time. And this time would create endless opportunities for memorable meetings, extreme fan antics, experimentation with drugs, and a strange encounter between myself and Brian Epstein.

Los Angeles, with its endless sunshine, was chosen again as a rest and recreation site for the Beatles. They avoided the Whisky A Go-Go, justifiably, and the strategy for safety was one of a tight security net surrounded by seclusion. They were staying at a ranch-style house in Benedict Canyon, an exclusive neighborhood featuring narrow drives and homes set on hilltops. It would take an army ranger to scale the cliffs and penetrate Fortress Beatles.

The Beatles had a longer stay in Los Angeles than in most places. Realizing that we in the press party were somewhat cut off from them because we were staying elsewhere, they invited a few of us to take a look at their private retreat. On the phone, Tony Barrow told me, "Larry, bring your tape recorder, and don't forget the bathing suit." This was the invitation I had been waiting for.

When I got to their hideaway, the sun was beating down on the concrete walkway around the pool. As I walked I heard some scuffling noises; something was moving on the other side of the retaining wall that prevented one from falling down the canyon. Press chief Tony Barrow flinched, and his neck turned. Together, we noticed a hand reaching over the top of the wall! A second hand appeared, and I moved very quickly toward the wall, where I discovered a girl dangling in agonizing disarray. She was out of breath but had the determined look of a tiger creeping through the grass.

Fearing a catastrophe, Tony and I helped the frightened fan over the top and to safety. Her face was smudged with fresh garden dirt from her climb up the steep grade of the house's backyard. How she made it all the way up was a mystery, not to mention a spectacular feat. By the time she landed on the beach chair next to Paul, tears were flowing down her face, mixing with the mud and making for a rather embarrassing sight. Face to face with her objects of desire—the four Beatles—the teenage intruder was absolutely paralyzed with fear and rendered speechless.

It was then and there that humanity and compassion prevailed, the kind of special behavior that most of the press never saw displayed by the Beatles. The police had approached the patio, ready to take the visitor away, when a smiling John Lennon intervened. He walked over to the girl and whispered something in her ear. Her smile was instantaneous. Then he gathered the others, snatched a pen from Tony Barrow and grabbed some napkin paper. One by one, they signed autographs for her, posed for pictures and sent her off with some hugs.

That same afternoon I walked into an embarrassing situation, at least for me. For others it would be a source of laughs. With the teenage intruder gone, John Lennon insisted that I go swimming. I had not brought a bathing suit, so he pointed to one of the rooms off the patio and said, "Larry, grab yourself some trunks. If the suit fits, wear it, Kane. Don't be a drag."

I slid the glass door open and saw some clothing laid out on a bed, including a men's swimsuit. Just as I grabbed it, the bathroom door opened and a woman emerged, draped in a loosely tied bathrobe. I was stunned; she was nonchalant. In a very soft voice, she said, "Hi, I'm Joan." I answered, "I'm Larry; excuse me."

Realizing I was looking for a place to change, she motioned me to the bathroom, where I slipped into the swimsuit, taking enough time for her to have a chance to get dressed. As I remembered her words, "Hi, I'm Joan," I realized that I had just come face to face with Joan Baez.

She left shortly after. At the pool, I never asked whose room that had been, or whose bathing suit I had borrowed. But the next night, I stood along the fence with Joan at Balboa Stadium in San Diego. We made eye contact. She said, "Hello again." I asked, "You came down here to see them?"

"Aren't they wonderful," she responded, staring intently at the stage, moving her head to the beat, clearly entranced by the band and the music. I would see Joan Baez again at the Cow Palace for the final 1965 concert. Here she was, an American star, following the Beatles as a fan, a real fan.

There was Bob Dylan, whom we had met in New York. There was Baez. And, of course, there was Elvis. For a man of twenty-one who had grown up with rolled-up cuffs on my Wrangler jeans and a duck-tail haircut, and whose teenage friends tried to be the living embodiment of the King of Rock-and-Roll, I found the prospect of the Beatles meeting Elvis thrilling. The Beatles were children of the music born in the forties, and they were nursed to maturity by the rock-and-roll and rhythm-and-blues of the fifties. As much as their fans idolized them, they had an obsessive idolatry for Elvis Presley. Of all the Hollywood happenings on the two tours, meeting Elvis would be the highlight in their eyes.

So we formed yet another motorcade on the evening of August 27, 1965. Three extra-size limousines traveled from the Beatles' vacation house at 2850 Benedict Canyon Road to the Elvis complex not far away, on Perugia Road in the Bel Air section. All cameras and tape recorders were banned, so we've all had to rely on mental memory to paint the picture. Luckily, for those who got inside, what transpired would be impossible to forget.

The Presley complex was a round structure with lots of glass, and there was plenty of land around it. To observers of the meeting, it appeared early on that Elvis was uncomfortable about the arrangements and the traveling party, which included Beatles regulars and a small group of reporters, all of whom waited outside the complex. The first few minutes were reportedly edgy, with Presley and the Beatles launching into some small talk. The situation was odd because most of us were watching from outside. Elvis's handlers insisted that no broadcast journalists would be allowed in. There would be no tape of this. All we radio guys saw was Elvis greeting the Beatles; that was it.

But several print reporters, including Ivor Davis and several veterans of the Hollywood beat, were given the green light to enter the complex with the boys. The stars didn't exactly have an intimate conversation, Davis remembers. "We stood a few feet away, trying not to make them feel like prize horses at stud being watched over the fence to see if they'll mate. To most of us, Elvis seemed disinterested. Finally, Paul reported later that Elvis said, 'Didn't you guys show up to jam?'"

Tony Barrow said that Epstein and Colonel Tom Parker, the Elvis boss, had spent days negotiating the "terms of engagement." The situation was so sensitive that Epstein had to fight for Tony Barrow to go inside. I asked Tony about the meeting recently:

BARROW: When they got there, it was almost anti-climactic. My take on the whole thing is that it was a bit of a flop. Until the music. Before that, they were talking a great deal of small talk. The Portland plane business came into it, and Elvis said he had a similar scare with a plane having engine trouble, all that kind of stuff. But it was very, very meaningless, until Elvis called for guitars and turned the sound on the television down for the first time. And they all sat around on this crescent-shaped sofa and started to sort of have a jam session, and sparkling conversation that had been missing in speech was now replaced by sparkling conversation in music.
KANE: So the conversation was awkward?
BARROW: Yes. Then, as I say, as soon as they got on their instruments, suddenly, that was a new kind of a conversation. They could converse in music where they couldn't . . .the conversation in music between them was strong. The conversation without any music was dull, was lifeless.
KANE: That's a very interesting observation, that they really communicated better by, with rock-and-roll and their own sounds.
BARROW: I gathered that the whole meeting was done more for Elvis Presley than for them. That was just my impression, because Elvis's career really needed a little bit of rejuvenation then.

It has also been reported that all four Beatles played billiards with Elvis, among other diversions. I did see a small group of women head into the house, apparently witnesses to the event, and possibly participants in it. The Beatles spent three hours with Elvis, talking up music, cars and the tribulations of touring. British journalist Chris Hutchins, who engineered the meeting, reported to us that Brian Epstein and Elvis's legendary manager, Colonel Tom Parker, played some roulette in a game room. Priscilla Presley was there, he said. The boys left the house with collections of Elvis albums and a few of his famous sequined jackets as souvenirs. They looked pleased. The next day we talked.

LENNON: We were all a bit nervous, Larry. It's embarrassing, meeting people for the first time—especially when you *want* to meet them.

STARR: I just loved it. We talked music and records. He liked ours. We liked his. We were all a bit nervous.

McCARTNEY: I sort of liked the guy. We tried to persuade him to make some new records, records more like the old sound. *If* he does, I'll be down at the record store with me shilling in me hand!

George was equally impressed. But it was two road managers who captured the magnitude of the moment.

ALF PICKNELL: Larry, I haven't gotten over the shock. It was like they had known each other for years. It was like walking into the mansion of a duke or something as he greeted us at the door. I work for the Beatles. I'm thirty-five and to me, Elvis was my idol, but to see the two top artists in the world together was great.

MALCOLM EVANS: We talked show business. The guys played guitar with him. I'm a member of his fan club, get the magazine every month. It was wonderful, Larry. I met me idol.

No one will ever know what Elvis thought of the meeting. Mal Evans said he launched lavish praise on the Beatles. What is known of Presley's disposition suggests that that might have been an exaggeration. But one thing was sure: The Beatles, individually and collectively, would cherish the visit to Elvis Presley and view it as a highlight of their visits to America.

With Elvis still fresh in our minds, we took the day trip to San Diego for the Balboa Stadium concert. This short journey provided some traffic fireworks. Beatles and company hired a twelve-seat, luxury bus to take them down the interstate to San Diego. Fans followed the bus out of Benedict Canyon and onto the freeway, where it was a chase scene all the way down. Five of us rented a car and made the trip ourselves, since there was no room on the bus.

The concert was impressive. As mentioned, I was fortunate to spend some time at the concert standing next to Joan Baez. As we watched from the sidelines, both of us broke into laughter when frenzied fans ran onto the turf and gathered up clumps of grass, an odd souvenir of the Beatles' San Diego concert.

The trip back was uneventful for those of us in the rental car, but the journey of the Beatles back to Los Angeles featured an unscheduled yet interesting stop. Tony Barrow later described a scene more suited to the Grateful Dead. The Beatles' chartered bus, facing mechanical difficulties, hobbled into the parking lot of a San Diego mortuary. The Beatles were forced to switch to limousines for the ride back to Los Angeles.

Once back in Los Angeles, the band played two Hollywood Bowl concerts on consecutive nights. The sound was so fantastic that some critics suggested they were lip-synching, mouthing recorded music. John Lennon couldn't believe that suggestion.

> KANE: There are reports that you really aren't singing during this tour because of the noise, that you're just lip-synching, more or less.
> LENNON: No. No, we're singing like mad. On places like the Hollywood Bowl . . . we were heard, y'know. Good acoustics, even though the crowd was wild. There's a couple of places we've been heard quite well. Y'know, better than we've been heard for years.

In fact, when you could hear it, the Beatles' sound was so brilliant, so clear, that it did seem like recorded music. Their ability to replicate their recorded sound was astonishing. George said the reason for this was rather simple.

> KANE: Have you ever had trouble replicating your sound on stage?
> HARRISON: No way, Larry. From the beginning, when we were taping, we always did it in one take. We never did any of that overdubbing and that stuff. We are what we are.

The Beatles' performances were real, indeed. But as on my visit to Nassau, more and more on the 1965 tour I was witnessing them as participants in the unreal world of drugs. At the pool in Benedict Canyon and in our post-Elvis interviews, it seemed that John and George were in a different state of awareness. Press chief Tony Barrow recently confirmed my impressions:

KANE: On the first tour, the strongest thing I ever saw was—
BARROW: —was pot. Right, exactly, but one year later they were quite happily in that Benedict Canyon house there—they were with members of the Byrds and Peter Fonda—and they were definitely on acid. One or two of them certainly were. George was and John was.

Tony Barrow also confirms the rumors and speculation over the years that Lennon and McCartney credited drugs with enhancing their songwriting talents. I asked for further clarification.

KANE: In what way?
BARROW: Now, rightly or wrongly, they say that it made them better lyricists, better musicians and better performers of music. And I remember Paul saying something like the brain was normally one-tenth in use and the other nine-tenths really ought to be put to use, and the way to do it was to take the right drugs at the right time and start using up the other nine tenths.

Despite their drug use, Barrow feels the Beatles knew the danger of drugs. He said they saw that in their own manager, Brian Epstein. "They could see Brian's drug use, to control his moods, as unsettling. They didn't mind feeling good, but in Brian, they saw fear and fright. So, they knew that some limits had to be set. They didn't want to become addicted, like him."

The Hollywood stay in 1965, with its free time and loose lifestyle, was conducive to the use of drugs. I believe this atmosphere also led to my own sad and infamous encounter with Brian Epstein.

Brian Epstein had taken the Beatles under his wing a few years earlier, transformed their appearance, instilled a sense of professionalism, and put them on course to achieve historic success. Just a couple of years older than the oldest Beatle, Epstein was quite a bit more serious and businesslike. First impressions could make you feel unwanted and ignored by this handsome young man whose fateful trip to a Liverpool nightclub had culminated in a business and personal relationship that would set a standard for decades to come. But he did not ignore the band in favor of the business. Watching Brian Epstein watch the Beatles in complete absorption was one of the most educational sideshows of both great tours. He truly loved their music.

Still, Epstein was the opposite of his charges. While John said in public what many people only thought in private, Brian was guarded in his comments and reserved in his expression. And while Ringo was as casual as a human being can be, the boss was the epitome of formality, a stoic figure of stereotypical British refined behavior. George read comic books; Brian read the *Financial Times*. Paul glanced at female beauty; Brian appeared uncomfortable in the presence of glamour.

Differences aside, however, Brian Epstein was the boss, and the Beatles, in their early touring, marched to his beat. From the moment I met him in San Francisco in 1964 to the final night of the 1965 journey at the Cabana Hotel in Palo Alto, I found it beyond obvious that Brian Epstein loved each of them. Despite reports over the years insinuating a romantic love, the quality of Epstein's presence suggested a relationship based on true pride and admiration for their work.

At a number of concerts, I stood with him backstage or in one of the musky corridors of some arena, watching his eyes, sometimes filled with tears, staring at the act, snapping his fingers in a subdued sort of way. He was a fan, but most of all, he was like a protective older brother, watching out for his brethren and obsessed about their personal security. He had reason to be.

During the inaugural concert at the Cow Palace, for instance, a barrage of jellybeans was hurled at John. The security staff was overwhelmed at the base of the stage, with hundreds of possessed teenagers closing in on their prey. Suddenly, Epstein ran forward in the crush of the crowd and, in a futile but brave effort, tried to stop the projectiles. Later, his tie disheveled and coat mussed up by the melee, Epstein looked over at me and some others and grimaced. He said, "If this is what the States are going to be like, we are totally and awfully unprepared. The promoters must act appropriately." The next day, press chief Derek Taylor advised me that Epstein had later called every promoter in every city to make sure they beefed up security, especially around the stage area of the concerts.

In Chicago's Comiskey Park earlier in the '65 tour, Epstein revealed to me his view of the Beatles' success and his unabashed feelings as a fan:

KANE: Why are the Beatles successful?
EPSTEIN: Well, there are four of them, you know. Four people to admire. Not just one but four idols, with four different levels of appeal. Each boy or girl can identify with a different Beatle.

KANE: Are you a fan?

EPSTEIN: I'm very much a Beatles fan. I've probably felt everything that any, um, male Beatles fan ever felt. All the various things I've liked, I think, is what the fans have liked, both in their music and their general manner. To me, in terms of popular music, the Beatles express a cross quality of happiness and tragedy. And this is basically what the greatest form of entertainment is made up of. They in fact do original things. Their songs are always new and different. So are their performances.

The polite expressions, formal style and air of kindness that come across in Brian's comments were sincere, yet Brian was also a shrewd and commanding businessman. In 1964, his authority was never questioned by the Beatles; but in 1965 he was beginning to show visible signs of insecurity. He was on edge, and his mood changes on the plane and at the concerts were dramatic. His authority over the Beatles' empire was never questioned, but it appeared to me that his one-on-one relationships with the Beatles weren't as warm as they once had been.

On a professional level, he was an expert image-maker. Image was very important to him. For instance, the boys were never allowed off the plane until all the press was in place, especially the photographers. These were the days before jetways that lead directly from the airplane into the airport, and the descent down the stairs onto the tarmac was always a favorite moment for the fans and the press.

In addition to the disparities between the businessman boss and his youthful, informal charges, there was another difference: Brian Epstein was a homosexual. His sexual preference was the talk of people on tour, even though he didn't telegraph his personal inclinations and they had no consequences on his work. Still, like anyone else, his sexual desires sometimes got the best of him and demanded expression. It was in one of these moments that I had an unexpected confrontation with his sexuality.

By the '65 tour, Epstein was feeling more comfortable around me—no small feat considering that he was a man who seemed uncomfortable in his own skin. And when Epstein invited me to join him for drinks in his cottage at the Beverly Hills Hotel, John Lennon thought it apparent that Epstein had more than just respect for me. "Watch out, Larry," Lennon said. "He wants more than your big nose."

Neither Lennon's droll warning or my second-hand knowledge of Epstein's sexuality kept me from saying yes to his invitation. I treated the invitation innocently enough—as an opportunity to get know Epstein better and maybe even to do some tape. I had no apprehension, just a curiosity and a hope to learn more about his relationship with the boys. As I made my way to Epstein's cottage, which he had chosen over the Benedict Canyon house so he could have some more privacy and do business in his down time, I didn't know that I would learn a lot more than I had expected to.

I never turned on the tape recorder, but I do remember my talk with Brian Epstein vividly and without question. He invited me into the living-room area of his cottage with a drink in hand, a warm smile on his face and an invitation to listen to classical music. We chatted for a few minutes about family and growing up. It was a natural, genuine conversation. I felt badly about having brought the tape recorder, so I set it aside in a coat closet, a sign that I wouldn't be using it. Epstein was candid about his feelings for the Beatles, especially for Lennon, who he described as a "genius with genius problems." He was especially concerned that John's growing political activism might divert attention from the main event—the men and their music. He felt like a father to John, whom he described as overly petulant and difficult to manage.

As the conversation progressed, I realized that I was serving as a depository for some pent-up, constrained feelings. I listened intently as he expressed concern that he was losing his grip on John and maybe the whole group and described his fear that, without his presence, the Beatles' unity would divide into four separate camps. His words would be prophetic, but he didn't imagine that his own death would be a catalyst in realizing those predictions.

I was surprised as Epstein described a growing paranoia. He looked pained when he described an awareness of the boys talking behind his back. He assumed that they were laughing at him. I told him I had never heard or seen anything like that. I could imagine that happening, but I was hardly an expert on their private behavior and of course didn't make any guesses with him.

I decided to shift the course of conversation, hoping to get him to lighten up. "Tell me about Liverpool," I asked. He described a decent childhood, work in the family store, and the exhilaration of seeing the Beatles perform for the first time. And then, much to my astonishment, he addressed a subject close to my heart—anti-Semitism. This scourge was commonplace in industrial Liverpool in the forties and fifties, he said, creating a cloud of resentment that he unmistakably felt, even around entertainers. "Are the Beatles anti-Semitic?" I inquired. "I don't think so," he said. "But it was always around them, so it may be in them." I never told him about the incident on the plane in 1964.

The conversation, and our visit, ended when he stood up to change the album on the turntable. It was then that he made his move. Epstein talked about my behavior and courtesy on the tours and told me he admired me. Innocent child of the fifties, I had no idea what he was talking about until he suggested that we become close friends. Even then, I thought he meant good buddies.

He raised his glass and said, "Here's to you and me." I raised my glass of Coca Cola and drank a sip. As the soda went down, I gulped extra hard. Suddenly I understood, and I hoped he couldn't tell that I was instantly petrified. The truth was that I really liked Brian, but not in a "you and me" way. I began to yawn and feigned exhaustion, insisting that I had to get back to my room to file my reports for the morning. I thanked him for inviting me and sharing his thoughts. Shaking his hand goodbye, I saw the strained look of disappointment and embarrassment on his face. The whole meeting had been awkward, and I felt sad about it afterward.

But Brian Epstein's actions toward me were always forthright and courteous after that, just as they had been before. I will never forget that he respected me enough to share his private thoughts. And I knew from hearing some of those thoughts that there was a big hole in his life. When word reached me of his death in 1967, I was upset and angry that the man who had delivered the talent of the Beatles to the world would never have the chance to see what an influence his "boys" would have on the twentieth century and beyond.

CHAPTER 30:
"We Are the Beatles, That's What We Are"

W as it the beginning of the end, or just the end of the beginning? That's the question I was asking myself in the place where this had all begun—that old exposition hall in San Francisco, the Cow Palace, scene of the living nightmare that was my first Beatles concert in 1964.

This time around, wisely, I stayed backstage and around the stage, avoiding the possibility of getting trampled in the seats and ending the second tour on a sour note. The Beatles were housed in a trailer again in the rear of the arena, where I quizzed them before the concert about the second tour and the future.

> KANE: So you liked this one?
> STARR: Yeah, especially Shea. These were fun days. No one had been there before.
> KANE: Will you ever be anything but the Beatles?
> McCARTNEY: We are the Beatles, that's what we are.

Those words would be repeated again in 1968 during an interview I would conduct with McCartney and Lennon in New York. "We are the Beatles, that's what we are." They would say these words in earnest, but in retrospect, they were pure fantasy.

By that final concert in 1965, the four young men from Liverpool were beginning to fortify a union with millions of people, one that has made their music one of the world's greatest shared experiences. As Paul prophesied, the four would always be remembered as the Beatles. But their individual lives would travel separate and signifi-

cant pathways. In the backstage trailer before the last Cow Palace concert, an air of relief reigned. The Beatles were tired but pleased. Tony
Barrow recalls how the band seemed on the plane afterward:

> BARROW: They were enjoying themselves. This was the huge
> difference between 1965 and one year later, when it was all
> over. The return journey in 1966 was a low-key affair.
> Nineteen sixty-five was their peak in terms of sheer enjoy-
> ment. They were kind of playing at being superstars at that
> moment. It was all smiles. There was a lot of drinking going
> on from plastic and cardboard cups on the plane. They were
> walking up and down the aisles and seat hopping. No ques-
> tion, the Beatles had their happiest year in 1965.
> KANE: So 1965 was fun, 1966 was work. Is that what you're
> saying?
> BARROW: Remember, the Beatles had an extremely short life
> as a touring band, 1963 through 1966. And I guess that if they
> stayed on the road giving concerts after that, that *Sergeant
> Pepper* might never have been made, because while they were
> touring they were allocating no more than a couple of months
> a year to recording. And that I would have thought would be
> altogether far too short a time to produce something of
> *Sergeant Pepper's* massive dimensions. They needed to come
> off the road.

In that backstage trailer, all four Beatles had given me the impression
that Cow Palace would be their final American concert. But a year later,
Epstein talked them into coming back, a decision they later regretted.

For me, that time in the trailer was poignant. I liked these guys, a lot.
The thought of parting was disappointing. Sometimes familiarity
between a reporter and the subjects of his reporting can breed contempt.
But it seemed that a second year of living the frenzy, chaos and trauma
of touring America had brought all of us together in a closer bond of
respect. I viewed them not just as "the Beatles," but as four very real
human beings. I could honestly say that they viewed me not just as a
trusted reporter, but also as a person they could relate to in their own
comfort zone. Were we friends? Perhaps in a professional sense. But the
Beatles and I managed to do our professional thing without compromis-
ing our respect for each other. That, to me, was a real accomplishment.

There was still time for goodbyes. First there was a concert ahead, and once again it was time to batten down the hatches. I had told Tony Barrow how bad that venue had been in 1964. He had remarked, "Can it get any worse?" It did.

Failing to learn the lessons of a year earlier, police did not deploy an adequate number of officers. The result: another trampling rush at the stage. I spoke with Barrow about it decades later.

KANE: Where you shocked?
BARROW: What I remember about that mostly is the dreadful crush of fans in front of the stage. It was this very high stage at the Cow Palace, very high, and kids towards the front were getting squashed against the front of the stage. Joan Baez was doing a kind of Florence Nightingale, and sort of holding kids up to safety and bringing them around the back there, laying them out on the floor.

Baez, after following the Beatles to still another location, behaved in an extraordinary way, braving the onrush to pick the injured children out of the crowd one at a time. Her strength was amazing. Thirty-five people were treated that evening for injuries. Without Joan Baez's heroics, the toll may have been higher and the results more disturbing.

The good news: The concert ended peacefully. The bad news: There was a second concert scheduled, with the potential for a mayhem double feature. In between the two performances, I had time for a chat with a relaxed John Lennon and Ringo Starr. The first subject was one that was becoming a favorite of John's—Vietnam.

KANE: John, President Johnson has asked for additional troops in Vietnam. Do you think there will be any way out of this?
LENNON: It's all rubbish, Larry. Killing goes on, you know, and who is the real enemy?
STARR: I just think it's unfair that you get a leader of each country and they force so many people to fight. It's all the young men in the world who get shot, bombed and blown to bits. It's unfair.
LENNON: Unfair, Larry. Unfair.
KANE: John, let's talk about your son, Julian. Financial needs are no problem. But the other thing, things that money can't buy?

LENNON: Well, I just want him to grow up happy. That's the
main thing.
KANE: What can you give him?
LENNON: Just love, that's the main thing, you know. He's
just going to be happy and know he's wanted. I'm not having
any of that boarding school or sending him away. He's going
to be with us all the time.

Lennon was twenty-four hours away from a return to his toddler
son and wife, Cynthia. Just one concert left.

Near the trailer, some more commotion erupted. Johnny Cash had
arrived. Ringo looked like a child on Christmas morning as he greeted the country music star on the steps of the trailer. He beamed, his
body language mirroring that of some of the fans with outreached
arms on the other side of the massive security at the Cow Palace.
Country and western was a favorite of would-be cowboy Ringo.

KANE: What were some of the influences on you as a
musician?
STARR: Well, been listening to American country songs since
I was a kid, y'know. Think all of us loved the sound. Maybe
John and Paul put a little of that in their sound, y'know.

Johnny Cash. Joan Baez. It was a regular goodbye party back in
the Beatles' trailer central, with food and gaiety. Policemen were coming back for autographs, and Mal and Neil were accommodating them
by shuttling them in and out of the trailer.

The second concert was much like the first—wild and unruly. John
looked surprised when a souvenir button was hurled at his chest. And
the crowd roared when John again tickled the ivories of his electric
piano with his elbow. All in all, it was a typical concert, but it was the
last, so it felt special. You would think that after so many concerts, I
would have gotten tired of it all. I was tired in the physical sense, but
emotionally, I was still very much attached.

Many of the traveling deejays and overseas reporters bid farewell
to the band and each other at the Cow Palace. I decided to stay on for
the final night at the Cabana Motor Hotel in suburban Palo Alto. It
was a wise choice. The hotel was away from the center of things,
which gave the Beatles the rare chance to enjoy a final night of relative
peace.

Shortly after we arrived at the hotel, Mal Evans and Brian Epstein invited me to a reception in a suite of rooms. When the door opened for me, I saw what looked like a classic cocktail party. Epstein was chatting with the promoters, and the Beatles were engaged in conversation with some invited guests.

I plopped down on a comfortable sofa and took it all in. John sat down next to me. He was smoking. He looked relaxed and offered me a cigarette. He said, "So where do you go from here?" I replied, "Back to work at the station, and maybe into the service. I think I may be drafted." He looked shocked. "Now why would you do that?" he queried. I answered, "Maybe no other choice." He looked disbelieving.

George and Ringo came over and gave me hefty handshakes. Paul wandered around and wished me well. There was no pretense to them at this party—just four human beings mixing it up with some local VIPs. I was relieved and relaxed now that the tour was over, yet sentimentality had taken over inside of me. I went over to the bar for a drink and was immediately joined by a mature woman in a low-cut black dress. She seemed to be about thirty and looked out of place in this crowd of older civic officials and record promotion types. She said hello, and we had a few minutes of conversation.

I returned to my room at 3 a.m. and scribbled out my final reports. I had a plane to catch to Miami at 9 a.m., but I knew sleep would not be easy. Propping the pillows up, I laid the tape recorder on my lap and played back some of the most recent interviews, which included the farewells:

LENNON: Nice working with you, Larry.
McCARTNEY: Great working with you. See you soon.
HARRISON: Larry, it's been great.
STARR: Fantastic working with you. Bye, Larry.

Once again, their friendliness touched me, and now it was all over. That morning of September 1, 1965, a bit of personal history was being recorded, not on my trusty tape recorder, but in the recesses of my memory. There are moments in your life that you begin to recognize as singular and distinctive. They can never be relived or duplicated, but they will, you know for sure, be permanently lodged in your memory bank. The Beatles' tours were filled with those kinds of moments. I knew that my travels with these remarkable young men—the sounds, the sights and the people—would remain in my soul forever.

As I lay there, I reflected on changes I saw in the Beatles on this go-round. They were more relaxed, more trusting, much more outspoken and, above all, molding their individual images. Because they seemed more independent, I wondered here, too, whether these changes were the beginning of the end or just the end of the beginning.

I drifted off to sleep, and was soon awakened at 7 a.m. by a knock on the door. I immediately realized I had overslept. Adrenaline was now surging. As the door opened, I saw her again: the woman in black from the cocktail party. She said, "I came to visit."

"Sorry, but I have to go, or I'll miss the plane."

She said, "Can I go with you to the lobby?"

"Sure."

Within fifteen minutes, I was shaved, showered, packed and ready to move. She had waited outside, and she traveled with me to the elevator. As I hailed a cab, she looked at me in an alluring way and, calmly, said, "There's only one thing I really want to know."

"What?" I said.

"Tell me," she said. "What were they really like?"

Little did I know then that I would be asked that question for the rest of my life.

EPILOGUE:
Beyond the Tours

My hair was just beginning to grow again after a stint of active duty with the United States Air Force Reserve when I walked into the locker room at Busch Stadium in St. Louis to join the 1966 tour, already more than halfway over. I was greeted by bear hugs along with sarcasm about the state of my hairdo. Ringo touched the fuzz on my head. John chided me furiously about my failure to refuse military service. "Don't give me that crap," I brazenly answered him.

Since I had last seen John Lennon, I had enlisted in the air force and finished basic training and some more active duty, with five years of reserve duty left. I didn't appreciate his comments. He continued to give me a piece of his mind, and I lashed back. He simply couldn't comprehend how I could wear the uniform. John was against all wars. He viewed my fulfillment of military obligation as a statement against peace.

Lennon's opposition to the war in Vietnam was a part of his general rage against authority. His attempt to humiliate Kansas City A's owner Charles O. Finley during the 1964 tour was early evidence of this anger. And his 1965 comments about American racism were another sign of the changes occurring in John. His defiance against the war seemed to give a deeper meaning to his philosophy of questioning the establishment. It seemed ironic that, fresh from basic training, I was encountering a man who would soon become one of the most visible opponents of the war in Vietnam, a conflict that would end just five years before his own death.

After joining the tour in St. Louis, I flew with the Beatles to New York City. My participation in this tour was just a short visit, a chance to say hello and goodbye. The Beatles, we would learn later, would tour no more as a group after 1966. But as a result of my career transition from radio to television, we would eventually meet again in the most unusual of circumstances.

My career took me to Philadelphia in the fall of 1966, first as a radio correspondent and, shortly thereafter, as a TV reporter and anchor. I kept in touch with Nems, the Beatles' management group, by letter and a few phone calls. After Brian Epstein discovered from my letter that I had moved to Philadelphia, I received the following letter from him.

Dear Larry,

Thanks for the letter. The reason for such a delayed reply is the fact that I was in the States up till a week ago. As it happens, I heard you had moved to Philadelphia. Thanks for letting me know, and I hope it won't be too long before we are associated again.

With all best wishes,
Brian

The letter was dated April 9, 1967. On August 27 of that year, Brian Epstein was found dead from what was described as an overdose of drugs. His death was officially ruled an accident, but speculation has remained over the years that he took his own life. What a waste it was that he left so soon, before watching the Beatles blossom even more as individuals and as a singular influence of contemporary culture. The man was brilliant, though obviously conflicted.

I had no contact with the band or its staff until May of 1968, when Apple Corps. Ltd, the Beatles' new corporation, notified me that John and Paul would be coming to New York to promote their new concept: a company dedicated to finding and developing musical talent. The invitation came from the Beatles' London headquarters, letting me know that John and Paul were holding a news conference in Manhattan and wanted to provide some private interview time for me. By this time, I'd been a TV reporter for two years. Gone were the days of interviewing the Beatles with a heavy audiotape recorder; I would be conducting this interview with the band on television.

Our May 1968 session at the St. Regis Hotel turned out to be the final joint television interview of Lennon and McCartney before the group split up. The following excerpts from the transcripts reveal how open they were about drug use by this time:

KANE: Paul, about a year and a half ago, there were quotes on the wire about your discussion of LSD. . . .
McCARTNEY: Yes, Larry.
KANE: It seemed to me from what I read that you had endorsed and condemned it.
LENNON: We were manufacturing it at the time.
McCARTNEY: Some . . . newspaper man came up, and he said, Have you had LSD? So I thought, Well, I'll either be cagey or I'll be honest, so I said yes.
KANE: What are your plans?
LENNON: We are still singing and all that. We're still doing all that. You know, nothing's changed. The only difference is we don't tour. But we might during the future, you know.
McCARTNEY: Yeah, we only stopped touring because there was nowhere to go.
LENNON: With all the rifles, the clubs and all that frighten me to death.
KANE: Will you ever cease being the Beatles, and going off and working on your own or even working together?
McCARTNEY: We are the Beatles. That's what we are.

Again, we hear those words from Paul McCartney. Yet in a year, the Beatles as we knew them were no more.

Soon after that New York City interview, I received an invitation from John and Paul to visit them in London. I set off for my first trip to England on the evening of June 4, 1968. The trip was supposed to be a vacation, but the news I received on arrival made it anything but. The plane landed in London at almost the same moment as Robert F. Kennedy was shot dead in a hotel kitchen in Los Angeles.

My station called from Philadelphia, seeking a story about British reaction. Tony Barrow and the Beatles helped me find some good London locations to get meaningful interviews. I didn't know the town, so their advice was invaluable. A few days later, Paul invited me to Apple's office, where he gave me a taste of the new company's mission.

In a sparse office in London's West End, he introduced me to a young woman named Mary Hopkin and played a tape of a song he had collaborated on with her. It was a catchy tune, a ballad based on a Ukrainian folk song. Watching Paul mentor the young lady was a joy. This first effort by Apple to find and develop new talent was a great success. Mary Hopkin's song, "Those Were the Days," eventually sold eight million copies.

My next contact with a Beatle came a year later. It was an interview with John, which I conducted by telephone from my Philadelphia studios on May 30, 1969. It was surreal. I was holding a phone and taping an interview with a superstar who was carousing half-naked with his wife, in a bed, in a suite at the Queen Elizabeth Hotel in Montreal.

A few weeks earlier, John Lennon and his bride, Yoko Ono, had spent their honeymoon in a public bed in Amsterdam. Their every move was photographed and filmed. Their "bed-in" for world peace had stunned the world. It was so well received that they decided on an encore in Montreal. Unable to fly up there and interview him, I decided to tape a phone call. When I reached John in Montreal, he was all pumped up.

> KANE: Are you putting on the world or just having fun?
> LENNON: We're putting on the world a bit, but we've dedicated the first week we've had off, instead of having it in private, we've dedicated to world peace, and we believe that sincerely. We stay in bed for seven days and seven nights, a protest against violence. The other part of the protest is called "hair peace." Instead of people smashing things up, the people just grow their hair as a protest. There are so many hairy people, they grow and carry a continuous sign of their protest.
> KANE: Is this somewhat of a message to the people?
> LENNON: We've sincerely dedicated our time to peace. If the worst thing is giving people a laugh, that's okay, too.
> KANE: Trying to make the world a little happier?
> LENNON: Everybody's getting a little serious about it, and although it is serious, you still need laughter, and we're here to provide laughter.
> KANE: Thanks, John.
> LENNON: See you next time, Larry.

As it turns out, next time would be in the next decade in Philadelphia. But the newlyweds' next day in Montreal would provide a clear theme for those years ahead. Less than twenty-four hours after my phone interview, John and Yoko sent the word out from their hotel room: Bring instruments to the room. The world's most unusual recording session was about to take place.

John and Yoko, intent upon making their mark, assembled an eclectic collection of band members—later listed as the Plastic Ono Band—to record a rather basic song with a direct message. That roomful of people included just one other professional singer, Petula Clark. A guitar was brought in for comedian Tommy Smothers, and the chorus included members of the Canadian Radha Krishna Temple. Drug guru Dr. Timothy Leary joined in, along with the Beatles' former press secretary Derek Taylor and Montreal's Rabbi Abraham Feinberg.

I learned from news photographs that the walls of the room were covered with some large words—oversized lyrics for the chant. When the session was over, the recording was pressed and released, and the song that John and Yoko had chosen to express their evolution made a significant contribution to the youthful revolution around the world.

The song, "Give Peace a Chance," was released as a single in July. It was an instant hit and became an anthem for nonviolent protest for years to come. And it would be the song mourners sang at nationwide vigils after John Lennon's death in 1980.

My next contact with John after the bed-in interview came in the spring of 1975. Lennon was in a bad place in the mid-seventies. He was living with Yoko at the Dakota Apartments on Central Park West in New York. He was, according to reports, despondent over a career that was going nowhere after the Beatles' breakup and over the campaign by the Immigration and Naturalization Service to oust him from the United States because of a marijuana conviction. The campaign against Lennon was hostile and heavy-handed. He needed help, and Philadelphians gave him some cover.

Almost at the same time as Lennon was fighting in the courts, WFIL Radio—the sister station to WPVI, the television station where I was working—was planning a "helping hand weekend," a marathon fundraising event to benefit a number of community organizations. The management at WFIL suggested that Lennon might want to come to Philadelphia to host the fundraiser. I got a note off to John with two main points: Part of the marathon would benefit multiple sclerosis, which had killed my mother; and his involvement in a major charity event could prompt some letters of support from public officials in reference to his deportation battle. Lennon sent word that he would be there, and we hastily made travel arrangements.

I met him at 30th Street Station in downtown Philadelphia. John, who was losing his hair, emerged from the train alone, looking for me. I was surprised that he was traveling on his own. He ran to me and we embraced. He said, "Larry, thanks a million for getting me out of the house." I replied, "Thanks for coming, and let's take a tour of the town!"

We drove to Independence Mall, where I gave John the quick tour, reminding him that the Liberty Bell was the symbol of our revolution against his native Britain. There and at other locations, there was a turnabout: My role as a news broadcaster meant that people knew who I was and wanted to meet me. I had become a celebrity in Philadelphia. Lennon got a kick out of watching people recognize me. "Man, you've done well," he said.

The radio marathon got underway at 5 p.m. Lennon was really enjoying the radio show, and his on-air introduction had already sparked a switchboard jam the likes of which hadn't been seen at the station in years. There he was, international superstar John Lennon, away from home on a weekend vacation, doing some real good and having a ball. But the real ball was yet to come; I got hit with a bolt of inspiration. Jim O'Brien, the weatherman, was off that Friday night. Whispering to John, I said, "How would you like to do the weather?" He grinned that devilish Lennon grin, the one that told the world he was up to something, and he said, "Groovy, baby. Let's do it, boss."

As the 6 p.m. newscast approached, producers prepared Lennon for the weather forecast, coaching him on highs and lows and cold fronts and the jet stream. He didn't seem to care but just sat on a chair in the corner of the studio, watching the newscast, his face wearing that daffy, weird Lennon look. There in the hot studio, I came to realize that the man who had set the world on fire with his music and his madness was thrilled to be back in the spotlight again.

When the time came, I introduced Lennon as our guest weatherman, and he started taking the magnetic weather strips bearing numbers and names of cities and tossing them indiscriminately at the weather board. "Well, there's a high here," he would say, flipping Denver onto the East Coast and rain clouds onto the Mojave Desert, "and a low there, and people everywhere are singing where is the blue, ha ha ha." He summed up the forecast by saying, "So the outlook is sunny, but the weather is funny, and you should find a yellow submarine." The people in the studio—cameramen and other news people—couldn't hold in their laughter. Lennon was a hit, but no one got the genuine weather forecast on Channel 6 that night.

Having finished his stint as weatherman, John retreated to his suite at the Marriott Hotel for some R&R. Then he returned to the radio station, where he hosted the rock-and-roll program till midnight, then returned to his suite. The sales department at WFIL Radio had promised to make John comfortable, but I got the sense that comfortable was a code word for something else altogether. I don't know what happened in that suite, but every time John returned to the station, he would whisper to me, "Larry, what a ball. Every one of them was gorgeous. Great weekend."

Despite the intrigue in the hotel, Lennon spent many marathon hours on the air through Sunday night, when we wrapped it up. He worked hard and made the deejays feel good about broadcasting with him, offering tidbits about his personal life and memories of Beatles experiences. He also talked about me, fondly and with great humor, among other things reminding everyone that his famous manager Brian Epstein had had the hots for me on tour. I asked John, "Were you jealous?" He answered, "Was there something to be jealous about?"

The weekend was a success. Thousands of dollars were raised for MS research. Once again I faced the memory of my mother's death, which had occurred just days before the 1964 tour began. And one of the men who had helped me forget during those difficult days in 1964 had come to Philadelphia to contribute to a cause in her memory. I was grateful. And, as promised, I secured some letters from legislators on John's behalf.

John returned to New York. His battle with the INS continued over the next five years, during which period we talked several times on the phone. He had fond memories of that weekend in Philadelphia and appreciated the letters on his behalf. Eventually he won his fight to stay in America, a place where he could walk the streets in freedom and have little or no need for personal security. In New York as in Philadelphia, John traveled without guards, enjoying the sights and sounds of his city. Fatefully, however, his desire to live without a screen of protection led to his encounter with a deranged fan, Mark David Chapman, who ended John Lennon's life with bullets in December of 1980.

On the night of his death, when I read the copy on the air, I was deeply saddened and disgusted. I also felt fortunate to have known the man who had defied convention and used his celebrity to inform people about the travesties of hatred and war. The memory of John Lennon always stays with me, especially when I hear his voice on Beatles songs and when I recall that magic weekend when John Lennon lost himself in Philadelphia.

John was gone, and for years my only connections with the Beatles came through the occasional request to be interviewed about my experiences with them and the offers over the years to write a book about the tours. And through a career covering politics, government, crime and punishment, a career that has included giving hundreds of speeches, nary a month has passed without someone asking me what it was like to travel with the Beatles.

Then, in the summer of 1989, I met with one of the band members again. My wife, Donna, and I traveled to suburban Milwaukee for a one-on-one interview with Ringo at his all-star concert. Ringo, with the help of producer David Fishof, had put together a tour combining Ringo's talents with those of six or seven other rock musicians, including Clarence Clemons, Dr. John and Nils Lofgren. We reminisced. And I saw Ringo again in 2000, when I interviewed him in Atlantic City. His memories of the sixties tours were hazy by then, but he remembered the fans:

> KANE: Do you remember playing in Philadelphia?
> STARR: Did we play in Philadelphia?
> KANE: Yes.
> STARR: I need people like you to remind me of things I've forgotten. Write it down, Larry.
> KANE: What was your favorite memory of the tours?
> STARR: Just the wonder of it all. Mostly the fans. We were just boys then, but it was so special, so very exciting, that surge of energy they gave us. It was great.

Aside from these occasional meetings, the Beatles have come and gone in my life in less direct ways. Every year or two, I get a query from someone doing a project on them. Some materials I gathered while traveling with them have been used in TV and book anthologies, because their surviving organization, Apple, had purchased the rights to use some of my interviews. Other than that, my recent contact with London has been minimal, except that I sent some packages of video and tapes as a courtesy to Paul, who is an avid collector of anything Beatles. Paul and I have had no direct contact, however, since the band split, and he has turned down my offers to interview him about his memories of the band's touring era.

Paul, of course, has had his trials in recent years—most notably the death of his wife, Linda. Both Linda's death and George's passing prompted press people to call me for reactions, especially in Philadelphia, where my Beatles history is well known. I did not know Linda McCartney, but like everyone else, I grieved for Paul and his family. And George's death brought back memories of his courtesy and calm in the middle of all that madness.

Given the significance of some of the other stories I've covered, the Beatles and their tours might seem to pale in comparison. To some, the combat in the Middle East, a superpower summit, a mayoral election in Philadelphia, a devastating earthquake, nineteen political conventions and even everyday stories of human conflict and achievement may appear more important than touring with a group of megastar musicians. But the events that began in America in 1964 were also major historical turning points, and the Beatles played a role in how our nation coped with its trials.

The Beatles arrived in America just months after the assassination of President Kennedy and in the same year that the civil rights movement was blossoming. The band's music was liberating, along with the band members' dress and style, and all of these dimensions helped bring young people toward the activism that came to define the ensuing years. Like the young people who adored them, John, Paul, George and Ringo evolved in a single decade from teen idols to serious musical poets of peace and protest.

Today, many of their teen fans are in their mid-fifties, baby boomers whose cultural compass was guided by the music they heard and the musicians who inspired them. Today, the Beatles' music is perhaps their most enduring legacy, music written primarily in a decade and lasting through the technological phases of vinyl, cassette, eight track, compact disc and now digital files. No other entertainment entity has crossed these generational and technical boundaries with such consistency and timelessness. The music of the Beatles in the early twenty-first century is as fresh and alive as the Beatles sounded in 1964. I'm not talking about the wonders of modern audio, but about the ageless vitality and beauty of the music.

It has been a pleasure to have known them and covered them, and to have watched their original audiences grow older and their contemporary audiences get younger and younger. I hope I've been able to convey what it was really like to be on tour with the Beatles as they made history.

Covering the Beatles was one of the greatest joys of my career as a journalist. And the assignment, although so long ago, still feels current. Unlike the many famous people I've covered, the Beatles' voices and music live on every day, in private homes and public places. Millions of people collect and listen to their music, and hundreds of thousands nurture collections of tickets, pictures and other souvenirs.

My collection is different. It's imprinted in the recesses of my mind and consists of memories of four men, their living music and the people who loved them. I had a ticket to ride, and what a ride it was. It's been a pleasure to take you along on that improbable, magnificent journey.

Appendix:

Complete 1964 and 1965 Tour Schedules

EARLY 1964

CITY & VENUE	DATE	SHOWS	ATTENDANCE
NEW YORK CITY : *The Ed Sullivan Show*	Feb 9, 1964	2	728 (ea., live audience afternoon taping for 2/23 broadcast plus live evening show)
WASHINGTON D.C. : Coliseum	Feb 11, 1964	1	8,092
NEW YORK CITY : Carnegie Hall	Feb 12, 1964	2	2,954 (ea.)
MIAMI : Deauville Hotel	Feb 16. 1964	2	2,600 (ea., rehearsal and show, 3,500 tickets reportedly issued for main show)

1964 TOUR

CITY & VENUE	DATE	SHOWS	ATTENDANCE
SAN FRANCISCO : Cow Palace	Aug 19, 1964	1	17,130
LAS VEGAS : Convention Center	Aug 20, 1964	2	16,816 (total)
SEATTLE : Seattle Center Coliseum	Aug 21, 1964	1	14, 382
VANCOUVER : Empire Stadium	Aug 22, 1964	1	20,621
HOLLYWOOD : Hollywood Bowl	Aug 23, 1964	1	17,256
DENVER : Red Rocks Amphitheater	Aug 26, 1964	1	7,000
CINCINNATI: Cincinnati Gardens	Aug 27, 1964	1	14,000
NEW YORK CITY : Forest Hills Tennis Stadium	Aug 28, 1964	1	16,000
NEW YORK CITY : Forest Hills Tennis Stadium	Aug 29, 1964	1	16,000
ATLANTIC CITY : Convention Hall	Aug 30, 1964	1	18,000
PHILADELPHIA : Convention Hall	Sep 2, 1964	1	13,000
INDIANAPOLIS : Indiana State Fair	Sep 3, 1964	2	12,413 & 16,924
MILWAUKEE : Milwaukee Arena	Sep 4, 1964	1	11,500
CHICAGO : International Amphitheater	Sep 5, 1964	1	13,000
DETROIT : Olympia Stadium	Sep 6, 1964	2	30,000 (total)
TORONTO : Maple Leaf Gardens	Sep 7, 1964	2	35,000 (total)

(continued)

1964 TOUR *(Continued)*

CITY & VENUE	DATE	SHOWS	ATTENDANCE
MONTREAL : Forum	Sep 8, 1964	2	9,500 11,500
JACKSONVILLE : Gator Bowl	Sep 11, 1964	1	32,000
BOSTON : Boston Garden	Sep 12, 1964	1	13,909
BALTIMORE : Civic Center	Sep 13, 1964	2	28,000 (total)
PITTSBURGH : Civic Arena	Sep 14, 1964	1	12,603
CLEVELAND : Public Auditorium	Sep 15, 1964	1	11,000
NEW ORLEANS : City Park Stadium	Sep 16, 1964	1	12,000
KANSAS CITY : Municipal Stadium	Sep 17, 1964	1	20,214
DALLAS : Dallas Mem. Auditorium	Sep 18, 1964	1	10,500
NEW YORK CITY : Paramount Theater	Sep 20, 1964	1	3,682

1965 TOUR

CITY & VENUE	DATE	SHOWS	ATTENDANCE
NEW YORK CITY : *The Ed Sullivan Show*	Aug 14, 1965	2	728 (ea., rehearsal and show)
NEW YORK CITY : Shea Stadium	Aug 15, 1965	1	55,600
TORONTO : Maple Leaf Gardens	Aug 17, 1965	2	18,000 (ea.)
ATLANTA : Fulton County Stadium	Aug 18, 1965	1	30,000
HOUSTON : Sam Houston Coliseum	Aug 19, 1965	2	12,000 (ea.)
CHICAGO : Comiskey Park	Aug 20, 1965	2	25,000 37,000
BLOOMINGTON, MN : Metropolitan Stadium	Aug 21, 1965	1	25,000
PORTLAND : Memorial Coliseum	Aug 22, 1965	2	20,000 (total)
SAN DIEGO : Balboa Stadium	Aug 28, 1965	1	17,000
HOLLYWOOD : Hollywood Bowl	Aug 29, 1965	1	17,256
HOLLYWOOD : Hollywood Bowl	Aug 30, 1965	1	17,256
SAN FRANCISCO : Cow Palace	Aug 31, 1965	2	18,000